A HISTORY OF DRUIDRY IN AUSTRALIA

A HISTORY OF DRUIDRY IN AUSTRALIA

A Collection of Perspectives

Edited by

Sandra Greenhalgh

&

Elkie White

First published in 2020 by Byrning Tyger
© copyright (as a collective work) Byrning Tyger 2020
Each author is copyright owner of their own contributed materials.

The moral rights of the authors have been asserted.

All rights reserved. Except as permitted under the Australian Copyright Act 1968 (for example, a fair dealing for the purposes of study, research, criticism or review), no part of this book may be reproduced, stored in a retrieval system, communicated or transmitted in any form or by any means without prior written permission.

All inquiries should be made to the Publisher

Printed in Australia
Cover design by pro_ebookcover

Disclaimer

Views or opinions represented in this publication are personal and belong solely to the individual author and do not represent the views or opinions of the editors or any people, institution or organisations that the author and editors may or may not be associated with in any professional or personal capacity.

Although the editors and publisher have made every effort to ensure that the information in this book was correct at press time, the editor and publisher do not assume and hereby disclaim any liability to any party for any loss, damage, or disruption caused by errors or omissions, whether such errors or omissions result from negligence, accident, or any other cause.

Some names and identifying details have been changed to protect the privacy of individuals.

ISBN 978-0-6482701-3-3

www.byrningtyger.com

We acknowledge and pay respect to the past, present and future Traditional Custodians and Elders of this nation and the continuation of cultural, spiritual and educational practices of Aboriginal and Torres Strait Islander peoples.

Dawn Blessing
Cherry Carroll

Frilly lizard proudly holds position in the North,
Standing for his fire dragon kin,
Whose ancient eyes survey the South,
Where echidna burrows in.
Eastward the cries of magpies sail upon the crystal air,
And in the West the mighty whale sings songs of oceans fair.

This is our land of fires and floods
A land of ochre hues,
Of ancient forests, wide blue skies
A land of endless views.

We gather on this sacred soil to greet the blushing dawn,
To ask a blessing for the land and protection over all.
Tendrils of mist caress the air,
As we circle here this morn.
Sharp cries of whip birds crack the peace,
Doves soothing with their calls,
Ribbons of laughter weave the lore,
As kookaburra declares.

This is our land of fires and floods,
A land of ochre hues,
Of ancient forests, wide blue skies,
A land of endless views.

But we stand silent in the Grove, our hearts too full for words,
Our love for all this beauty seems almost too much to bear.
Then magically our voices swell in concert with the birds,
And inspiration fills our hearts,
As the power of Awen soars.

This is our land of fires and floods,
A land of ochre hues,
Of ancient forests, wide blue skies
A land of endless views.

CONTENTS

Foreword I by Philip Carr-Gomm	xi
Foreword II by Rev. Jean (Drum) Pagano	xiii
Foreword III by Philip Shallcrass	xv
Introduction	**1**
Part I - DRUIDRY IN AUSTRALIA	**3**
Background to *A History of Druidry in Australia*	4
Timeline	**6**
Timeline of Druid groups and significant events in Australia	6
Interstate Australians of different traditions at DDUNG in 2018	10
Representatives from Australian and New Zealand Druid communities	11
Personal Experiences of Druidry	**12**
Awen Through the Lens of Indigenous Culture	13
Reflections on the Early Years of Druidry in Australia	15
My Druid Journey	26
Southern Hemisphere OBOD Assemblies	**30**
The Second Australian OBOD Assembly	31
Wyeuro and the 2003 OBOD Assembly	33
NEWSFLASH...Hedgie flushed out: enjoys himself at Assembly!	35
Fire archway from the 2016 Assembly	36
Welcoming the Chosen Chief to Western Australia in 2000	37
Inaugural Australian Druid Assembly Promotion	38
The Inaugural Australian Druid Assembly Program Notes	39
Photo of the camp at the Inaugural Australian Druid Assembly	40
Pre-ritual at the Inaugural Australian Druid Assembly	40
Inaugural Australian Druid Assembly Program of Events	41
The Second Australian Druid Assembly Notes	42
Second Australian Druid Assembly Program (Friday and Saturday)	43
Second Australian Druid Assembly Program (Sunday and Monday)	44

SerpentStar	45
Timeline of *SerpentStar* editors	45
The first editor of *SerpentStar*	46
The middle years of *SerpentStar*	48
The current editor of *SerpentStar*	49
Front cover of inaugural edition of SerpentStar	50
Front cover of Beltane 2019 SerpentStar	51
The Inaugural Druids Down Under National Gathering (DDUNG)	52

Part II - DRUID GROUPS, SEED GROUPS AND GROVES   53

Overview	54
New South Wales Druid Groups	55
Druids Down Under	55
Druid Pilgrim	65
The Living Nemeton	75
The Song of the Eastern Sea	76
The Urban Druid	77
Wollemi Seed Group	78
South Australian Druid Groups	79
Adelaide Seed Group, *Wind Harp* and South Australian Druidry	79
Green Man Grove based at Rosedale, South Australia	82
Image adopted by Wind Harp Seed Group	82
Cooringal Grove	83
The stone circle at Cooringal Grove, during the third Assembly in 1999	84
Druids of OZ and the *English Ale*	85
Druids of Oz image	85 & 86
The Golden Wattle Seed Group	87
Golden Wattle Seed Group pendant	89
Queensland Druid Groups	90
Australian College of Druidry	90
Macadamia Grove	95
Macadamia Grove banner design	103
The Chair of Caer Witrin	104
Victorian Druid Groups	105
The Melbourne Grove	105
The first OBOD Tutors meeting in Australia	107

The Melbourne Grove banner	119
Silver Birch Grove	120
Silver Birch Grove banner detail	123
Silver Birch Grove banner	124

Western Australia Druid Groups

Western Australia Druid Groups	125
Druid Journey	125
Dreaming Tree Grove	127
Gaelic Druid Order	128
Ganieda Grove	129
Silver Eyes Seed Group	130
The Silvereyes Seed Group logo	131
Western Australia Druidry	132
Silvereyes Seed Group's Wheel of the Year	133
The ritual to celebrate the 50 year OBOD anniversary	.134

Part III - THE AUSTRALIAN DRUID HISTORY PROJECT   135

Preferred terminology and is Druidry distinct from other Pagan groups   136

Preferences regarding terminology	136
Is Druidry distinct from other Pagan groups	139

History Project Questionnaire Responses   141

Cherry Carroll	142
Chris Parker	146
Chris Pingel	150
Janine Hartley	153
John Jordan	156
Julie Brett	161
Kacey Stephensen	170
Marigold	176
MS	178
Michael V	181
Morphett Vale	184
Murray Barton	188
Narine	192
Sandra Greenhalgh	194
Vicki Minahan	201
United Ancient Order of Druids badge and vest	204

Part IV - FRATERNAL DRUID LODGES IN AUSTRALIA 205

Australia's First Druid Lodges 206
A Timeline of Fraternal Druid Lodges in Australia 207
What became of the AOD and UAOD? 212
Druids Cricket Club 213
    Images of UAOD building in Melbourne 214
    UAOD Druid's Hall in Geraldton, Western Australia 215

Ancient Order of Druids – a personal connection 216
    UAOD Arch Druids Charge proficiency certificate 217
    UAOD Grand Lodge Office Past Arch rank certificate 217

Part V - APPENDICES AND ACKNOWLEDGMENTS 219

Appendix A: The original *Australian Druid History Project* Questionnaire 220
Appendix B: Promotion in *SerpentStar* 223
Appendix C: Additional *SerpentStar* section 224
Appendix D: *SerpentStar* Update 225
Appendix E: The Wild Hunt Response 226
Acknowledgements and Credits 229
Key Contributors 229
Editor Biographies 233

Limited Glossary – common abbreviations
OBOD - *The Order of Bards, Ovates and Druids*
BDO - *British Druid Order*
ADF- *Ár nDraíocht Féin: A Druid Fellowship*

Foreword I

WHEN I ATTENDED THE SECOND OBOD Australian Assembly in 1998 how could I have known that this very special gathering under the southern stars would continue to be convened every year thereafter? That's an extraordinary achievement! And now, twenty years later, it's time for a history of these events, and more widely of the story of Druidry's development in Australia in recent times.

I've just read this history, and what strikes me most is the sheer humanity in it: all these voices talking about their personal experiences of Druidry: their discovery of community and of connection with the land and their ancestry that has changed their lives - sometimes in small ways, sometimes in profound ways. This book feels like a film of an eco-system: a flourishing world of colour and movement.

Reading it made me think about a moment at an OBOD camp in the UK when I asked the 120 or so people gathered there in the morning circle why they were at camp. I had assumed it was because either they wanted to spend a week practising and learning about Druidry or they wanted to spend some time living closer to the land, or a combination of both these motives. But I was completely wrong: all but one person said they were there for community. It was only then that I truly took on board the importance of this need within most of us to come together - to make connections, support each other, build relationships.

And this is what I see in this book. Of course we follow Druidry to deepen our relationships with all of nature, to learn the Old Ways, to grow familiar with the Otherworld too, but somehow a basic impulse is also this need for connection and community. And this book is a manifestation of this. It is a record, the story of Druidry in Australia, told through many different voices that reflect the way that this particular stream of spiritual culture has developed here in recent years.

As I write this, the fires burn close to Sydney, and the world is finally waking up to the realities of the climate crisis and mass species extinction. It's hard not to feel pessimistic, and yet like travellers crossing the desert we can still come across oases, we can find flowers blooming in the desert, and this book encourages us to be optimistic - to find those flowers, and to find support on our individual journeys.

Stephanie and I, and I know Damh and Cerri too, have so many fond memories of the gatherings and rituals we attended in Australia, of individual members and their generosity, of special moments we shared: too many to recount here! They will live in our hearts forever. May Druidry continue to grow and flourish in Australia!

Philip Carr-Gomm, Chosen Chief of *The Order of Bards, Ovates and Druids* (1988 to 2020)

Foreword II

AR nDRAIOCHT FEIN (ADF), A DRUID FELLOWSHIP, was founded on Samhain, that is Beltaine in Australia, 1983. Based in North America, this branch of Druidry spread to Australia with our first member on 9 May 1988. Today, we have a Grove and a Protogrove, both in Melbourne, and members in New South Wales, Queensland, South Australia, Victoria, and Western Australia.

ADF is an offering-based religion that is Indo-European in character, encompassing hearth-cultures from Connacht in the West of Ireland to the Indus River valley in India, and all points in between where Indo-European languages spread throughout the world in pre-Christian times.

I am the sixth ArchDruid of ADF and I was blessed to visit our Grove in Melbourne and attend the Mount Franklin Festival in 2015. It was a pivotal experience in not only my Druidry, but in my understanding of the global nature of the phenomenon that we call "Druidry". I was received with great kindness and boundless hospitality, such that I am so looking forward to my return to this blessed continent in the very near future.

I celebrated Samhain in North America and then just a few days later I celebrated Beltaine with Silver Birch Grove, ADF, nestled in the bosom of the Earth Mother inside Mount Franklin with 100+ attendees and the blessings of good weather, a gentle breeze, and good omens. I saw the Southern Cross and the Moon as I had never seen it before. It left an indelible mark on my psyche and on my practice.

I came to see that the Earth Mother, she from which we come, she on which we flourish, and she to which we return is not a sleeping or waking entity, but a vibrant life-force and spirit that is in motion constantly on this blue planet.

I see Druidry in the same way: nascent, in its infancy, and embracing the Earth Mother and Spirits of Nature where ever they are found and it is everywhere just like they, the Earth Mother and the Spirits of Nature, are evident in forests, in cities, in the hearts of the planet.

We are a proud part of the History of Druidry in Australia and I like to think that the History of Druidry in Australia is a part of me. It was born in me in October 2015 and continues to grow in me and call to me as it reminds me and calls me home again, and, hopefully again thereafter. I look forward to this volume of work not to see me in its pages but to see its pages in me and the pages will turn like leaves in the wind, telling the stories again and again. It is a story worth telling and retelling, a new lore that is seed for the present and a promise for the future.

The blessings of the Earth Mother, the Ancestors, the Spirits of Nature, and the Shining Ones of our people and yours on this work. May these stories be told for many years to come.

Blessings,
Rev. Jean (Drum) Pagano
ArchDruid, ADF
16 November 2019

Foreword III

"… *A Covenant Bringing Bright Prosperity* …"
AS A BRITISH DRUID, IT IS impossible to ignore the legacy of colonialism. For Indigenous peoples encountered during the period of colonial expansion, the results were frequently devastating. The arrogant assumption that the British way of life was superior to any other resulted in our ancestors attempting to wipe out indigenous cultures and peoples.

Now, in the 21st century, more of us are waking up to the fact that the culture our ancestors exported to the world is creating global warming, industrial pollution and the mass extinction of species. This reassessment of our colonial legacy is occurring in tandem with the growth of a Pagan Druidry having its roots in the radical consciousness-expansion movement of the 1960s. In the *British Druid Order* (BDO), we look back further, to 2,000 years ago, when Druidry was the indigenous spirituality of a large part of Europe, and beyond that, to its roots in Bronze Age Britain and its deeper roots in a 'shamanic' world-view originating in Central Asia perhaps 40,000 years ago. This inspired our creation, or re-creation, of Druidry as a Pagan, animistic, 'shamanistic' way of interacting with the spirits of the world around us, our ancestors, and the old gods of our lands. This understanding of Druidry allows us to interact with spirit workers in other indigenous cultures, not with the patronising paternalism of Empire, but from a place of equality, mutual respect and shared understanding.

At a Druid camp* in the 1990s, a Native American, John Two-Birds, spoke of a future in which indigenous spirit workers of the world come together to work for our Mother Earth, or Grandmother in his tradition. He saw Druids, Wiccans and Heathens as vital to this process, being the indigenous spirit workers of our post-industrial nations. This is a vision I work to promote through the BDO. We are part of a global family brought together by The World Drum, made by a Sami drum-maker, which has travelled the world since 2006, uniting people across cultural, spiritual, political, generational and racial boundaries with its message of peace and ecology through shared fundamental beliefs. We have shared ceremonies with Native Americans, Sami, Shintoists and others. One sunny afternoon in the 1990s, following a ceremony among the ancient stone circles of Avebury in Wiltshire, a young Australian Aborigine who had taken part said he loved what we were doing, adding that "the old folks back home" would recognise, and rejoice in, our words and actions.

We can't rewrite the past but, working together, we can create a better future for ourselves, our children, and our world. I rejoice that the vibrant Australian Druidry portrayed within these pages is playing its part in this most vital of projects. May we create a world, in the words of the Irish Druid, Mogh Ruith:

> *"...mead-flowing, stream-flowing,*
> *heavenly half with well-ordered game,*
> *spreading bird-song, growing inspiration,*
> *hostings where the sun shines on the multitude,*
> *a covenant bringing bright prosperity..."* **

So may it be!

Philip Shallcrass, a.k.a. Greywolf, chief of the *British Druid Order*

[Editor's comments: * Druid camp = the second OBOD Summer Camp held at West Sussex. **Greywolf's translation of 'The Siege of Drom Dámhgháire,' from the 15th century Book of Lismore.]

INTRODUCTION

Sandra Greenhalgh

THERE ARE MANY COMPELLING REASONS to create a historical account regarding the practice of Druidry in Australia. The land on which we live shapes our experiences and interactions with it, and with each other. In Australia, we have unique flora and fauna, found nowhere else in the world. Additionally, being 'down under the equator' makes it nigh impossible to impose Northern hemisphere sensibilities onto our climate and seasons. Australia has its own histories, cultures and stories.

Some people felt that a record of Druid history should be the scholarly endeavour of a highly qualified historian in order to gain the credibility it deserves. Yet despite these lofty ideals, this publication was undertaken by two women with a wealth of lived experience as Australian Druids. We are not trained historians; however, we bring our passion and deep love of Druidry to this edited collection. We felt that this was such an important initiative, that it just had to be done… so we did it. Doing what needs to be done is a concept which underpins contemporary Druidry.

With the exception of the Forewords, which were kindly provided by leaders of world-wide Druid groups, contributions in this book are from Australians who identify as following a Druid path. To enable the creative and idiosyncratic voices of the contributors, most of the submissions have been only edited lightly when required for clarity. Elkie and I feel that any quirky 'imperfections' in the contributions give the project life and personality.

This book has been organised into the following sections:
- Forewords by leaders of three influential modern-day Druid groups
- An explanation regarding the background to the *Australian Druid History Project*
- Significant personal stories about Druidry in Australia
- Timeline of major events in Australian Druidry from the 1980s onward

- Southern Hemisphere *Order of Bards, Ovates and Druids* (OBOD) Assemblies
- Publication history of the *SerpentStar* magazine
- Druid Groups, Seed Groups and Groves. These have been sorted alphabetically by Australian State and then by group name
- Preferred terminology and details from the *Australian Druid History Project*
- *Australian Druid History Project* questionnaire responses, which have been sorted alphabetically by the first name of the respondent
- Information about Fraternal Druid Lodges in Australia
- Appendices which include communications relating to the *Australian Druid History Project*.

You will see that there are no upfront descriptions regarding what Druidry 'is' or any lists or renditions of Druidic practices. This is quite deliberate, as we believe that any descriptions are best expressed through the explanations provided by the contributors. These are their stories, and their interpretations of Druidry, as they chose to share them.

Part I

DRUIDRY IN AUSTRALIA

BACKGROUND TO A HISTORY OF DRUIDRY IN AUSTRALIA

The Project's Beginnings
Elkie White

SHORTLY PRIOR TO THE 2017 *Order of Bards, Ovates and Druids* (OBOD) Assembly in Sydney, Josephine Winter, a founding member of the Pagan Collective of Victoria, sent out a series of questions for an article that she was putting together for *The Wild Hunt*. First on the list was, *Tell me about the history of Druidry as a spiritual practice in Australia.* I explained to Josie that that this 'question' was not one that I could answer in 24 hours (the turn-around time) and offered to create a questionnaire which I would then take to the Assembly. With 50 plus Druids in attendance, it was too good an opportunity to miss! My motivation for initiating this project was a simple one: I wanted to ensure that the stories were not lost.

Julie Brett had published *Australian Druidry: Connecting with the Sacred Landscape* a few months before Josie's article. Julie commented on the *Druids Down Under* Facebook page that she was tempted to include a history of Druidry in Australia but decided against it because she was not an historian.

I agreed with Julie that this project should be steered by an historian and contacted my friend, Dr. David Waldron – author and Senior Lecturer in History at *Federation University*.

I devised the questionnaire, hoping that lots of Bards, Ovates, and Druids would participate, so that the rich diversity of expression of Druidry in Australia could be heard and appreciated within its greater context. The questionnaire was adjusted along the way, but it was only ever intended to act as a springboard.

People were invited to ignore it and write their contribution as the Awen moved them—as an essay with photos, poetry, music and musings. They were informed that they didn't need to be an experienced Druid to have a crack at the questionnaire or a personal essay. I further hoped that as well as personal accounts of individual Druids, the histories of Australia's Groves and Seed Groups would be included along with *Druids Down Under* and other expressions of Druidry active in Australia today.

Before the 2017 Assembly, I sent David Waldron the questionnaire and asked him for his thoughts on it. Specifically, *Have I omitted questions that a historian might have wished were there when it comes to compiling the information*? David suggested that I add: *Do you think that Druidry is worth seeing as distinct to other Pagan groups?* It was a question that people would readily respond to.

The response from OBOD members at the Sydney Assembly was sufficiently encouraging to warrant taking the project further, and so I took it to the *Druids Down Under* National Gathering (DDUNG) in March 2018. Again, it was received enthusiastically, this time by a wider audience. At DDUNG there were Druids from the *British Druid Order* (BDO) and *Ár nDraíocht Féin* (also known as *A Druid Fellowship* or ADF) as well as some who were independent of these teaching orders.

There was another exciting development over the DDUNG weekend. Sandra offered to help compile and publish *A History of Druidry in Australia*. And, several months, drafts, and emails later, here it is!

TIMELINE

This timeline provides an overview of significant events in Australian Druidry, commencing in 1988 through to late 2019. Information about fraternal Druid Lodges has been included in a separate section. While the following list may not be complete, it was developed with the best information available at the time of publication. Groups are currently active unless identified otherwise.

Timeline of Druid groups and significant events in Australia

Year	Event	Details
1988	OBOD reopened and correspondence course made available	A.B. and S.G. were the first two Australians to join OBOD in December 1988. J.G. was the third person to join in 1989.
1989	*Sgiath an Fhithich* Grove (also known as Ravenswing Grove) commenced	Originally based in Western Australia. Currently active, now based in Scotland.
1991	*The Chair of Caer Witrin* commenced in Queensland	Based in Melbourne. Inactive.
1992	*North-East Arbor (N.E.A.) Grove* commenced	Year of Seed Group formation. Based in NSW.
1992	*Cooringal Grove* commenced	Year of Seed Group formation. Based in South Australia.
1997	1st OBOD Assembly near Wiseman's Ferry, New South Wales	Hosted by the North-East Arbor Grove on 19-21 September. Inaugural Australian Druid Assembly.
1997	*SerpentStar* first published.	Still in production.

A HISTORY OF DRUIDRY IN AUSTRALIA

Year	Event	Details
1998	2nd OBOD Assembly at Wiseman's Ferry, New South Wales	Hosted by North-East Arbor Grove on 18 – 21 September. Attended by OBOD Chosen Chief Philip Carr-Gomm.
1998	*Macadamia Grove* commenced	Year of Seed Group formation. Based in Queensland.
1998	*The Melbourne Grove* commenced	Year of Seed Group formation. Based in Victoria.
1999	3rd OBOD Assembly near Port Lincoln, South Australia	Hosted by *Cooringal Grove* in September.
1999	*The Gaelic Druid Order of the Southern Cross* commenced	Based in Western Australia. Changed to *Gaelic Druid Order* in 2007. Closed in 2016.
2000	4th OBOD Assembly in Albany, Western Australia	Hosted by *Ganieda Grove* in September. Attended by Philip and Stephanie Carr-Gomm and their two daughters
2000	Emma Restall Orr visited Australia	Hosted by *The Gaelic Druid Order of the Southern Cross* to Australia (West Coast) and by Zan and Akkadia, of *North–East Arbor Grove*, to the East Coast.
2001	5th OBOD Assembly in Yulara, Northern Territory	Hosted by Elkie at the Winter Solstice.
2001	*Corona Australis* commenced	Foundation Druids simultaneously chartered across Australia. Inactive.
2001	*Australian College of Druidry* commenced	Based in Queensland. Inactive.
2001	*Hermetic Druidry* commenced	Based in New South Wales, established by Akkadia and Zan.

Year	Event	Details
2003	6th OBOD Assembly at Punyelroo, South Australia	Hosted by Vyvyan Ogma Wyverne and Nellie on 22-23 November.
2004	7th OBOD Assembly at Kingaroy, Queensland	Hosted by Cherry and Denis Carroll on 25-26 September.
2005	8th OBOD Assembly at Currarong, New South Wales	Hosted by Carole Nielsen and Wayne Clarke on October 28-30.
2006	9th OBOD Assembly at Port Lincoln, South Australia	Hosted by *Cooringal Grove* from 29 September – 1 October.
2007	*Silver Birch Grove* commenced	Based in Victoria, part of an international Order (ADF).
2007	*Druids Down Under* (DDU) Facebook group commenced	National online based.
2007	*Ashby Grove* commenced	Based in Western Australia. *Daughter Grove of Ravenswing*. Closed in 2016.
2010	*Silver Eyes Seed Group*	Based in Western Australia.
2010	10th OBOD Assembly at Cockatoo, Victoria	Hosted by The Melbourne Grove on 23-26 April.
2010	druidryaustralia.org website went live	Active.
2010	*The Grove of the White Cockatoo* commenced	Affiliated with the Melbourne Grove. Closed in 2013.
2011	*The Adelaide Seed Group* commenced	Based in South Australia. Inactive.
2011	11th OBOD Assembly at Port Lincoln, South Australia	Hosted by *Cooringal Grove* on 6 – 10 October.

A HISTORY OF DRUIDRY IN AUSTRALIA

Year	Event	Details
2012	*Dreaming Tree Grove* commenced.	Based in Western Australia. Originally named *The Perth Hills Druid Grove*. Affiliated with the *British Druid Order*. Closed in 2018.
2012	12th OBOD Assembly at Beltana, South Australia	Hosted by Ngatina on 25 – 29 October.
2014	13th OBOD Assembly at Binna Burra, Queensland	Hosted by Elkie and Ngatina on 24 – 28 January. The year of the 50th OBOD Anniversary. Attended by Philip and Stephanie Carr-Gomm.
2014	*Golden Wattle Seed Group* commenced	Based in South Australia.
2015	14th OBOD Assembly at Mt Hyland, New South Wales	Hosted by Michael V, Elkie and Debs on 1-5 May.
2015	*Wollemi Seed Group* commenced	Based in Newcastle and Hunter NSW.
2016	15th OBOD Assembly at Bribie Island, Queensland	Hosted by *Macadamia Grove* on 14-18 October.
2016	*The Song of the Eastern Sea Seed Group* commenced.	Based in Central Coast, NSW.
2017	16th OBOD Assembly at Pennant Hills, New South Wales	Hosted by *The Song of the Eastern Sea Seed Group* on 10-15 August.
2017	*Wind Harp Seed Group* commenced	Based in South Australia.
2017	*Urban Druid* commenced	Based in Sydney.
2018	Inaugural *Druids Down Under National Gathering* (DDUNG)	Hosted by Julie Brett and *Druids Down Under* in March.

Year	Event	Details
	at Pennant Hills, New South Wales	
2018	17th OBOD Assembly at Glenhaven, South Australia	Hosted by the *Golden Wattle Seed Group* on 10 - 14 August.
2018	*Druid Pilgrim Grove* commenced	Based in Australia and Aotearoa.
2019	18th OBOD Assembly ("SHOBODA") at Tatum Park, Leven, New Zealand	Hosted by *Grove of the Southern Stars* on 17 - 22 January. Attended by Philip and Stephanie Carr-Gomm and the Chosen Chief–in Training Eimear Burke.
2019	*Living Nemeton* commenced	Based in Sydney.
2020	19th OBOD Assembly at Gembrook in Victoria (pending)	To be hosted by *The Melbourne Grove* on 24 – 28 April.

Interstate Australians of different traditions at DDUNG in 2018

Photo credit: Pete Blake.   *Pete Blake, BDO Druid, Sandra Greenhalgh of Macadamia Grove, Julie Brett of Druids Down Under, Elkie White of The Melbourne Grove, Shaz Cairns and Ang Bausch of Silver Birch Grove (ADF).*

Representatives from Australian and New Zealand Druid communities at the Southern Hemisphere OBOD Assembly (SHOBODA) 2019

Photo credit: SHOBODA 2019
Julie of Druids Down Under, Pamela from Grove of the Summer Stars, Sandra, Nina and Linda of Macadamia Grove, Ben of Urban Druid, Chris of The Song of the Eastern Sea Seed Group, Michael and Danuta of Druid Pilgrim Grove, Cait of Wind Harp Seed Group, Kacey of Golden Wattle Seed Group and Elkie of The Melbourne Grove

PERSONAL EXPERIENCES OF DRUIDRY

This section includes three different contributions which provide a valuable and diverse overview of Druidry in Australia:

- GGM Kate Wood-Pahuru shares her perspective of being an Aboriginal person and a Druid.

- Akkadia and Zan hosted the first two Australian OBOD Assemblies. Here they share information about the early years of Druidry in Australia, from the mid 1800's onwards, and provide reflections on the current status of Druidry. Their account includes background to the first two OBOD Assemblies and the beginnings of the *SerpentStar* publication.

- Trudy Richards is a long-term and current member of Australia's Druid community. She describes her personal journey, which includes crossing State and international boundaries.

Awen through the Lens of Indigenous Culture
GGM Kate Wood-Pahuru

TO BEGIN, I WOULD LIKE to say that this is my personal experience as an Aboriginal person. We all have our own perspectives and journeys and what I write relates to mine. Some will see themselves in these words and some will not. As a mixed blood Aboriginal, the world and myself are viewed differently at times but there are no rights and wrongs if you honour your being and your path.

To be Aboriginal and a Druid seems to confuse people at times. I've seen the same reaction with other practices I undertake that connect to voodoo, Paganism or the lifestyle of Reiki. Perhaps it is my light coloured skin that is more confusing than my practices? There are many times I find that I need to explain Aboriginality first so I will do so here, and this will assist in explaining my connection to Druidry.

I am fair-skinned and green eyed, as were my Welsh ancestors, throw in some Scottish and Irish heritage, as well as a full-blood Aboriginal grandfather on my father's side and another on my grandmother's side, and you have me. As a woman, I follow my mother's lineage in colouring.

Any Aboriginal person who has felt the call home to Country and is practising their culture will tell you that it is not about colour but about what is in your heart and your mind, how you practise your beliefs and how you understand Mother Earth and all She gives us. Combine that with a further call, to me, from Mother to heal Her land and Her people and you get a powerful life purpose that, in part, is fulfilled with Druidry, a connection to my Welsh culture, past lives and current destiny in this lifetime.

I was born in Australia and, because of this, I am always Aboriginal. This does not change. It is my heritage, and Druidry is my practice. If I lived in Wales as my forebears did, I would live my Druidry and practise my Aboriginality.

From my perspective, Druidry is a way of giving identity by acknowledging culture and connecting to ancestral memory. I believe we are called to Druidry; we do not choose it. Druidry is part of my identity, it is part of me.

Over time, I have been blessed to be called to many practices in which I have gained an understanding that the underlying purpose of all is very similar.

I work and practise to honour all my cultural parentage by connecting to the indigenous source of all, the original knowledge from which all knowledge, practices and beliefs spring. This allows me to openly practise without confusion between the Earth Spirits of Aboriginality and the Nature Spirits of Druidic ancestry.

Although the practices of each may differ, the purposes are identical; honour and heal Mother Earth and all she brings in Her seasons, Her cycles, Her deities, and Her elements. Each must be acknowledged and understood to assist in these practices. How this is done is not as important as the fact that it is done.

Having said that, for those of us that are called, we are shown by the spirits and deities, often through the teaching of others, how they would like us to do this, it may be different from person to person, and then we must do so to the best of our current ability. This honours our gifts and our knowledge and assists in bringing back the practices of old, the power and magic that once was commonplace on this Earth as the connection of mortal to immortal, and in returning our identity.

Druidry is as old as time. Aboriginality is, was and always will be. They are the same, but they are different. As long as the core of purpose is sought, they are one. Division only occurs through a lack of knowledge of core purpose. Practices do not change the purpose; they are the right way to connect to this. Each person may have a different spiritual connection, and this is right. If you are called to Druidry, it is right. If you are not, it is right. There is no wrong in this, the only wrong can be to deny the call, deny your identity and deny the power and practice of connection to Mother Earth through your culture(s) and through the practices of your calling, in my case, the call of Merlin, the Nature Spirits and Druidry.

This is a perspective of an Aboriginal person born of many ancestries to undertake her soul purpose of healing through cultural knowledge and medicines of Mother Earth and the practices that honour Her ways.

Reflections on the early years of Druidry in Australia
Akkadia and Zan

TO CONTEXTUALISE THE SIGNIFICANT EMERGENCE of Druidry in Australia, particularly the beginning and growth of *The Order of Bards, Ovates and Druids* in the Southern Hemisphere, it is important to identify that there was a proliferation of Western Mysteries and Paganism in Australia since the late 1950s, with a focus upon British forms of witchcraft and traditions of Wicca (Alexandrian, Gardnerian), a growing presence of Northern European traditions of the Asatru, and a strong presence of Western ceremonial Orders, all drawing a diverse and eclectic range of participants.

For many an aspiring creative seeker living in an urban centre (Sydney) during the late 1980s, the connection point into the Western Mysteries was either through esoteric bookstores, where the occasional business card for a group may have been furtively inserted into the cover of a book, or through personal contact with an existing group or initiate—remembering these were days long before the internet. Wicca was the predominate Celtic–based tradition that had migrated to Australia and Druidry was relatively unheard of.

In making this observation, it is not implied that Druids and Druidic groups were not already present in Australia and the Southern Hemisphere throughout and prior to those years. There is evidence that Druidry was active in Australia from the mid–1850s, with a lodge of the Ancient Order of Druids opened in 1851 (https://ramblingwombat.wordpress.com/2017/11/02/united-ancient-Order-of-Druids-in-adelaide/). This is of immense significance to the current cycle of Druidry in the Southern Hemisphere. From 1882–1932 the name *United Ancient Order of Druids* was adopted, growing increasingly active in Australia and extending Druidry to Aotearoa (New Zealand) (http://www.Druidicdawn.org/node/1987).

On a journey to Aotearoa in 1997 we were overjoyed to discover first–hand the active presence of Druidry from the early 1880s, with a lavishly hand painted Charter of an Arch Druid documented at Larnach Castle in Dunedin. Druidry was an enduring presence in Dunedin, continuing half a century later, when ceremonial activities were announced in the nightly local newspaper The Evening Star on March 15, 1932, with an entire column devoted to "Druidism", including a report that "during the evening two candidates were initiated into the mysteries of Druidism", with a "bards report" following.

There is also evidence that *Caer Witrin*, a Red Druidic group drawing upon Welsh traditions, hence a 'Red' branch, as a parallel to the 'White' branches of Druidry from Albion, has been present in Australia since the mid–1980s (refer to section later in this volume). This was soon to be joined by *The Order of Bards, Ovates and Druids* (founded in 1964) becoming active in Australia soon after the rekindling in 1988 as evidenced by a comment made by Philip in the 'Foreword' (p. 13) to *The Book of Druidry* that was published in 1990; the Druid Clan of Dana (connected to the Fellowship of Isis) from 1992 (http://www.Fellowshipofisis.com/dcd1.html), and the British Druid Order, founded in 1979 (https://www.Druidry.co.uk) all became active in Australia from the early 1990s. They were later to be joined by the *Gaellic Druid Order of the Southern Cross* initiated by Ruiseart and Ceit, who were members of both the BDO and OBOD.

As in many places around the world, initiates in Australia were often members of one or more groups, or knew of each other. This history is not intended to be an exhaustive list of all the variations of Druidry that may have been practised in those years, only referring to the major groups that were publicly active in Australia and reflecting the Druids and groups with which we regularly interacted with in Australia during those years. This included training and initiation of members into OBOD, who were already initiates of Druidic groups and who kindly shared what could be spoken of the differences between OBOD and other groups.

In 1990 a High Priest and High Priestess from a Sydney wiccan coven presented us with a handwritten list of contacts to initiates and groups in the UK and Ireland, as we were about to travel overseas to Africa and Europe for an extended period. This precious list of contacts included luminaries now passed in the Western Mysteries with whom we were blessed to spend time, including to the Founders of the *Fellowship of Isis* in Ireland at Clonegal Castle and a note about an open Pagan pub moot in central London called *'Talking Stick'*, and this is where the journey into Druidry really begins...

Birth of the North–East Arbor
Seed Group (1992), then Grove (1994) entwined with the origin of the Druid Assembly in Australia.

It was during our three-month stay in London that we had regularly attended the new pagan moot *'Talking Stick'* (which started 2 weeks after we arrived in

London), held downstairs in a dimly lit and atmospheric pub called *The Plough* in central London (just around the corner from the British Museum). A rare time in the Western Mysteries when all the main traditions gathered informally to share experiences, to share a drink and most importantly to listen. Over these months, we heard representatives from a diverse range of Western Mysteries speak about their paths.

We have clear memories of hearing C. P. speak about London as a living sacred place before Roman occupation, and inviting all present to journey in heart and mind to the old forests on each side of the banks of what was once called the River Isis (now the Thames), a place where deer and bear roamed. We listened attentively as leading practitioners shared their knowledge and skills. This naturally led to invitations to participate in private conversations, meetings and rituals, and by the time we left London we had regularly participated in a range of the Mysteries, from Spring ceremonies in public woodlands, to private ceremonies in council flats.

It was during one such night that we heard the Chief of *The Order of Bards, Ovates and Druids* (OBOD) Philip Carr–Gomm speak on Druidry. Years later Philip told us, it was the only time he had spoken at Talking Stick. What he said and the open and grounded way in which he presented the tradition and practices of Druidry touched our hearts so greatly that upon return to Australia we wrote to the Order in the UK and enquired about the possibility of commencing training in Druidry, in Australia. It may be asked why did we follow Druidry of all the traditions that were presented? It was because it was the one tradition out of the many that spoke to our ancestral hearts, the epigenetic memory of the Oak. During this time, we also found a copy of the recently published *The Book of Druidry* in a London bookstore. This book became inspiration and nourishment upon the budding quest. Far from the centre of Druidry and Groves in the UK, would the Order accept our request to be trained?

We eagerly checked our mailbox each day and week and finally, about a month later, a letter arrived, accepting our request to be trained and enrolling us in the emergent OBOD correspondence course, which we began immediately and were initiated into the Bardic Grove at Alban Heruin 1991, in the North–East of Australia. In this way, our first experiences of Druidry and more specifically, of Druidry in the Southern Hemisphere, were directly connected to OBOD. Following initiation, our time as Bards was tutored directly by the Chief Philip Carr–Gomm and this continued throughout our Bardic year. We were told later that we were the third and fourth initiates in Australia (and in the Southern

Hemisphere) within OBOD, at a time when we knew of only one other in Druidry in OBOD (MB was an early Australian OBOD member) when distances could not be bridged by email, or SMS, or websites, remembering it was 1991.

As the correspondence course was printed and mailed by air once a month, we waited with increasing anticipation each month for the next package of gwersi to arrive to facilitate moving forward with our training. We were trained throughout these years during the same time periods. In 1992, we formed a Seed Group, the North–East Arbor reflecting the geographic location of where we were at the time: in the North–East and the most Easterly point of Australia, but also the ceremonial point of solar renewal in the seasonal cycle, all of which fitted the sunshine location where our seed group was born. In time this blossomed into a Grove after our Druidic initiation, the first OBOD Grove on the East Coast of Australia, called the *North–East Arbor Grove*, founded at the same time as the Order authorised a Grove in Western Australia (run by T. T.).

When the time eventually arrived to be initiated as Druids at Alban Heruin 1994, we were initiated in Sydney by a UK Druid, who himself had also been initiated by Philip, a member of the *College of Caer Lud* (an inner college of the Order that ceased to function in the late 1990s) who had recently moved to Australia. Subsequently, we were then tutored throughout the Druid training by Philip.

First Assembly (1997)
The early history of OBOD Druidry in Australia is connected to the *North–East Arbor Grove* and to our work as young Druids: you can see us robed in the photo on the cover of the first issue of *SerpentStar* on the right–hand side of the image. Our Grove inaugurated the Druid Assembly in Australia for OBOD in 1997, inspired by the annual OBOD Assembly that was held in Glastonbury in the weeks leading up to Alban Heruin. The First Druid Assembly in Australia is a significant milestone in the history of Druidry. This was the first time in the 20th Century that any Southern Hemisphere OBOD members had met in person. Some travelled from as far as New Zealand to attend. Ceremony, feasting, initiations, festivities, workshops and skill sharing took place on private property at Wisemans Ferry, within a serene bushland setting with a fresh water flowing creek. The hearth fire was ceremonially lit at the start of the Assembly and kept alight throughout.

As the location of the Assembly property was off-grid (not connected to electricity), this central fire became a focal point for ceremony, feasting and warmth, literally and philosophically, keeping everyone warm at night with temperatures dropping to 9 degrees Celsius and providing an active spiritual centre. Participants bush–camped in tents, or simply rolled out a swag sleeping under the starlit skies or slept in their vehicles. The atmosphere was uplifting, enthusiastic and you could feel the joy of people meeting for the first time, it was very much the atmosphere of spring and emergence, and was specifically timed for Alban Eiler.

It was at this Assembly that we met members who continued to work with the *North–East Arbor Grove* for many years, including J, whom we later initiated as a Druid. OBOD members, including Sandra Greenhalgh, shared their enthusiasm and energy for Druidry, and we felt an immediate kinship with those present that has lasted throughout the years. As we write these reflections, the warmth of the tinne burns in our hearts and has held what the eye and ear gained. It was at this First Assembly in 1997, that the idea for a newsletter was mooted around the central fire, again the first ceremonial fire that all Order members in the Southern Hemisphere had gathered around (and there is a photo of this fire also in *Serpent Star*) and Druid Zan Co–Chief of the North–East Arbor Grove named the newsletter *SerpentStar*. An OBOD member, C. N. (a Bard at the time), offered to perform the task of compiling and mailing the newsletter out, and this is clearly visible on the reverse side of all the early newsletters.

SerpentStar

The concept for the newsletter was clear from the beginning, to be, as the Order newsletter *TouchStone* was in the Northern Hemisphere, an open forum for all OBOD members to communicate their experiences of living Druidry, this time in the Southern Hemisphere and from this, to learn from each other and to develop understanding of how Druidry existed in these lands, beside the pre–existent Indigenous cultures and ancestral traditions. The newsletter was one of those rare moments when time, space and participants align to create something of lasting value. The early copies were hand typed and photocopied, placed into envelopes and posted by mail, very much like the early years of the gwersi. As *SerpentStar* has now been produced for over twenty years, it is clear that it met, and continues to meet, an ongoing need.

Second Assembly (1998)

The First Assembly was such a joyous and inspiring experience and with the beginning of regular contact and personal expression between members enabled through *SerpentStar*, it was logical to continue this forward momentum and plan for a Second Australian Assembly. With long distances between Australia and the UK, and for many travel to the UK out of reach due to the low currency exchange with the Australian dollar, it also seemed logical to ascertain whether Philip would be interested in travelling to Australia, to spend time with members, to present workshops, ceremonies and initiations. As Philip was supportive of this idea, our Grove hosted the visit of Philip Carr–Gomm to Australia to attend the Second Druid Assembly in 1998, raising the funds through members generously donating a $50 contribution each along with a nominal fee to cover hire of a venue and catering for the Assembly to be held.

All activities of our Grove were (and have always been) provided freely (without charge) and the Assembly was established on a minimal cost only basis, with members working throughout the Assembly days to provide the comforts of fire and food for all. I have a beautiful memory of seeing C in the kitchen stirring a cauldron of plenty pot of oats one crisp morning for breakfast. Whilst the accommodation was rudimentary, as the venue was alternately used as a Scouts camp and as an outdoor fitness/leisure facility, our hearts were all uplifted and filled with Awen. At this Assembly, we also met OBOD members who continued their work with the *North–East Arbor Grove* for many years, this included T, who has gone on to be a world leader in environmental studies.

The Second Druid Assembly was located at a larger and more public venue than the First Assembly (which was on private land), a decision that was made to reflect the growth of interest in attendance with Philip's participation and the necessity for accommodation, kitchen facilities and bathrooms for attendees. For historical accuracy, we note at this point that Philip landed in Western Australia and met with OBOD members connected to the Grove run by T. T., before continuing on to the East Coast and the Second Druid Assembly.

Prior to the Assembly, we hosted a public presentation by Philip and hired a beautiful heritage–listed venue, the Lions Gate Lodge in the Botanical Gardens in Sydney, for the workshop afternoon. Following the formal presentation inside, we all headed into the gardens and beneath the boughs of a mature spreading Oak, we all sat on the grass as Philip shared further teachings with all present. Throughout the Second Assembly, Philip led ceremonies, initiatory Groves for each Grade and shared teachings via presentations. At night, feasting, mead and wine flowed and the conversations lingered late into the night. Our Grove continued to perform private ceremonies and initiations on the land where the First Druid Assembly was held for a number of years after and we gratefully acknowledge the generosity of L and S who provided free access to their land for our Grove and for OBOD use.

As their relationship to Druidry deepened, we were subsequently invited to celebrate their wedding through a full Druidic marriage ceremony, a glorious union, where as a marriage celebrant legally recorded the marriage, our Grove in full ceremonial form led L and S through the fires of love as sixty or more of their family and friends formed an outer circle around the ceremony. Later, wheelbarrows full of barbequed salmon from an open firepit were wheeled to long feasting tables under a fairy-tale marquee in a field of tall trees. A renowned jazz band played throughout the afternoon heightening the festivities. In time, we were also invited to arrange a baby naming when their first child was born and this ceremony was performed in conjunction with other OBOD members and led by the Druid who had initiated us.

As interest in Druidry in the Southern Hemisphere was growing, with attendance doubling between the 1st and 2nd Assembly, and now with the established presence of Groves and qualified Druids in many locations around Australia, at the culmination of the 2nd Assembly we ceremonially passed the light of the Assembly on to Cooringal Grove in South Australia, with the intention that the Assembly would move each year around Australia. As the Assembly has continued on to this day in a journey embracing both Australia and Aotearoa, this also has proved to be a wise decision.

Following Years

In subsequent years we continued our work in the worlds within and without and in the millennial year 2000 our Grove hosted the visit of Emma Restall–Orr, at the time Joint Chief of the *British Druid Order*, to Australia and like Philip in 1998, Emma stayed with us at our home in Newtown, Sydney. Emma's visit marked the beginning of new horizons; we learned of new approaches deepening our connections to Druidry. This included of the *British Druid Order* (BDO) apprentice system and of the passionate wildways of BDO Druidry that mingled approaches of craft and Druidic lores. Given the history of Wicca and the long friendship between Gerald Gardner (founder of Gardnerian Wicca) and Ross Nichols, founder of *The Order of Bards, Ovates and Druids* and interconnected esoteric work, including in the Ancient Druid Order and collaborations on the Gardnerian *Book of Shadows*, we could sense in the BDO work a continuation of an undercurrent in contemporary Druidry and a generational shift in mingling anew of the currents of witchcraft and Druidry. We recently found in our Grove archives a rare filmed interview recording that we made at Newtown of Emma discussing Druidry.

We have both always been keen scholars, training and completing a range of University degrees. This natural curiosity echoes the intellectual life of many foundational Druids, including Ross Nichols and Vera Chapman (first Pendragon of OBOD), distinguished as one of the first women to enter Oxford University and founder of the Tolkien Society. Our perception of Druidry throughout time is that it elevates heart and mind and nourishes the many worlds in which initiates live; the inherent trainings of Druids and the sustained enquiries into philosophies of nature draw a particular temperament.

In this intellectual/scholarly/esoteric environment, in the context of our Grove, which was public throughout the 90s and into the early 2000s, we have met a wide range of people, from a scholar with a doctorate in Icelandic witchcraft through to initiates researching and restoring Celtic arts and practises. We spent a lengthy time pursuing metal crafts, including studying bronze casting and the creation of ceremonial objects including hand–making our Grove sword. Our eager pursuit of Art, Culture, Science and Philosophy has led our lives. These times filled with passionate engagement and inter–traditional interactivity provided fuel for the tinnes of our lives that have continued to illuminate our paths.

A Druid College was formed with the intention to work though relevant matters, called *Corona Australis*, with Foundation Druids across Australia from a number of Druidic traditions (including ourselves, OBOD and BDO) but Druidry in these lands is not easily syncretised, or perhaps not at all, so correspondence on this ceased. Well–qualified Druids have remained silent, whilst those newer upon the path grapple with many matters, for outside the framework of the established correspondences, all else are simply personal ways of working, with inherent philosophy of Druidry as a foundation.

After a decade of very public activities and service within OBOD, including seven years as an Ovate tutor, around 2001 we changed our focus to more inner work and continued our lives as Druids, through regular journeys–continuing–to the old lands of Ireland, England, Scotland and Wales and through a working we named *Hermetic Druidry*, to reflect the inner path of the spiral.

In 2011 we celebrated the important milestone of our twenty years in Druidry on the summit of Dun I, on Iona, Scotland. A place of profound meaning in Druidry, and for many years was the location of an annual OBOD retreat and the place from which we were gifted at the time of our Druidic initiations. In 2013, while attending the Druid Conference in the UK and staying with OBOD/BDO Druids nearby, we finally were able to meet Philip Shallcrass and the opportunity to see Emma after so many years, which was beautiful.

At the time of writing this contribution (Imbolc 2019), we now have twenty–eight years of experience in living Druidry within the Southern Hemisphere and more particularly, in Australia; of these years, having passed through the twenty–year milestone so significant in the ancient cycle of Druidic training, we now have twenty–five years lived as initiated Druids. Throughout all these years we have remained organically in touch with various OBOD and BDO members, and it has been amazing to see where those trained in Bardic, Vatic and Druidic lore have made their way in the world.

We have often reflected upon the challenges of Druidry as a tradition in lands so far from the old countries and where the sacred trees grow in only few places and then where some simply do not grow at all. The vast distances that Druids traverse in these lands and, indeed, to gain access to the lands and sacred places of our ancestors, is profound. Having no recourse to established sacred sites or standing stones, we have had to start as Druids in this land from the beginning, learning the lore of our ancestors in the lands of the ancestors of other peoples. We made the decision at the outset, continuing to this day, to not attempt to syncretise the customs of Australian Indigenous peoples, nor to use their lore or sacred places in workings of Druidry. This decision, which was criticised by some in the early years, has proven to be the path in tune with the Spirit of this land and time.

This has been especially evident in the North–East of Australia where both our Seed Group and Grove were born. As recently as 2019, Elders and representatives of the Bundjalung nation have publicly stated that they do not want non–Indigenous people using their lore and symbols joining a worldwide initiative to protect First Nations customs called *'Culture Aware'* (http:/cultureaware.org/about; http:/cultureaware.org/statements/aunty-delta-kay). This initiative centralises Indigenous agency and their ancestral rights as living custodians to control their sacred heritage, whilst inviting other people to be in 'right relationship' to First Nations peoples through not appropriating culture. This also meets a time when the custodians of Uluru have continued to assert their sacred connection to this place and are closing off access to the public desecration through a ban that will finally end climbing of Uluru from 26th October 2019 (https:/parksaustralia.gov.au/uluru/discover/culture/uluru-climb/).

From the outset of our lives as Druids, we intuitively knew that for our path to be a vital and living reality in these lands. We needed to respect that we are guests here and that our practices of Druidry must not interfere with the existing Indigenous lore. Over the years, we have had the opportunity to sit with, listen to and learn from Elders from Australia, Africa and to journey and dream upon the lands of Navajo peoples, to open our hearts and minds to what it means to practise ancestral ways in the twenty-first century.

One of the mysteries that has been revealed is that the Spirit of this Time has called all to embark upon a quest to reclaim and remember ancestral ways as an antidote to environmental crisis and species extinction–whether Druids, First Nations, Australian Indigenous peoples–there is a recognition of the immense disruption and desecration of colonialism upon Indigenous ways and what this has cost the earth and elemental worlds. This recognition must include the intergenerational oppression that was wrought upon the ways of our Irish/Scottish/Welsh ancestors–who were indigenous to the lands of their ancestors–and who also lost land, language and heritage through colonial invasion and oppression. The enforced starvations of the Great Famine in Ireland, the centuries of cultural imperialism enforced upon Wales, with her language and culture being actively undermined by the British State, and the highland land clearances in Scotland, all caused the necessity to migrate far from our homes to new lands, beyond what must have seemed the ninth waves.

In 1990 we sailed from Le Havre in France towards Rosslare Harbour in Southern Ireland, our first journey home. We were filled with the sense of our Irish ancestors' grief and the realisation that this is what they would have seen – but in reverse – the last glimpses of the lush green Eire their homeland slipping away forever, never to return. So, we have made that journey for them, for all our ancestors. We are the ones who have returned, who have made the homecoming, who have lit the tinnes at Alban Heruin and who have walked the lands anew. We are the ones who have protected the tinnes in our hearts and minds and who speak publicly about this quest with deep respect for that which has been given over the years.

So, what does that mean for us as Druids in Australia? The profound experiences of living as Druids over these decades, has necessitated continual learning and practises, of planting sacred Groves, engaging in multiple ecological restoration projects to restore littoral subtropical rainforest, of watching the cycles of these trees rise and fall with the seasons; of learning the lore of star and stone in this land and in the old lands of our ancestors, and never forgetting that beyond time, Druidry exists.

As we write this necessarily brief history of the early years of Druidry in Australia, we are mindful of the Past–Present and Future aligning and that this will be published in a collection in 2020, the same year that the current OBOD Chief Philip Carr–Gomm will pass the Chieftainship to the next Chosen Chief Eimear Burke. We express thanks to Elkie and Sandra for embarking upon this collection of Australian Druidic writings and for the invitation to contribute. At this time, we would like to express our deep gratitude to Philip for the courageous and tireless work that he has performed since 1988 in bringing Druidry to all of us, and on a personal note, for his central role in our earlier training. Our wishes for the continued successes of OBOD and Awen and Imbas for the incoming Chief Eimear and to all future Chiefs in continuing the line of traditions for the next generations are offered. With such deep well–watered roots we have been able to grow and to sustain our lives, as not only Druids living in Australia, but as Druids and for this,

By Star and Stone beannacht.

Akkadia & Zan / | \

My Druid Journey
Trudy Richards

I WAS HAVING A MASSAGE WITH a woman I'd met at a Psychic Awareness and Tarot Workshop when she suddenly stopped and said, "Oh my god, you were a Druid in a past life!" Well, I went all goosebumps and tingles, it was like a bell ringing in my head and electricity sparking through my body; I knew instantly that it was true. And so, I began my Druid journey.

I'd heard of Druids before, but didn't really know much about them, apart from that it said in the bible that Jesus had gone to study with them. I'd been brought up in a family that was involved with the Salvation Army, but I was dissatisfied with the limited view of life that Christianity portrayed. I was exploring different perspectives of the world and opening my eyes to a different reality to what I had been brought up to believe. I bought a book, *The Modern-Day Druidess* by Cassandra Eason, which just happened to be in the current catalogue of my book subscription. And at the back of the book was a reference to OBOD. I enrolled into the Bardic Grade soon after.

I started receiving *Touchstone* and saw an upcoming event in Australia, an Assembly at Kingaroy, Queensland, but I didn't have available funds to attend. There was a Grove in Melbourne, and I made contact with Elkie White through email. I didn't meet her then though, and as I was living at Trentham, nearly two hours away from Ferntree Gully, I didn't go to any *The Melbourne Grove* (TMG) events. I was quite happy studying my gwersi and doing ritual on my own. The course was everything I'd been looking for, the subject matter intriguing and relevant to me in a way that was new but also familiar in other ways. The more I learnt, the more I wanted to learn, and that is still true for me.

The next year the Assembly was being held at Currarong, south of Sydney, and I decided I was ready to meet other people who were studying with OBOD. Within five minutes of meeting Carole, who picked me up from the nearest train station, I realised that I had found my family. Over the next few days we shared ritual, made a dragon, wrote a song, cooked, ate, drank mead, made a spiral out of seaweed on the beach and sang, drummed and chanted our way around that spiral while dancing with the dragon. Such fun!

On my return to Melbourne I finally attended a Melbourne Grove event, *Caving at Cape Schank*, and have enjoyed many Melbourne Grove events since.

Celebrating and sharing ritual with like-minded people is satisfying and nurturing for the soul.

I moved to Kyneton (still two hours away from TMG) and rented a farm of forty acres. It was mostly cleared land with quite a few trees and lots of rocks and boulders in the paddocks. Before long, I had rolled some of the rocks to a special area in between a gum tree and a hawthorn tree and made my own sacred circle, complete with a fire in the middle. This was overlooking Lauristion Reservoir, which was conveniently to the West.

There were lots of birds on the farm, as the owners used to feed them, and they kindly continued to provide the seed for me to keep feeding them. The white cockatoos were regular visitors, and would perch on the branches of the dead gum tree near the clothesline while waiting for their food. In the mornings, if I was taking too long to feed them, one would fly up to the guttering of the house and perch above the window near the kitchen sink, turn around and look in at me upside down, as if to say, "Well come on then, we're waiting!"

One evening, I noticed one down on the ground in the driveway, and it didn't fly away when I approached, just shuffled around behind a tree. I wanted to check it closer, but each time I got too close it squawked and got upset, so I let it be. In the morning, I couldn't find it anywhere, but when I got home from work it was dead under another tree in the driveway. I picked it up and cried and cried and cried. Then I took it into my sacred circle, dug a hole, and buried it in the East, under the rock I had placed there. (In my personal rituals, in the East I call the white cockatoo into my circle when opening the quarters.) And so, the Grove of the White Cockatoo was birthed.

I'd travel to Melbourne to share ritual with *The Melbourne Grove*, but I'd also begun hosting some of the seasonal celebrations at the farm. It was wonderful having so much space and privacy, and people were always welcome to stay overnight before or after a gathering. For Lughnasadh, I organised the inaugural Melbourne Grove Lughnasadh games, which involved challenges such as gumboot throwing, three legged races and a 'tossing windfall apples into the bucket' competition. My two sons attended and had a lot of fun with us. For Beltaine, I collected lots of wood and made two large bonfires to walk between during the ritual. Spring Equinox was celebrated in the early morning with the sun rising in the East while the moon was setting in the West. We celebrated a Samhuin enclosed within a grove of gorse, and a Winter Solstice with another bonfire that was full of dancing dragons. The only ceremony I didn't host at the farm was Imbolc, because Brigid's Well, in the Dandenong Ranges, where TMG usually celebrates Imbolc, is such a special place, and the presence of the divine goddess when we do her ritual there is inspiring, supportive, loving and unforgettable.

A highlight was when Damh the Bard and Cerri Lee stayed overnight, after Damh's very first concert in Melbourne. What a wonderful day that was! Elkie and I, and a few other Melbourne Grove members, met Damh and Cerri at the airport, enjoyed their company for a few hours, then had the best concert with the wonderful Spiral Dance, followed by Damh the Bard himself. It was my first experience of being in a room with so many people all singing along to my favourite bard's songs... amazing! The next morning, I got my mandolin out and had a bit of a jam with Damh on his guitar, and showed him and Cerri around the farm, before they left to fly to Sydney.

OBOD assemblies have become the highlight of the year for me, and I try to attend them all. After Currarong, I travelled to Port Lincoln, South Australia for the Assembly at Cooringal, was there when *The Melbourne Grove* hosted at Lady Cu's at Cockatoo, then attended Binna Burra, Bribie Island, Sydney, Adelaide and New Zealand. I attended the Druid Camp hosted by the Wind Harp Seed Group in South Australia in 2019. Spending time with my Druid family has become one of the most important things in my life. I can be myself, talk about Druidy things, get excited about finding an unusual stone, or a pretty feather, gaze in wonder at the moon and the stars or the setting sun, and no one looks at me like I am weird. Because we are all pretty much on the same page and understand each other.

I lived at the farm for about five years, until the owner sold it and I was forced to move. This was very hard for me. I'd completed my Bardic and Ovate grades by now, and had started Druid grade. As I dismantled my fire circle and rolled the bigger stones away from the outer circle, I had tears in my eyes. I'd slept overnight by the fire in that circle, watched eclipses and sunsets, drummed under the full moon, shared mead with Pan and got drunk… I still have one of the smaller stones from the outer circle. The rest were just too big to lift and carry. One day when I am settled with my own place, and know I won't have to move again, I'll build a new circle of standing stones, and maybe start an OBOD Seed Group.

I put all my stuff in storage and travelled for 4 months, to Northern Ireland, Wales, Scotland, England, Brittany and Majorca. I explored ancient megaliths and stone circles, climbed legendary mountains and swam in mythical seas. On return to Australia I lived in a pokey flat in Daylesford as there was nothing else affordable, then a year later I moved to Cairns in the far tropical north of Qld.

The heat was at times oppressive and unbearable, at other times stuffy and insufferable, and for a few short months each year, pleasant and enjoyable. I developed a great all over tan, while experiencing amazing skyclad rituals in the privacy of my backyard at Clifton Beach, around the corner from Palm Cove, all year round.

I experienced at least six distinct seasons, all completely different to any I'd experienced in Victoria. I developed relationships with unusual birds and trees, mountains and rivers, and learnt how to grow exotic tropical food. I volunteered at the Cairns Turtle Rehabilitation Centre on Fitzroy Island and fell in love with an amazing Olive Ridley sea turtle called Lou. And it was while living here that I completed the Druid Grade. I travelled back to Victoria a few times each year, to see family, share a ritual with the Melbourne Grove when possible, and experience a bit of cold weather. I journeyed to South Australia to share Samhuin with the Golden Wattle Seed Group at Wyvern's property, Wyeuro, in the Mallee. And another year I celebrated Beltaine with Macadamia Grove at their site at Mt Coot-tha, near Brisbane.

After four years I returned south to Victoria, to be closer to my family. It was an epic road trip down the East coast of Australia, from Edmonton to Trentham. I've been staying with an old friend at Healesville in the Yarra Valley and house sitting at various locations in the mountains East of Melbourne since. It's been fantastic to again share ritual and ceremony more regularly with *The Melbourne Grove*; I really missed the company of fellow Druids, as much as I enjoy being solitary at times. And now I'm looking for my new home where I can really put down my roots and begin the next chapter of my life. No matter what, I know that I will continue to practice my Druidry. It's a part of me as much as my blood and my bones.

SOUTHERN HEMISPHERE OBOD ASSEMBLIES

Southern Hemisphere Assemblies hold a special place in Australian Druid history, as these events often brought people studying *The Order of Bards, Ovates and Druids* (OBOD) course together in person for the very first time. Assemblies have been significantly formative for the spiritual and physical landscapes of Druidry in Australia for over twenty years.

This section includes personal experiences relating to attending or hosting an Assembly. Other accounts of Southern Hemisphere Assemblies are available in contributions and questionnaire responses throughout this publication particularly in the following pages:

- The timeline of groups and significant events (page 6)
- *Reflections on the early years of Druidry in Australia* article by Akkadia and Zan, which includes background to the first and second OBOD Assemblies (page 15)
- *SerpentStar* Article by Carole Nielsen (page 46)
- *The Melbourne Grove* article by Elkie White. This article includes information about all Assemblies (page 105)

The Second Australian OBOD Assembly
Sandra Greenhalgh

IF I WASN'T SUCH A RULE BREAKER, I'd write about attending the 1997 inaugural Assembly as being my first experience with OBOD members in Australia. That weekend had me moving out of my solitary Australian Druid status to meeting with other 'real life' Aussie OBODies. But that first Assembly, wonderful as it was, is a blur of rain-drizzled memories. Only a few clear glimpses remain, such as key people and features such as camping in a Birch tree grove; the 'all hands in' approach; sitting around the porridge pot under a small tarp; the inclement weather; and wearing an Akubra hat to shield the ritual script from the rain.

So, I will speak of the Assembly in 1998. Perhaps that is more apt anyways, as the second Assembly marked the first Australian visit by Philip Carr-Gomm, the OBOD Chosen Chief. Compared to the anxiety I felt at attending my first Assembly, by my second Assembly I was an old hand. This time I flew down instead of undertaking the mega-drive from Brisbane to Sydney and stayed the night before the Assembly at Akkadia and Zan's apartment in Newtown. Staying in that part of Sydney in the 1990s was an eye opener in itself, as I experienced the hodgepodge cauldron of diverse cultures which was so different from my Brisbane home town.

Then it was off on a wild grocery shopping trip with Zan before heading up the mountains and into the bush. We also bought a beautiful candle lantern, which could help shield and disperse the light from this Assembly to the next one, which was to be held in South Australia.

How lovely it was to greet those OBODies I'd met for the first time at the inaugural Assembly! How lovely, also, to meet and make new friends. Despite wonderful and special rituals and workshops, to me, it's always the people, my fellow OBOD family-tribe, who are the cherished aspect of my experiences with Druidry in Australia. And of course, there was the delightful bonus of spending time with Philip in my home country, after first meeting him in England in the late 1980s.

Thankfully, the accommodation was a bit more luxurious than that of the first Assembly, being bunk houses rather than soggy tents. We also had an undercover meeting place with a roof, rather than a tarp stretched between the trees. And we had a kitchen as well as the great fortune of having an OBOD member who was a proper cook. This person was able to turn the selection of groceries into a series of wholesome and yummy food for us all.

Yes, there were the amazing and deeply felt shared ritual experiences, including Initiations, which are a feature of our Assemblies. Workshops there were aplenty, presented by a range of people including Philip and yours truly. I spoke of the differences and similarities between witchcraft and Druidry, which was very well received by the attendees.

We also enjoyed the Eisteddfod and costumed dress-up event, which featured the 'tradition' of an inspired speaker who presented an over-lengthy tale. Nowadays, there is usually a time limit placed on Bardic presentations to minimise the chance of this occurring… though of course the 'Master Bard of Australia', Michael V, is exempt from such timing restrictions.

My shinier memories include those shared experiences which weren't part of the program; singing chants with Elkie and some other OBODies as we washed the dinner dishes; sharing a bottle of honey mead with Carole; the happy laughter and deep conversations; chatting with Tuan about *Macadamia Seed Group* (which is now the flourishing *Macadamia Grove*); having my numerology forecast completed by a very gifted attendee; and exploring the trees and features of the glorious surroundings.

After the Assembly, I 'chucked a sickie', which is something that I rarely do. This terminology is Australian slang for taking a day off for reported ill health although you are perfectly healthy. Fortunately, I was able to reschedule my Brisbane flight home for the next day. This meant that I spent the night back in Newtown with my OBOD kin, drinking black Sambuca and reminiscing about the joy filled, wonderful, inspirational weekend we had spent together.

Wyeuro and the 2003 OBOD Assembly
Vyvyan Ogma Wyverne

IN THE YEAR 2003, THE late Helen Sutanovic and I had the honour of hosting the fourth OBOD Australian Assembly. I'd finished the Druid grade and Nellie was not far behind, enjoying the Ovate grade. I must admit to having had some misgivings—neither of us had ever done anything like it before, and Wyeuro seemed an unlikely place for it. We had no facilities, no hot water, not even solar power back then, so no electric lighting, hay bales for seating and no protection from rain should it occur.

But everything conspired to bring our plans to fruition, all the omens were good and, after all, the thirty-three hectares of unspoiled native Mallee and sandalwood scrub seemed likely to compensate for any shortcomings. Nellie quickly put herself into a supporting role, and I was very grateful to the wonderful Elkie White for her assistance and quick thinking around a number of quite significant glitches at the time. The weather helped by being nigh on perfect, with only the lightest of short-lived sprinklings of rain.

Not many more than a dozen people came to Assemblies in those days, and we had the privilege of hosting the first tutor convention, as tutor coordinator Susan Jones came from England with her husband Ian to address us all, particularly the tutors. The presence of these delightful people was a true blessing.

Lacking rooms and facilities, the whole Assembly was outdoors, under the orchard trees or round the campfire, with the wide-open spaces and our abundant wildlife setting the scene for the Druid ceremonial and Bardic performance. The days were cool enough to make the campfire a pleasure to sit around, but not too cold for comfort when away from it.

Highlights included performance on the harp by the immensely talented Rafayard; her daughter's bardic initiation which made her the youngest ever OBOD Bard at age nine; three other Bardic initiations; my own re-naming ceremony; the launch of *Southern Echoes*, our first poetry anthology, which Murray Barton and N.E. presented for us—a beautiful production and still worth reading; lots of enthusiastic campfire singing—we even wrote a song together under Raf's kindly guidance; talking circles in which we shared our thoughts and feelings about our Druidry that brought forth some very articulate ideas which were thought-provoking and sometimes deeply moving, and encounters with friendly kangaroos and multitudes of birds. Queensland artist, Cherry Carroll, brought some of her amazing hand-made character bears to raffle for charity.

Because we were working on a small budget and in primitive conditions, we weren't able to provide catering, but all pitched in with ingredients and recipes and shared some wholesome home-cooking, and even made soda bread in our hand-built mud-brick oven.

As with any Assembly of like-minded people, the success of the event was assured by the goodwill and enthusiasm of the people themselves, many of whom met each other for the first time, and some of whom were attending their first Assembly. People came from as far away as Queensland and Western Australia, and from NSW and Victoria and all over South Australia, all contributing unstintingly to the magic of that Assembly.

Wyeuro was not quite a Grove at that time. When Nellie finally became a Druid, we often considered registering as a Grove, but never felt quite ready. However, we did host a highly successful weekend camp for Samhain in 2017 for the Golden Wattle Seed Group, where Kacey Stephensen thrilled us with his music and we all contributed to ceremonies sparkling with all the exciting magic that comes from commitment and the inspiration of the Awen.

Now, since Nellie's tragic early death, Wyeuro has only one Druid again, and so cannot become a Grove. Fortunately, there are now some much better equipped Seed Groups in existence, so I've joined the Golden Wattle Seed Group, which celebrates the seasons with the Wind Harp Seed Group, which holds them at Greenman Grove in Rosedale and puts on a splendid show for us. But the future is a long time, and there's no knowing what good things are in store!

NEWSFLASH...Hedgie flushed out: enjoys himself at Assembly!

Jeremy Runnalls

I KNOW MOST HEDGIES, and perhaps others, will take this headline as typically sensational and misleading, however, if you have the time or inclination, please read on. I've been a Hedgie for many years now, and passing through the grades found my Druidic journey to be enlightening and comfortable, in that it effectively agreed with and helped define my beliefs and rose to be commensurate with my thoughts and need for spiritual growth. The key aspect was that it enabled me to have a personal and private journey without interruption or the need to perform to others' pace or expectation, which after many years in a quite regulated and performance related industry was refreshing and exactly what I needed.

I had wondered on occasions about attending an Assembly but dismissed it more for personal preference rather than logistics. Reading the accounts in *Touchstone* or other sources, the reviews of wonderful experiences (made lasting friends, was amazed at people's talents, felt loved and amongst family etc) seemed either like the expected responses or codified compliments that come so easily to the English tongue, yet have not been mastered or really understood by Australians. I won't bore you with repeating them albeit that they, surprisingly, all turned out to be oh-so-true for me. So, I decided with trepidation to go to an Assembly hinging off the most obvious and believable comment of 'met like-minded people'

Having decided, I procured appropriate dress and emailed the organiser with an offer of participation, expecting minimal involvement as I was unknown to the Grove. The answer returned thanking me, and informing me that I would be involved in 'all' the initiations and rituals. Hedgies and introverts will understand that hollow feeling I felt on receiving this news.

My journey began, a myriad of excuses that ran through my head almost reduced in desperation to the oldie-but-goodie 'I think I can hear my mum calling me', however as she had passed over some years ago it lacked credibility now, and besides my wife has heard it before. I arrived and obtained a personal space away from the bunk rooms and main camp, a safe haven I thought, until a fellow camper arrived and effectively amalgamated our camps into one. My initial horror and dismay soon turned to joy and appreciation. This was the first of many instances that proved the truth in all those supposed rhetorical responses I had read.

Ceremonies, rituals, lectures, discussions, Eisteddfod and the most magnificent Beltane celebration crowned with an enormous and fierce fire arch, created by our own Valkyrie. Eight Bardic, six Ovate and two Druid Initiations later I was exhausted physically, mentally and spiritually. Although the assault on my senses and no doubt that of any introvert or Hedgie was immense, but in the same token uplifting and extremely special.

People of 'the tribe' had travelled thousands of kilometres, from Cairns to Adelaide and even New Zealand, it's so hard to explain the benefits and feelings but I urge anyone who has not attended an Assembly and could possibly do so, please do and almost regard it as a must in your Druidic journey. Which now leaves me with not understanding how to differentiate truth from requisite politeness of the codified compliments and comments of the English tongue - perhaps that is a mystery we antipodean cousins will never know.

Fire Archway from the 2016 Assembly

Photo Credit: Linda Marson

Welcoming the Chosen Chief to Western Australia in 2000
Tiki Swain

I'D SAID I'D MEET PHILIP, Stephanie and their daughters at the airport when they came here for the 2000 Assembly in Albany. I wanted to greet them each with a flower - the State flower, the Red and Green Kangaroo Paw, *Anigozanthus manglesii*.

Unfortunately, it was just a little after their season—maybe only by two weeks, so after about ten phone calls I finally found a florist that had a few in their freezer and could give me four. They barely charged me because they were worried the flowers wouldn't be any good.

It was a very warm day and the plane was marked as running late, so I put them in my fridge and found something to do. Then I got a call from Philip and Stephanie very politely asking where I was. The plane was early, not late! I grabbed the flowers and went to the airport. They were wilting badly in the heat by the time I got there and had lost a lot of their iridescence.

I remember everyone being very polite and a little confused. Especially when I explained that these flowers were very symbolic of the country they had come to, because while traditionally one might draw a red flower on a green stem, these were in fact green flowers on a red stem. They carefully looked at the buds, some open and some not in the way of k-paws, and Philip asked what colour the flowers would be when they opened.

They were quite surprised when I said "No, that's it, the colour you see there, that's the flowers open." I had momentarily forgotten that people from other countries expect more petals on their flowers! So, it was a good introduction to things being a little upside down from what they were used to.

Inaugural Australian Druid Assembly Promotion

Order of Bards, Ovates & Druids
Presents
Inaugural Australian Druid Assembly
Alban Eiler, Fri.19th, Sat.20th, Sun. 21st September 1997

Assembly Update : Dear Member,
   Due to the majority of responses to the initial Assembly invitation being from the Eastern States of Australia and from New Zealand, for practical reasons the location of this event has been changed. It will now occur at a private location in N.S.W. and not in Western Australia as was previously stated. The site for the Assembly is now a 50 acre property near Wisemans Ferry, which offers a beautiful forest and river setting for our celebrations.
   If you did not respond to the initial invitation because you thought you would be unable to attend due to the distance previously involved; please register your interest in participating as soon as possible .
Any member wishing to contribute to the Assembly's activities by offering a talk, workshop, ceremony, music or with practical aspects in setting up etc. please send your proposal (idea/draft) now.
As this will be the first time all Order members in Australia & New Zealand will have had the opportunity to get together, the Assembly program is open to input from all members, as much as you wish to contribute - it is *your Assembly*.
   Please take some time to reflect on the benefits that participation in both the Assembly and the Chief's visit in 1998 will have for you and your Druidic work and attend this important Inaugural event.

Proposals are sought from Seed Groups, Grove and individual members who are interested in offering Workshop, Ritual, Meditation, Music, Performance, Poetry or a Presentation on a topic relevent to Druidry. For further information and to submit proposals for the 1997 Assembly

N.E.A. Grove

Image credit: Sandra Greenhalgh

[Editor's comment: it cost $45 to attend the inaugural Assembly]

The Inaugural Australian Druid Assembly Program Notes

Program Notes:

It is with joyous hearts that we welcome all participants to the 1997 Assembly - the first time in the Order's history when members of all Grades & from all states of Australia & New Zealand - will have gathered together to celebrate the Light of Druidry. The workshops being offered will give unique insights into the diverse range of talents within the Order and also, the skills which encompass being a Druid today.

As is the Order's custom, all members of the Bardic, Ovate & Druid Grades are invited to participate in welcoming new members into the Bardic Grade at the Initiation and all Ovate & Druid Grade members are likewise invited to participate in the Initiation of the new Ovates : please note these are the only items in the program *not open* to non-member/spouses - & we request, in advance, that you respect this by being aware of the need to leave the Ceremonial area for a couple of hours after the Opening Ceremony - whilst this is in progress.

Eating With the Elements - with Carole .... : through analysis of what we eat, elemental strengths & deficiencies in our diet may be detected & rebalanced; in this workshop the concepts behind eating consciously & in harmony with the elements will be introduced. This has important ritual applications & enables us to select specific foods which correspond to each of the elements Earth, Water, Air, Fire & Spirit.

Celtic Chess - with .... : this will mainly focus on three games of the Caryl group of Indo-European games anciently played by the Celts of Ireland & Britain, if not all Celtia. The Irish games Sidchell & Brandub, the Welsh Gwyddbwl & Cawlbred, the British Cawlbort. The mythology concerning these games - the Thirteen Treasures of Britain, the Three Treasures of Ireland, the Game of Owain versus King Arthur, the Game of King Conchabar, the Invention of the game by Lugh the Celtic Mercury, the Battle Between Light & Dark, Danann & Somer, Celt & Viking, the Cultural aspects of the Game - what it tells us about Celtic Chieftainship & land ownership, the Board's relationship to the Land and the Eightfold Calendar. In addition to this, the numerological aspects of the Games & their relationship to magickal squares & grids and the 4 Axe of Light will be examined. A Game will be played after the Workshop & J. ...... has generously offered to donate a Gameboard to the Winner. His company - ...., makes these boards & they will be available for sale during the 'Village Market' part of the Assembly. Prices range from $10-$20 for a cardboard or cloth board, up to $300 for an intricately carved wooden board.

Australian Native Tree Essences - with R .... : be introduced to these Essences & learn a comprehensive natural system which includes the essences of certain Australian Native Trees, the Wisdom & Counsel of the animal, mineral, insect, bird, plant & Devic Kingdoms, Colour & Sound influences, as well as lunar Cycles, all focused on correcting imbalances & assisting our own intuitive knowledge to create self-growth & increased well-being - not only for ourselves, but also for the Planet. Rosemary has been involved in the research & development of these powerful Essences for the past five years.

Village Market - members are encouraged to bring along handicrafts of a Celtic nature to either barter or sell during the Assembly weekend; examples are handmade incenses & candles; ritual jewellery & items; sacred artwork; herbal essences etc. This is a good opportunity to also network our collective skills & specialities for future reference.

Open Forum - in this important part of the program all members are invited to raise Issues of concern/relevance to the practise of Druidry today, as members of O.B.O.D. A 'Talking Stick' will be used to enable members to be able to individually speak out, be heard & debate these issues. Some Topics worth raising when we are all gathered include ; how to fund the proposed 1998 visit to Australia of the Chosen Chief, Philip & the continued development of the Australian practise of Druidry & our Community. Please think in advance about this Forum and the Topics you would like to raise.

Image credit: Sandra Greenhalgh

Photo of the camp at the Inaugural Australian Druid Assembly

Image credit: Carole Nielsen

Pre-ritual at the Inaugural Australian Druid Assembly

Inaugural Australian Druid Assembly Program of Events

Order of Bards Ovates & Druids - Inaugural Australian Assembly Program Alban Eiler 1997

Day 1

10:00-2:00pm
Arrival:
setting up camp

3:00pm
Welcome Ceremony

4:00pm
Bardic Grove:
Bardic Grade Initiations

6:00pm onwards
Evening Feast:
Celebration of new Bards with music, poetry, food & storytelling.

Day 2

10:00am
Join together for
Light Body/Awen

Workshops

10:30-11:30am
'Eating With The Elements' with Carole ..

12:00-1:00pm
'Celtic Chess' with J

1:00-2:00pm
Lunch & 'Village market'

2:00-3:00pm
'Australian Native Tree Essences' with R.

4:00-6:00pm
Bardic Grove:
'Australian Bush Regeneration & Tree Identification skills' with S.
Ovate Grove:
Ovate Grade Initiations

6:00pm onwards
Feast, celebration of new Ovates.

Day 3

10:00am
Light Body/Awen

10:30-12:00pm
Sacred Grove:
Tree Planting Ceremony

12:00-1:00pm
Lunch

1:00-3:00pm
Open Forum

3:00pm
Preparation for Equinox & closing ceremonies.

4:00pm
Alban Eiler Ceremony

Sunset Closing Ceremony
Feast & Departure.

Image credit: Sandra Greenhalgh

The Second Australian Druid Assembly Notes

Program Notes : What To Bring

Welcome to the Second Annual Australian Druid Assembly !

We extend the warmest of welcomes and a hearty Druidic Blessing to all participants in this year's exciting event – for us in Australia a most important occasion, when for the first time in the Order's history the current Chosen Chief, Philip Carr-Gomm will be visiting our beautiful country and participating in the four days of the Assembly. The significance of having a Chief Druid present to lead the Groves and Rituals at the Assembly represents a 'coming of age' for O.B.O.D. here, or perhaps we should say a 'home-coming' for us all.

Whilst distance has always presented us in Australia with its own particular difficulties, we see at this pivotal junction in human history, with the Twenty-First Century rapidly approaching, that Druidry is reawakening in these distant shores and developing at an exciting pace. The events of this year's Assembly and the Chosen Chief's visit, will no doubt go a long way to increasing and inspiring that momentum; as last year's Assembly also did in its own way. In this we each have a part to play; for our own spiritual-magickal progress, for the Tradition which we love and for the Land in which we practise it.

May hearts unite in joy and peace to celebrate all we have and that which we shall retain long after the Assembly has ended for another year: that wondrous experience of the deep peace of the Grove and the Unity we have as Members and as *friends*, our lives enriched and lit by the Awen we intone beneath the Southern Stars.

North-East Arbor Grove, Order of Bards, Ovates & Druids ...
/|\

Essential items to bring with you :
Robe & Tabard
Alban Eiler Ceremony of Bardic Grade
Grove Openings (if you have them from last year)
Musical Instruments, Poetry, Sacred Songs
Your 'Celtic Hero' (something to say as well as wear!)
Sleeping requirements (pillow, sleeping bag or doona, torch)-the bush-huts are not equipped with any sleeping gear, except a small bed-mat, we recommend bringing an air bed or extra bed-roll for extra comfort. Tents are welcome, most members have requested a bush-hut and we have allocated these as you booked; campsites are plentiful, so if you prefer your own tent, bring it. BYO Mead/Wine (note-there is no mead at Wiseman's Ferry Pub!)

Image credit: Sandra Greenhalgh
[Editor's comment: the last line states:
"*note - there is no mead at Wiseman's Ferry Pub!*"]

Second Australian Druid Assembly Program (Friday and Saturday)

Second Annual Australian Druid Assembly
In Celebration of the 10th Anniversary of the Order's Refounding &

Program : FRIDAY, Sept. 18th

10am-2pm: Arrive at Castle Mountain Settle in/set up Campsites.

2.30pm: OFFICIAL WELCOME OF CHOSEN CHIEF TO AUSTRALIA & OPENING OF ASSEMBLY in Bardic Grove.

3.00pm: INTRODUCTRY WORKSHOP "Following the Druid Path Today" by Philip Carr-Gomm.

6.00pm: EVENING FEAST with "Toning Circle" discovering Sacred Sound led by Lesley

SATURDAY, Sept. 19th

10am: CIRCLE OF LIGHT Morning Light-Body Exercise & Orientation to day's Program.

10.30am: CIRCLE OF LIFE Special Meditation led by the Chief.

11-12: "Druidry & Wicca" by Sandra

Midday-1pm: LUNCH.

1.00-4.00pm: "BRIGHT KNOWLEDGE: The Search for Wisdom in the Celtic & Druid Tradition" by Philip Carr-Gomm.

4.30pm: OVATE GROVE.

6.00pm: EVENING FEAST "Trekking the Southern Skies: Star-Lore"
Akkadia   Zan
& J   will lead an evening of stellar exploration.

Photo credit: Sandra Greenhalgh

Second Australian Assembly Program (Sunday and Monday)

Alban Eiler September 18th-21st, 1998.
the historic First Visit of the Chosen Chief, Philip Carr-Gomm.

Program: SUNDAY, Sept. 20th

10am: CIRCLE OF LIGHT

10.30am: "Druid Magic In a Changing World" by Philip Carr-Gomm.

Midday: DRUID GROVE & Druid Grade Initiations.

Whilst the Druid Grove is in Progress for all other participants there will be:

12.00-1.00pm: LUNCH

1.00pm-4pm: "Unleashing the Legendary Self Mask-Making Workshop" led by Carole

Also time for some canoing & bush-walking before dinner.

6.00pm: EVENING FEAST & CELEBRATION OF NEW DRUIDS WITH A SPECIAL GORSEDD "Come As Your Favourite Celtic Hero!" Music led by Carrl. BYO Mead!

MONDAY, Sept. 21st

10am: CIRCLE OF LIGHT

- VILLAGE MARKET -

12.00-4.00pm: ALBAN EILER CELEBRATIONS: ALBAN EILER CEREMONY

Formal Celebration with Lunch as the Feast at Conclusion of the Ceremony; followed by the CLOSING TALK "The Well of Segais" *by the Chosen Chief.*

4.00pm: CLOSING CEREMONY: FORMAL PASSING OF THE ASSEMBLY to LESLEY GENTILIN OF CORRINGAL GROVE *who will serve as Host for the Third Australian Assembly.*

DEPARTURE.
Until Next Year, May the Spirits of the Grove & the Guardians & Guides of Our Order Bless, Protect & Inspire Us All & May We Each Journey Safely to Our Homes.

Image credit: Sandra Greenhalgh

SERPENTSTAR

SerpentStar was the first *Order of Bards, Ovates and Druids* publication in Australia. It was originally published in 1997 and is still in circulation as of late 2019.

This section includes a timeline listing the editors of *SerpentStar*, as well as personal reflections from three *SerpentStar* editors: Carole Nielsen, Vyvyan Ogma Wyverne and Mandy Gibson.

Timeline of *SerpentStar* Editors

Alban Hefin 1998 to 2002 - inaugural editor	Carole Nielsen
Alban Arthan 2002 to 2007	N.E.
Beltane 2007 to 2010	Wyverne
Beltane 2010 to 2012	Kimmy Morley
Imbolc 2012 – 2013	Wyverne
Beltane 2013 – 2014	'Richard'
Beltane 2014 – 2015	Martin
Imbolc 2015 - current editor as at December 2019	Mandy Gibson

The First Editor of *SerpentStar*
Carole Nielsen

FIRST MY FIRST EXPERIENCE WITH OBOD.

My daughter and I went to a *Mind Body Spirit* Expo at Darling Harbour in Sydney. We came across a weekend in Wiseman's Ferry for a Celtic Spiritual experience and decided to go. It was a great weekend and there were some Druids there - not OBODs - who lived around Wiseman's Ferry. We had a talk to them and had a couple of ceremonies with the general group and met someone who told us about OBOD. So, we contacted OBOD and decided to do the Bardic Grade.

We got our pack and went up to the Blue Mountains. We drove around letting our instincts draw us to the beginning of the Megalong Valley and initiated each other. It was very exciting, and I suppose that was our first OBOD experience. It was also noteworthy that whenever my daughter and I organised a little ceremony for ourselves it would storm. It happened consistently for about six months, and we both had a lot of dreams during that time. The dreams were very much a part of the OBOD experience.

I was contacted by some OBOD Druids not so long after that to help at a wedding, also at Wiseman's Ferry, where I stood in the West while other more experienced Druid members of OBOD officiated. It was wonderful, and after the ceremony I had to go away for a little while and sit in the bush and digest the magic that was generated. Of course, as we all know, the first and second Assemblies were later held at Wiseman's Ferry, so that place was very special to Druidry and OBOD at the time.

What inspired you to become part of *SerpentStar*?

The first Assembly was in 1997 and was a wonderful, if wet, affair. People came from all over Australia and New Zealand. We huddled under makeshift shelters and made circles in the paddock/meadow and pitched tents and swags in the woodland. We were a group of people who had never met, yet we slotted together like family.

At the end of that weekend, not wanting to lose the connection, I suggested we have a newsletter. Elkie immediately said, "Yes, what a good idea, it should be you!" That wasn't something I anticipated, but I said yes because I thought it was important.

There was some discussion about the name, and I think it was Akkadia who suggested *SerpentStar*. This was thought to be a good name as it didn't appropriate any Indigenous spirituality but covered the Southern Hemisphere on an astrological plane.

> *"The aim of this newsletter/notice board is to inform and draw together members in the peace and light of the grove, and to support and nourish each other in our quest for strength, understanding, knowledge, justice and love. Let's work together to achieve this aim."*
> [excerpt from the inaugural *SerpentStar* publication]

What was your favourite part of being editor?

I have to first talk about the least favourite part of being editor. I was just learning about computers, and my son was helping me. So, I decided to use word processing to do the newsletter. It was a nightmare! Getting a newsletter layout into a Word document and getting the pictures to sit in the right place was so hard for a beginner. I was also working two jobs, and *SerpentStar* would often be finished at two or three in the morning, after some catastrophic fail that inevitably happened during the production of the newsletter, usually at the deadline for posting. There were spell check failures that I didn't see. It could take hours to print because I always tried to use the best resolution for the pictures. I was wanting to get the whole thing perfect with hardly any computer skills.

I remember posting out the first newsletters, I was so focused on the content that when I actually got a response saying thank you and how good it was, I suddenly realised that I had posted it to real people, all over Australia, most of whom I had never met!! The immediate response was of course wonderful. Finding the pictures for the banner for each edition was always a meditation I enjoyed. The articles, the sharing of wisdom of the different roads people were walking in the OBOD family, and the love so obviously offered. It was wonderful to be part of all that.

However, I realised that *SerpentStar* needed to be shared to grow, needed to move through many hands to unite us with renewal and regrowth. So, one weekend I went up to N.E.'s home and sat with her, while she took over that responsibility and rebirthed *SerpentStar*. It was a loss for me, but it was exciting too, to know that *SerpentStar* would move among members and draw from them the creativity they had to offer, revealing the different prisms of our groves and members, and the facets of our Australian Druid wisdom that were being revealed so generously.

The middle years of *SerpentStar*
Vyvyan Ogma Wyverne

When were you editor of *SerpentStar*?
I took over the editorship of *SerpentStar* in Beltane 2007 and was editor for three years, handing over to Kimmy Morley at Beltane in 2010. Kimmy handed it back to me at Imbolc 2012, and it stayed with me until Imbolc 2013.

What inspired you to become part of *SerpentStar*?
Living on a remote farmlet with limited access to transport and animals to care for was making it hard for me to attend OBOD events, so editing the newsletter was a great opportunity for me to participate, stay informed and maintain contact with fellow OBODies. It also gave me a chance to improve my publishing skills and learn a lot about the internet.

What was your favourite part of being editor?
I loved seeing Druidry taking hold and growing, with more and more people beginning to strike up the courage to send in their contributions – poems, articles, stories and thoughts - that revealed along with their amazing talents and wisdom the steadily evolving spirit of Druidry in the southern hemisphere. I've also enjoyed watching *SerpentStar* going from strength to strength under the masterly editorship of subsequent editors who have really brought it right up to standard as a newsletter to be proud of.

The current editor of *SerpentStar*
Mandy Gibson

I FIRST TOOK OVER EDITING of *SerpentStar* in 2015. At the Mt Hyland Assembly, an announcement was made that the current editor needed to step down and was looking for a replacement, and as I had publishing experience and the necessary software I stuck my hand up.

The first one to go out with me was Imbolc 2015, as of writing this the Imbolc 2019 edition has just gone out so I've just chalked up exactly four years! In those years, I've put out sixteen editions myself, but also put together the Twentieth Anniversary edition which was a special one done for Alban Hefin 2017.

To coincide with that I assembled an intrepid team who helped me hunt down, scan and put together electronic copies of all the previous editions of *SerpentStar*, right back to the beginning, which are now all hosted on a special archive page on the *SerpentStar* website. To enable this to happen, *SerpentStar* is now being hosted by the *Druidry Australia* website which also hosts bookings for the Assemblies each year. It was such an exciting project, and really shows how far that lovingly crafted little mag has come.

The last four years have also seen changes to the editorial guidelines, so that all content is now submitted by OBOD Southern Hemisphere members only, except by invitation (as it's always nice to have contributions from members of the OBOD HQ) - a little wave from home base - especially if they travel DownUnder. We now have a regular section from New Zealand members, entitled Aotearoa, and carry free advertising for businesses and events run by OBOD members in the region. Cover and editorial pages often come from my home *Macadamia Grove*, although I'm always on the lookout for great seasonal-relevant images or photos from our travels. Travelling is an especially big deal in a part of the world where we're scattered over such long distances and in many cases only see each other once or twice a year.

SerpentStar has gone electronic too! We now publish exclusively online - which allows flexibility with page numbers, completely free and open subscription and the ability to link to online resources within the magazine. I do still, as a nod to those who like a hard copy, lay the magazine out in a print-friendly format. And in June 2019 we launched the *SerpentStar* YouTube channel, which currently hosts the *Druids Down Under Discuss Everything* ('DDUDE') talk series and will in the future feature video contributions to tie in with the seasonal releases of the magazine.

As of Imbolc 2019, *SerpentStar* is read by around 800 people every quarter, from Australia and New Zealand to as far away as Wales! I've been so proud to be part of it, and to have contributed to our shared journey and memory.

Front cover of inaugural edition of Serpentstar

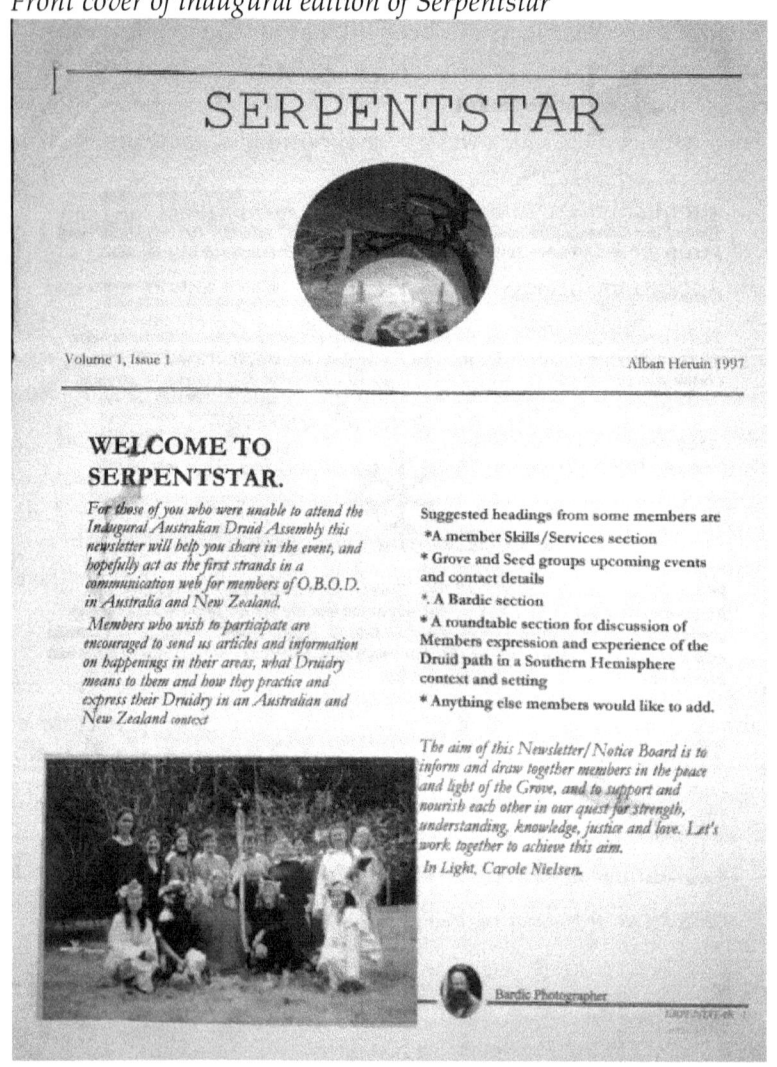

Front cover of Beltane 2019 SerpentStar

[Editor's comment: This is the current version of *SerpentStar* available at time of editing.]

The Inaugural Druids Down Under National Gathering 2018

Part II

DRUID GROUPS, SEED GROUPS AND GROVES

Overview

While *The Order of Bards, Ovates and Druids* (OBOD) appears to have the largest membership in Australia, it certainly isn't the sole Druid group active in Australia. This section includes information regarding current and active groups such as *A Druid Fellowship* (ADF) and *Druids Down Under* (DDU) as well as a range of Druidic activities, past and present.

Groups have been listed in alphabetical order firstly by Australian State, and then by group name. Information about fraternal Druid Lodges is available in a separate section, commencing on page 205.

Some groups have been described as Seed Groups rather than Groves. *The Order of Bards, Ovates and Druids* differentiates between OBOD Seed Groups and OBOD Groves in the following manner:

> *"A Seed Group can be formed by any member at any point in their studies. Each group is free to develop its own style of working, with the aim of making meetings informal and relaxed - giving members the opportunity to meet and meditate together, and to discuss Druidry and topics of mutual interest. Many Seed Groups celebrate the seasonal festivals together.*
>
> *A Grove is a group which meets regularly, and which is led by at least two members who have been initiated into the OBOD Druid Grade. A fully functioning Grove will celebrate the eight festivals, and may also give initiations, hold Groves in each of the three grades - Bardic, Ovate and Druid - and arrange other activities such as retreats, workshops and camps."*

Above information sourced August 2019 from
https://www.Druidry.org/community/groves-groups/treasures-tribe-guidelines-obod-seed-groups-groves

NEW SOUTH WALES DRUID GROUPS

Druids Down Under

Status: commenced in 2007 and currently active. Based in New South Wales, with an Australia-wide focus.

Julie Brett

DRUIDS DOWN UNDER IS CURRENTLY a Facebook group with about 3000 members (2019). I started it in 2007 when I was living in Glastonbury in England. I had started learning about Druidry through Morgan Rhys Adams, who ran *The Gorsedd of the Bards of Caer Abiri*, at Avebury. She and the Gorsedd were associated with the *British Druid Order*.

She also lived in Glastonbury, and was mentoring me on a one-to-one fairly casual basis over tea, walks in the forest and visits to talks and other events around town. We were friends. I had been a solitary practitioner in 'green witchcraft' for eight years beforehand, so Celtic Paganism wasn't new, but Druidry was. I learned about Awen, the roles of the Bard, Ovate and Druid, the function of the Gorsedd and the Eisteddfod in ritual, the function of the ancestors, nemeton space, the three realms of Land, Sea and Sky, and other significant teachings.

The Round of Amergín was a common part of the rituals that Morgan held. She had created it herself through inspiration of the Song of Amergín. We discussed the Mabinogion in the teaching and the rituals always had a Welsh mythic focus. Under Morgan's encouragement, I was initiated with *The Gorsedd of the Bards of Caer Abiri* at Lughnasadh in 2007 and then again at *The Gorsedd of the Bards of Cor Gawr* at Stonehenge close to the winter solstice, also in 2007. At the winter solstice gathering, I stepped forward and pledged to take what I had learned of Druidry back to Australia to share it with others there.

While in the United Kingdom (UK), I also met Emma Restall Orr at the launch of her book *The Apple and the Thorn*. The launch was at Chalice Well in Glastonbury. Emma and Morgan knew each other as Morgan had been her student, and Emma along with Philip Shallcrass had run *The Gorsedd of the Bards of Caer Abiri* before Morgan. At that meeting, I asked Emma what she thought of my book idea and she was encouraging. When I returned to Australia, she asked me to be the Oceania coordinator for *The Druid Network*. I did this for a few months but was not able to continue due to other commitments with my university studies. Emma would eventually come to edit my book and give me a great deal of good advice on how to present the information in it.

Before heading to the UK, I knew nothing of Druidry, but I did have this idea about making my Pagan practice more Australian and I had the first inklings of my ideas for the local Wheel of the Year I would end up developing when I returned. I wanted to go to Britain to see what the traditional Wheel of the Year felt like in its homeland, so that I could make comparisons to the Australian landscape. I thought I would be doing this in terms of witchcraft, but I ended up finding Druidry was a wonderful fit for me, and it spoke to me very deeply.

During my time in the UK, I was curious to find out if there were any others looking into 'Australianising' their Druidry practice. Facebook was very new, and I looked around for Australian Groves or Druid groups. I couldn't find anything, though I did come across a group in Sydney called *Ostarian Grove*. Being curious as to the possibility that they might be Druids, as Druids often call their groups 'groves', I started a discussion thread about Australian Druidry. It turned out they were not a Druidry-focused group but were more eclectic in their practice. However, they were welcoming of me, and through their group I met some interesting people who became and are still active members in the *Druids Down Under* community.

I was also told about the OBOD forum, where I was able to discuss the concepts further, though I didn't become a member of OBOD until 2009 when I returned to Australia. I also discussed my ideas about the Wheel of the Year and Australian seasonal, plant and animal symbolism on the *Witches Workshop* Facebook group.

On the OBOD forum I was eager to talk about these ideas in a Druidry context. I basically was interested in revolutionizing ritual and Wheel of the Year celebrations to be more Australian. I was met with a good deal of enthusiasm, but as I wasn't a member of OBOD at the time, I did feel I might have been a bit out of line discussing this there. Suggesting that an Order I wasn't a member of change its ideas certainly felt inappropriate, even if the discussion was interesting. I was learning quite a different system of ritual practice with Morgan and the Gorsedd and wanted to keep that up and didn't want to offend anyone with what seemed like radical ideas at the time. I was also interested in learning about other Druidry groups in Australia that might already be doing what I was looking for. I thought there might be a hidden group somewhere already practising a more Australian form of Druidry, and I just needed to find them.

I didn't continue discussing it on the OBOD forum a great deal as I was wanting my own space to guide discussion that was open to members from any Order, or none, where people could share information and ideas, resources, and rituals and perhaps even get together in person when I returned to Australia. The focus was most certainly from the start: Australian Druidry and not any Order or particular teaching. This way there was space for the radical ideas, as well as acknowledging when members preferred to hold to the ways things were presented in their Orders.

The *Ostarian Grove* group which included Pip, Brendan Hancock, Kristin Aplony, and others had encouraged me to set up my own Facebook group to further discuss the ideas that I had brought up initially in their group, and so I did. I called it '*Druids Down Under*' almost as a joke. It sounded a bit cheesy and silly, and that perhaps was a mood that would continue as I will explain. I never expected the group would have more than a few people interested in the topic, but as I write this today, there are nearly 3000 members, twelve years later.

There was always an undertone of fun and not taking ourselves too seriously right from the beginning. The group was always friendly, kind and encouraging of personal choice, right from the start. We started to get an idea of the diversity of different ways that people in Australia were approaching Druidry, from learning about the different Orders here, to finding out about the many different ways people adjusted their rituals to 'make more sense' to them and the places they lived. We also got to know some of the differences between the different Orders. There were many reasons and rationales for both changing our practice and maintaining tradition, and it was fascinating to see the diversity come into view through these many different experiences.

When I returned to Sydney, I began working on constructing a Wheel of the Year for the local area I had grown up in in Sydney's Northern Beaches. I decided to run some gatherings to explore and develop this idea further with others. I met with some of the people I had met online, including the *Ostarian Grove* members along with Stacey Wilson, Sal Lavallee and others. They were some of the first to come along to my circles. Stacey was a long-time member of OBOD already and became an important person in *Druids Down Under*, helping with the Facebook group, the workshops in Sydney, and eventually DDUNG. Sal is an Aboriginal woman of Ngarigo and Yuin descent who has been immeasurably helpful in my gaining a better understanding of the relationship between Druidry and Indigenous culture. She has been an advisor to me on this for many years, always happy to help and to share.

I had a rough idea of the wheel sketched out and the circles I ran were not meant to be teaching circles, but more exploratory and experimental to see what would work and what would not. Our rituals celebrated the land we were in and we tried quite a few different forms of ritual to see what would feel right for us. This included visiting different sites, asking the land what we should do, playing with natural elements like ochre or bringing different plants to represent the seasons to the ritual, we also considered our connection with deities, spirits of place and the ancestors to make sense of how to welcome these and respect their energies as well as we could.

I held these events around the Northern Beaches from February 2008. The first I held was going to be a bushwalk, but it was timed with what I called 'Storm Festival' in my local wheel of the year, and of course, it bucketed down with rain, so we ended up holding the ritual in my home. I found some confidence at least in that what I was mapping out was relevant! It was the first of many public gatherings I would hold over the next few years to deepen my understanding of this new wheel idea.

The rituals were always in the structure taught to me by Morgan and that were used in *The Gorsedd of the Bards of Caer Abiri*, though we were very experimental in terms of nature symbolism and what that meant for the ritual. Morgan had encouraged me to be experimental – to listen to the land and to see what worked. So, we tried many different things searching our way through the seasons to see what markers spoke to us and what each part of the year presented to us as a cause for celebration. And through this exploration the Wheel of the Year for coastal Sydney began to come into being.

In May 2008 I met Tom Byrom at one of Tim Hartridge's Witch Camp retreats. We had a great time over the weekend and became good friends. Later, in 2009, his interest had him sign up for the OBOD Bardic course. I listened to his introductory material and decided I would join up too. I remember we were sitting in Sydney Park one evening, on the hill, just us and one other friend and together we told her the story of Taliesin in great animation, and I knew this was an important and wonderful path to be on. Tom and I also took Irish Gaelic classes together at the Gaelic Club in Sydney and he came to many of the *Druids Down Under* rituals I held.

It was in conversations with Tom that the idea of the Three Ancestors really developed. Though it does come from a welcome to the ancestors in *The Gorsedd of the Bards of Caer Abiri* ritual, where the ancestors of our bloodlines, our tradition, and the land are welcomed, Tom and I realised how this triple group of ancestors could be really useful for welcoming the ancestors when these are not all Celtic. Australia being a multicultural society, we have diverse bloodlines. Welcoming them all felt right. This being a modern era of freely available information, many of us are not only influenced by Druidry, but by other paths as well, and it can be wholesome to welcome those teachers in ritual. And the ancestors of this land seemed in serious need of recognition by us, but with a need for sensitivity, without appropriation or disrespect. Acknowledging all three brought a balance to our rituals that felt very good.

In 2008, I had started studying a Bachelor of Arts degree at Sydney University. I majored in Studies in Religion. I became interested in the course as it offered subjects such as Witchcraft, Paganism and the New Age with Carole Cusack. I took many of her classes and enjoyed Studies in Religion a great deal, as it offered me an opportunity to look at Druidry through an academic perspective. I also took minors in Anthropology, Celtic Studies, Philosophy, Linguistics, and Sociology. I took a summer course in *Magic, Religion and Spirituality* with Doug Ezzy and Nevil Drury at UTAS in Hobart as a part of the degree. This introduction to Doug meant that later he would come to help with the editing of my book. I was really drawn to the role of the Bard as history keeper, storyteller and myth keeper, so I studied as many subjects within these areas as I could. I wanted to learn what I could of the history for the book on Australian Druidry that I was beginning to form.

At the end of my degree, I was pregnant with my son Lugh and he was born three months after I finished my last exams. In between finishing university and his birth, I was able to take a quick trip to Victoria to visit *The Melbourne Grove* for the first time. I met with Elkie White and other members and we celebrated Imbolc together. Elkie would eventually come to be a presenter at the *Druids Down Under National Gathering* ('DDUNG') and to be a part of the ritual team for that.

I was hoping at the time to collect information on the history of Australian Druidry for my book, but I realised it was far beyond my abilities at the time and a much bigger subject than I had anticipated. The trip did, however, help forge stronger friendships across the States, and over the years I would come to meet more and more members of Druidry groups from around the country that were part of the *Druids Down Under* group online. While I was visiting Elkie, she explained to me her mapping of sacred sites around where she lived that *The Melbourne Grove* used for their rituals. She came to speak on this topic at DDUNG, helping others to see how they too could map out sacred landscapes.

At the *Australian Wiccan Conference* (AWC) in 2012, I gave a presentation on my Australian Wheel of the Year and despite my tiredness for being at the gathering with my six-month old son, it was well received. It was there that I met Adrienne Piggott from *Spiral Dance*, and she tells me it was that talk that got her thinking about what would become the song *Goddess of the Southern Land* that I was lucky to be able to include in my book. Adrienne would also come to be a presenter, performer and ritualist at the DDUNG gathering.

Around the same time, I started holding pub meets at The Gladstone Hotel in Chippendale. It was a convenient and quiet location and we could meet in the beer garden on a Monday evening and my son could snooze away in the stroller while we all had a pub dinner and chatted about Druidry. It was a passionate group of people who had interests and membership in all three of the main Druidry Orders as well as those learning independently.

It was in these pub meets that we came up with the idea of holding a *Druids Down Under National Gathering* (DDUNG). Continuing our love for the mildly silly, tongue in cheek way of not taking ourselves too seriously, this was the name we decided to go with. We reasoned it is from DDUNG that many things grow and flourish. One might even argue this irreverent reverence or combination of silliness and seriousness is a tradition in modern Druidry. It could be compared to Orders such as the *Secular Order of Druids* (SOD), the *Glastonbury Order of Druids* (GOD), or even Damh the Bard (pronounced 'Dav' not 'damn').

This pub meet also led to a series of workshops through 2012 that were held at locations near Holsworthy where we experimented with the Wheel of the Year I had been developing to further see what worked, what didn't, and what we might change. It was in these workshops that we collectively came across the idea of the wheel of two lifetimes that I explain in my book, where both the summer and winter solstice are seen as 'death and rebirth' times. Members of this group included Rebecca Pickard, Lisa N, Stacey Wilson, and Rowan Fenton who would all help with the running of DDUNG in 2018. The Wheel of the Year work was very affirming and I became more confident in the idea being shared.

In 2013 and 2014, I was not very well and my Druidry work was fairly slow but I did continue to hold public circles, mainly around Narrabeen, and made some close friendships, such as with Amanda Davis whom I taught one on one a lot about the Gorsedd style of ritual. Amanda played an important role in DDUNG as a presenter and ritualist. I also met Chris Parker when he came to my circles. He went on to begin the *Song of the Eastern Sea OBOD Seed Group*. I met Ben Hopkinson via the Sydney *Gliding Seal* Beltane gathering in this period too. Ben and I were Beltaine King and Queen that year and we got to know each other well, I encouraged him to look into Druidry and he joined OBOD as a result. Ben now holds events in Sydney under the name of *The Urban Druid*.

In May 2016 I attended the English Ale in Adelaide and then the AWC in Canberra. At these events I met Kacey Guy Stephensen who had been a long-time member of *Druids Down Under* and would end up playing an important role in the DDUNG gathering both in the ritual, as a presenter and as a performer. Kacey is a talented musician. We both enjoy the bardic circles at camps and have had many conversations on the nature of Awen and how to go about connecting with the land for creativity.

At DDUNG, along with Adrienne Piggott, Kacey taught a workshop on these ideas. I was very keen to see them both share their creative talents with the group in this way. In the workshop participants created a chant song for the land with the chorus *The Awen I sing, from the deep I bring it*. This process has been used a few times since at OBOD Assemblies in Australia and New Zealand to connect with different lands and create songs for those places.

I met Shaz Cairns at the Mount Franklin Gathering at Beltane in 2016 and she agreed to come and talk at DDUNG about ADF and their ritual practices. She also came to be a contributor to the writing of the DDUNG ritual which included aspects of OBOD, ADF and *British Druid Order* (BDO) ritual forms. Shaz taught a workshop at DDUNG, giving many people an introduction to ADF practices for the first time.

In 2017 I released my book, *Australian Druidry: Connecting with the Sacred Landscape* through *Moon Books*. It included information on my studies of the Wheel of the Year and the work that the various rituals and workshops I had led had come across. It was the result of much collaborative work in the community and sharing information both online and in person. It included concepts of the elements in Australia, native plant and animal symbolism and how to create more, an exploration of the three ancestors idea, a sharing of the round of Amergín in an Australian context, and an explanation of ritual practice that helps all of these concepts come together to encourage Awen and creativity in a Gorsedd style of ritual. My many conversations with Australian Druids from many different persuasions allowed me to explain the diversity of the tradition while also sharing my own ideas about practice and theory.

After releasing the book, I was invited by Adrienne Piggott to host the *Druids of Oz* talk at the English Ale. It was a two-hour talk and I discussed the process of writing it, my travels to the UK and how the groups in Sydney had worked towards developing the ideas. We also discussed possibilities for a Wheel of the Year for Adelaide. While there I also met Unanyntji Scales who would come to present at DDUNG too. She would speak about her experiences growing up with Aboriginal family members and the connections between these experiences and Druidry.

She ran this workshop along with Amanda Davis who I had met through *Red Tent Australia*. We spent a fair amount of time together and I shared with her a lot of the ideas I had learned with Morgan about Gorsedd style ritual. Amanda also lived and worked in a remote Aboriginal community in the Northern Territory for some time. The workshop she ran with Unanyntji was about their sharing these experiences, and the lessons they had learned through them.

A lot of preparation went into DDUNG. I began learning about how to run big events by offering to help with the *Gliding Seal* Beltane events which were largely organized by the *Applegrove Coven*, along with Mark Hepworth as administrator. Through them I learned about how to run meetings, how to set up a schedule, how to allocate tasks to team members, and many other organizational aspects. Mark would go on to play an important back-of-house role in the set-up and running of DDUNG. Rhiannon Icasuriaga-Correa and Janett Icasuriaga also helped with administrative tasks at the event.

Through 2017 the ritual team for DDUNG formed including myself, Elkie White, Shaz Cairns, Pete Blake, Stacey Wilson, Lisa N, Rebecca Pickard, Adrienne Piggott, Kacey Guy Stephensen, Amanda Davis, and Unanyntji Scales. These were also the people who ran workshops through the gathering. The focus of the gathering was to explore the various Orders' approaches to Australian Druidry, and also to explore who we are collectively as Australian Druids. We looked at experimental themes in Druidry and asked questions about our relationships with Indigenous Australia, as well as the land, its seasons and symbols. The gathering was a celebration of our community, our diversity, our connection to the land, and our creativity.

The workshops included theory and practical elements what would help attendees to tap into their creativity. The rituals focused around community coming together from diverse places and influences, and bringing in the Awen to help us express that story. The weekend ended with an Eisteddfod where attendees could share how this journey had brought that about in them through some kind of creative performance, and what people shared was just wonderful.

The Order of Bards, Ovates and Druids (OBOD), and The *British Druid Order* (BDO) were represented in the workshops and in the writing and leading of the rituals. There were many members from OBOD in attendance, a handful of members of *Ár nDraíocht Féin* (ADF) and BDO, and also quite a few people who were interested in Druidry more generally and independently. For some it was their first experience of Druidry. I held two workshops, one on the Gorsedd style ritual as I was taught it and as we use in the circles I hold, and one on the Wheel of the Year. Other workshops included one by Lisa N about the three elements (calas, gwyar, nwyfre) and soapmaking, a morning meditation by Pete Blake, and there was an Awen space organised by Stacey Wilson where attendees could take some time to get creative.

The rituals over the weekend centred on the concept of Land, Sea and Sky, and the representations of these as the Three ancestors Land, relating to Land ancestors, Sea relating to our bloodline ancestors, and Sky relating to the ancestors of our traditions and inspirations. We symbolized our coming together as a community from many different lands by each bringing a small stone to represent Land and some water to represent Sea from our home lands, each person was also given a small bag of native bird seed to represent Sky.

These were ritually combined on a central altar to symbolize our coming together as a community. Over the weekend we shared a lot about our different paths and explored different ways to work with creativity in Awen and our connection with the land. The final outcome of which was a dance and chant and blessing of the seeds, water and stones, which we then redistributed out to the group for people to take home or give to the birds and trees. The symbolism of it all was the coming together of our different paths, our sharing of creativity and our connection with the land and ancestors.

There were fifty-seven attendees in total. It was held at the Baden Powell Scout Centre from 2nd March to 5th March 2018 with attendees mainly staying on site. I hope to be able to run future events and to help support events in other

States.

Since that time my focus has been on my personal practice, but also in creating content online which is a great way for the community to connect when we are living long distances from each other. I set up my podcast series *Forest Spirituality with Julie Brett* in 2016, and though it began with a vague idea of sharing my thoughts and talking to interesting people, it has progressively become more specifically focused on creating and sharing conversations within the Druidry community. I regularly share these with the *Druids Down Under* community and many of the people I interview come from that group.

I also hosted two sessions of *Tea with a Druid* for the OBOD Facebook page in 2019 and this inspired me to begin something similar on *Druids Down Under*. Continuing the theme of irreverently reverent titles, I named the series DDUDE (*Druids Down Under Discuss Everything*). In them, the host of the episode takes twenty minutes to discuss a topic important to them in a live video which can be viewed later. *Druids Down Under* has many experienced members with their own stories to tell in exploring Australian Druidry, and it's a great way for them to be able to share their ideas.

The *Druids Down Under* group has also branched off into a couple of Facebook sub-groups. *DDU Bardic Circle* Facebook Group provides a safe and supportive place for budding Bards to share their creative work with each other. It provides a place for us to share when we can't attend events due to long distances. *Druids For Peace and Justice* Facebook Group was also set up as politics and Druidry often overlap but not everyone wants to discuss politics. As such we made a space specifically for it to maintain the spiritual focus of the *Druids Down Under* main group. There may be space for more sub-groups in the future.

I could tell a thousand more stories about these experiences and about the people mentioned here and many others who have been important along the way. Every conversation we have opens us up to more ideas and possibilities for things we can create. Every moment is a possibility. Every connection is a potential doorway to greater understanding. Who knows where we will go next? We will just have to let the Awen guide us.

Druid Pilgrim

Status; currently active. Based across Australia and New Zealand.

Danuta Electra Raine

Why *Druid Pilgrim*?
DRUID PILGRIM IS A REASONABLY NEW sapling borne of a richly developed forest of Druid activity within Australia and founded upon the growth of numerous Druid Orders such as OBOD and BDO and the outreach work of community focused Druid groups, such as *Druids Down Under*. Started in October 2018, it offers a way of engaging with the practice of pilgrimage within druidry. *Druid Pilgrim* recognises the deep mysticism that infuses the world around us: the mysteries of natural environments and sacred heritages; the mysteries that grow from long periods of human practice and intention. We see these things in all manner of sacred spaces, which are often known as nemeta within druidry.

Australians are an amalgam of many different nations and their ontological beliefs and knowledge. To belong here is to make sense of conflicting webs of being in a place that is so different from that of most of our forebears that we often feel alien. To sit and think deeply about self and belonging in Australia not only leaves us to wrestle with deep layers of acceptance and origin, but it can leave us unable to position ourselves within our environment. The very stories that would cement our belonging do not always belong to us, and the stories that belong to the webs of our incarnations often exist somewhere else. Pilgrimage can be essential to resolving many of these tensions.

In visiting the origins of our history and beliefs, we are subtly readjusted in a way that repositions us on returning to our homes. Pilgrimage is a key to sovereignty and stewardship. Pilgrimage empowers our ability to create deep and lasting community. In standing on the sites that inform the self, we retune ourselves and, in retuning our inner beings, we begin to make the music that resonates with the places and spaces we are called to serve.

About the Founders
Druid Pilgrim was a natural expression of my conversations with Michael Vlasto about the central importance of pilgrimage to druidry. I come from a family with questions surrounding heritage. My father spoke of me being seventh generation Australian, yet the thread of those generations has been tangled and knotted by

different possible paths that trace back through the centuries. My mother is a child immigrant, a survivor of eugenics atrocities of World War II. I had spent nearly a decade researching and writing a PhD that revolved around questions of identity and self, of transgenerational and intergenerational trauma. A pilgrimage to Europe had been central to that work, so when Michael began speaking about pilgrimage and Druidry, his experiences resonated with my own.

Michael Vlasto has been involved with druidry all the way back into the early 1970s. To say he had been born to it would be an understatement. There is a song within Michael that has slowly unwound the workings of this lifetime to reveal an ancient understanding of how people and societies work. His unusual education and background in Southern England and Scotland have given him a personal experience of the sacred sites of Great Britain, of England, Cornwall, Scotland, Wales and Ireland, that have been fundamental to his identity. His years within marginalised communities in Australia have interwoven with this early life to develop a wisdom that could only have been embodied by somebody like him.

To be open to unique experiences and representations of self is key to the role of the druid. Only those who create the possibility to hold hidden wisdom within themselves can serve as repositories of wisdom for others. This is a persistent and active process for Michael Vlasto. Daily behaviours and disciplines of openness and integrity have earnt him the right to stand as a storybearer and storyteller. This integrity has been one of the wells from which *Druid Pilgrim* has drawn.

We had recognised the deep work we had both done when we first met, and that formed a comfortable bond that has grown over the last few years. Our days have been easy, sharing story and understanding, and like a sword drawn against a stone, we seem to have sharpened each other. We have supported each other to write for the wider Australian druid community, to attend conferences and events, to run workshops on myth, story and sovereignty, and to support the nurture and development of local community. *Druid Pilgrim* has been formed out of our work together.

What does *Druid Pilgrim* do?

Druid Pilgrim centres around the *Druid Pilgrim* Facebook group. We encourage those interested in pilgrimage and druidry to share experiences and support each other through their reflections and inspiration. Currently, we engage about ninety people from about half-a-dozen countries. We now have a team of four moderators, including myself, Tina Merrybard, Lisa N. and Rebecca Pickard. Michael Vlasto does not connect as a moderator because he is not comfortable with information technology, but this has slowly changed since experiencing a *Tea with a Druid* webcast with Philip Carr-Gomm in late 2018.

Druid Pilgrim began with a series of interviews between Michael Vlasto and I as we made various pilgrimages in 2019 around Australia and New Zealand. It started with some rough and ready conversation and storytelling while at Hungry Head, NSW at the end of 2018. I was motivated by a desire to share Michael's insights with others in our immediate community within *The Order of Bards, Ovates and Druids* in Australia. Michael was motivated to interview me in order to "detect the tears in the web".

We have matured in our use of technology as we have taken this journey. Salem Shaw supports our online, video and webcasting work. Our interviews are expanding from the Druid folk that we meet while travelling to members of the wider community. We hope to create a visual repository of people's thoughts and experiences of pilgrimage and Druidry that can serve as inspiration and support for those exploring pilgrimage as a part of their broader engagement with life.

We wish to facilitate opportunities for pilgrimage in the coming years. We would like to encourage our members to suggest pilgrimages that others can attend, or where people can meet up together along the way. Pilgrimage is often an opportunity for interconnection outside the structures of our everyday life practices, offering us a different way of knowing ourselves and others.

We are also interested in creating opportunities for people to engage their creativity and intellect with the key questions of *Druid Pilgrim*. We have a number of ideas on the drawing board and are excited to see what will finally manifest.

Druid Pilgrim Grove

One of the early off-shoots of *Druid Pilgrim* was the birth of *Druid Pilgrim Grove* (*DPG*). Michael and I were on our first intentional pilgrimage to the *Macadamia Grove* in Brisbane, staying with Sandra Greenhalgh. She suggested that it would be easier for us to do pilgrimage to various druid groves and seed groups if we were affiliated as a seed group ourselves.

The underlying tenets of DPG are to:
- stimulate a love and respect for both the inner and outer worlds of druidry, particularly through the practices of ritual observation and pilgrimage
- support active inclusion of a diversity of practitioners from different orders and disciplines

- engage a geographically diverse membership of peers who encourage and support each other's growth and vision
- work individually and as a group to build a deeper sense of community and a richer appreciation for Nemeta within the wider community.

Druid Pilgrim Grove grew from a seven-person OBOD affiliated Seed Group in December 2018 to an eleven person OBOD affiliated Grove spanning both Australia and New Zealand by the end of February 2019. We drew together a geographically disparate group of people, our original membership coming from Sydney, Lake Macquarie, Newcastle, Dorrigo and Brunswick Heads, New South Wales. By the end of February, we included Druids from Palmerston North in New Zealand, Victoria and Western Australia. Today, in August 2019, we are fourteen strong, and include more members from South Australia, Western Australia and New South Wales.

While OBOD affiliated, this group includes well respected representatives from several different orders, including Ady Chapman, an Elder with the *British Druid Order* (BDO). Three of our members have undergone training within the BDO. Two of our members are not affiliated with any official Druid Order. Six of our company are members of the OBOD Druid Grade. We also represent a diversity of ages, with our youngest member having just turned 19 and our eldest member being almost 70. We are family and community oriented, so we embrace the immediate and broader connections of each of these members beneath the canopy of our grove.

We are like nodes on a wide and beautiful web, offering a structure for more detailed webs of creation to be formed around us. The role of the grove is to empower its membership to richer and deeper manifestations of druid life so that we can further enrich all those with whom we connect. From this perspective, *Druid Pilgrim Grove* is motivated to energetically empower the stability and growth of the wider druid community. We do this through a deepening appreciation of the role of pilgrimage in forming connections between the individual, community and sacred space by developing the web of love between us. It is a gentle, organic process that has been woven over a number of years—some of our relationships are more than thirty years old—but has only recently coalesced in the form of the *Druid Pilgrim Grove*.

The key to this growth is diversity and the opportunity for each one of us to represent ourselves as a living tree within the deepening light that we create together. To that end, our membership was approached so each of us would have the opportunity to write a few lines about our connection with *Druid Pilgrim Grove*. Responses are included in the order they were received.

A, Unaffiliated
I don't believe in organised spirituality or religion. I don't like giving the expression of my spirit over to the control of another person. I cannot abide the hierarchies of the self-appointed who say they speak for the divine and intercede on our behalf. The control, arrogance and hypocrisy are unpalatable and repellent. And so, I find myself at the edge of a Druid Circle, in my friend's quiet and simple garden. I can hear and speak with like-minded people, verbalising gratitude to the Earth; speaking with respect and care to the One who nurtures us, taking the time to acknowledge precisely what we have gained and are grateful for. The voices harmonise and my voice blends in, so I don't need to be a card-carrying member.

K, OBOD
The night glows blue, filtering down from the layers and layers of near emptiness, pinned together with minute sparks called stars. The roots grow deep, burrowing through layer upon layer of condensed earth before it too becomes one, preserving the fragments of the past. Here, between the two, between the stars and the earth, we strive, observe and protect. We are the Druids, the bards, the ones who listen, the ones who remember, the ones who connect.

E, OBOD, Mason
There is unbelievable power and security in being able to say a Druid's oath, and any oath for that matter, and honestly and firmly believe that you mean what you say. Oaths that unite and share the spirit of your intentions with a group of like-minded people create a harmonious well that can be drawn upon to create, heal and bestow. We do this when we share the Awen. We do it when we hold hands and share one of the many oaths of unity and compassion that Druids of different orders declare. It is in the solidarity of the statement, in the integrity of the union in the circle, that we manifest magic into being, and call the spirits to inhabit the sacred space which is called into being.

The ability for closeness, communication, and veto in a closed group allows my membership and my Awen to remain in its integrity. The magic of the circle is that participation and is by ethereal invitation. Joined in spirit of pilgrimage, joined in hospitality.

Jasmine van Aalst, Unaffiliated

One of the most notable things about practising Druidry in Australia is the alchemical transformation of a suburban backyard into a sacred grove. The cups of tea and banter wind down to a hush as we gravitate to take our places in the circle. Each of the directions is honoured, the elements and guardians are called forth and represented by each unique participant. We are academic, farmers, single mothers, students … We are ranging in age from 18 to 69 … our shared passion for ritual and magic, practised with sincerity and skill creates a rich container. There is a Celtic structure and flow that melds with the Indigenous wisdom and connection of our own land with its opposite seasons and particular terrain. As we set our intentions and charge our sacred objects, nature spirits are invoked. The mother hen is summoned. The kookaburras go quiet, the summer sun goes behind a cloud and the breeze picks up and envelopes us all, surrounding the potent cauldron of our creation.

Tina Merrybard, OBOD

When I went to my first Assembly and connected with so many lovely people, it was such a joy. But, when they began to head for their homes across Australia and New Zealand, it felt like little parts of my heart were being torn away, and I could feel the light of their souls moving away, away. I knew that we would always be connected by golden threads, and that was a comfort, but *Druid Pilgrim Grove* has allowed me to strengthen those threads. It is a blessing for someone who lives on a very isolated side of this huge country.

We are doing our best here to grow our community, but I've missed the counsel of other Druids in this endeavour, and *Druid Pilgrim Grove* has given me the chance to communicate via letter with some wiser and more experienced heads than mine! This has helped me both in my role as facilitator of local Druid events, and in remaining connected to my own path in deeper and deeper ways. I love getting my real letters in the mail, and I love that sense of our connection across such a wide part of the world and knowing that every now and then we will be able to come back together physically too!

Ngatina Sylvanius, OBOD

To live pilgrimage
To leave questing footprints on this ancient land.

To listen to the songs the mountains sing.
To sink into the serpentine waterways and to stand in the headwinds.
To immerse yourself in ecology… Learn the lessons of nature from tree to beetle.
To travel within and discover the land waiting there.

Trudy Richards, OBOD
Druidry in Australia to me is the same as Druidry all over the world. You know from deep within that this is who you are. It's the way you connect to the land beneath your feet, be it in Australia, Albion or Europe. The trees might be different and our seasons upside down or back to front, the Solstices opposite and equinoxes reflecting a changing light, but my connection to Gaia is there regardless of this.

    I've been lucky to have travelled to the United Kingdom, Ireland and Brittany. I've been compelled to walk the land, visit the sacred sites and stone circles. And my connection to land sky and sea is always there, no matter which country I am in. I celebrate the changing seasons and turn of the Wheel of the Year because the land beneath my feet is a part of the land of the whole planet. Even when I lived in tropical far north tropical Qld and was celebrating a Winter Solstice skyclad, it was still the Winter Solstice. The climate was unique to the location, but the Solstice was still occurring as part of Earth's cycle around the sun.

    I've lived in many places, in different towns and in different States. As a Druid, I am able to offer an alternative perspective and interpretation of life to the people I meet. I know I am guided to walk the land and I am always in the right place at the right time, even if I don't know that until after the event. Every location has its own unique energy and nature spirits. Australia is an ancient land and the energy here is felt within the core of my being. It's in the very dirt, the Earth, and the ancient rocks, mountains, trees and rivers. Going on a pilgrimage is being open to receive the messages given to me, and then pass on the advice and wisdom gained. In helping others I help myself achieve my life purpose. Every journey I make is a pilgrimage, because I do it with intent, an open heart and mind, while listening to and connecting with the Spirit of the Land around me.

Rebecca
Many years ago, I discovered what a Druid was … and then a few years later, I actually met some.

It was in a pub - a dark dingy hole in the wall in Sydney. I'd been travelling for an hour and a half, having left work early to go home and get changed and hop on a train into the city. I was excited, nervous, and full of energy as I was about to meet a Druid, a real live Druid.

I had found a Blog call *Druids Down Under* and realised after many years of thinking Druids were 'over there on the other side of the world' or in books, that there were actually people living in Australia who were not only interested in Druidry, but living it and doing it: bringing down the Awen! From the blog I found the Facebook page, and on the Facebook page I found what would become my community.

It was at that first *Druids Down Under* pub meet that I crossed paths with a handful of people who would become very close to my heart. In particular Julie Brett and her now-husband Matt, Stacey, and Lisa, who I am very proud to say is one of my best friends in this life (and I'm pretty sure others too). Together with some other like-minded folk we spent a year exploring and developing the local wheel of the year, building our understanding of the landscape and its changing face, and workshopping the changes we observed and experienced within ourselves as well as upon the land.

It is with Lisa that I found a true partner in Druidry. Since that time, we have worked together in Druidic practice, and although we are quite different, we get along very well when it comes to the way we see the world through Druids' eyes. We have shared so many experiences over the years - from travelling to Celtic festivals nine hours away in the depths of Winter, to hunting down local areas to drum and howl at the moon without causing too much fuss from the neighbours. We've done our own pilgrimages to special places including the Northern lands of our ancestors, as well as remote Australian landscapes of deserts, waterfalls, ancient forests, giant boulders, blackwater rivers, mossy groves, views for days, and so many places to simply sit and contemplate the nature of things. Visiting one particular special place many times together, developing a relationship with this land in particular and the spirits of this place, has had a big influence on our Druidry and our understanding of the Australian landscape and how we fit within it.

More recently, we have been drawn towards exploring the concept of the Nemeton; that Sacred Space that lies Within as well as Without.

Holding a ritual, developing purpose and intent and setting the scene for the ritual to take place is one way to experience the feeling of a Nemeton. But there are many other ways to engage with the natural world - be in all of it, be part of it, learn about it, and show it respect. One way that we do so is by making our annual pilgrimage to a distant wildflower garden rich in natural and Aboriginal heritage that opens for only six weeks of the year in spring. Another is to gather the leaves of different trees, soak them in water for weeks, arrange them meaningfully on mordanted fabric and wait for the alchemy of the trees to make prints that you can wear, forever reminded of the spirit of those trees.

Finding sacredness in daily life is important to us both, because we are very busy people. We each work in professional roles that require a lot of our attention and energy. Being able to connect to our inner world and feel a special sense of connection to Spirit is fundamental to the way we experience Druidry. Awareness of the world around us, and awareness of the world within us.

Lisa Nemeton

I was furiously hermiting during my last personal '7' year when I discovered Druidry. I was reading Philip Carr-Gomm's lovely book *What do Druids Believe?* when suddenly there it was, laid out clearly in black and white. Armed with a word to guide me on my search for like-minded souls, this discovery changed my life.

The wheel has turned and goes on turning, and as I reach the end of my subsequent personal 7 year, I reflect on my journey since I discovered who I was. The doors that Druidry has opened for me, giving me a language and a community and the knowledge of Awen, has enriched my life beyond measure. I have learned to create so many beautiful things, my hands taking on a life of their own as the Awen flows through them. With my hands, I have literally poured out rainbows. I recognise and embrace the Awen flowing through me as I speak confidently, and with pleasure, about matters I am passionate about.

I am blessed to have made many lifelong friendships through this community. I recall hosting Julie Brett's Wheel of the Year workshops, where over the course of a year, a group of us reflected on the changes taking place around us, seeing cycles within cycles and seasons within seasons. As our insights into the local landscape developed, so did our friendships, which will always be part of my life. I am proud that I was able to contribute to developing a deeper understanding of our local wheel of the year, and to what would become Julie's excellent book, *Australian Druidry*.

Druidry, and the journeys and pilgrimages it has taken me on, led to one of the most intense love stories of my life. Travels with my Druid friends, the places they took me and the conversations we had, inspired me to seek out a particular landscape – a land of sweeping green plains, endless skies, lavender hills, looming granite, wild winds, powerful storms, deep quiet waters, thick winter mists, snows, fierce summer fires and nights with a billion stars. A land of contradictions. A stark and windswept land so strongly reminiscent of the lands of my ancestors, and yet so quintessentially Australian.

The land found me quickly, almost as soon as I knew we were looking for one another. I have since made hundreds of pilgrimages to this place, sometimes with friends who appreciate its primal majesty, but far more often, alone. How can one describe knowing that they are the only human creature for miles, with no artificial light as far as the eye can see? What magic it is to sit under the moonless night of a million stars in a circle of boulders atop a ridge, before a sacred fire whose flickering flames adorn the stones, in complete silence apart from the crackle of wood and the cry of an occasional night creature. To feel like this could all have been happening 2, 5, 10 thousand years ago, that there is no time, that this is time out of time and to know that as the descendant of those who sat before such fires and saw such stars before me, I too am ancient.

My Druid journey gave this to me. It gave me the eyes to appreciate it, the deep listening to really feel it, the open heart to love it deeply and the understanding to know, as we sang at the inaugural *Druids Down Under National Gathering* (adapted slightly, and with grateful thanks to Gabby and Julie who penned it):

I am the stones, the earth and the bones;
I am the seed to the sky that breathes.
I am the sea and the river's child,
I am one with the wild.

Rebecca is of course my ally in Druidry. We have had a thousand adventures, and we shall have a thousand more. Now, together with Rebecca, I have commenced the next chapter of my journey – a journey to honour our tribe and our land, to develop and nourish a deeper connection to the place we inhabit in this time and place, to join with others in deeply listening, and cultivating the sacred space within ourselves. A journey to develop *The Living Nemeton*.

The Living Nemeton

Status; currently active. Based in Sydney

Rebecca Pickard and Lisa Nemeton

THE LIVING NEMETON, A COLLABORATION between Rebecca Pickard and Lisa Nemeton, is dedicated to exploring and honouring the sacred landscape and living traditions of Druidry in the Australian context. Inspired by our Celtic ancestry and our love of this land, we arrange events and gatherings in and around Sydney for people interested in Druidry or on similar paths. We seek to foster a sense of community, create opportunities for others to share our journey, and to develop our tribe.

While between us we are members of *The Order of Bards, Ovates and Druids* (OBOD), the *British Druid Order* (BDO) and *Ár nDraíocht Féin: A Druid Fellowship* (ADF), our events are non-denominational. All who identify as being on a Druid path (and Druid-friendly people interested in nature spirituality) are welcome.

'Nemeton' is a Celtic word meaning sacred grove or ritual space. Typically, this was a circular space in a natural area, such as a clearing in a grove of trees. However, 'nemeton' is also used to describe an energy field; the energy band of trees, of rocks, of the land … and of each of us. Just as we can visit an existing 'nemeton', by engaging with a new place on a deep level, we can create one. And just as we can visit a physical 'nemeton', we each carry our own 'nemeton' with us. The 'nemeton' in all its forms is and always has been, an evolving, ever-changing thing.

Our events are designed to develop this 'nemeton', nourishing a deep spiritual connection with the land and the changing seasons. We achieve this through various activities, from informal yet thoughtful meanders through the bush to weekend-long retreats and rituals to celebrate the turning wheel of the year.

We have found that the turning of the wheel is sometimes best experienced by returning to special places from season to season, from year to year, and listening deeply. In this way, we form the hub of the wheel, attuning to the natural world and gaining insight into our own inner worlds as the seasons turn and turn.

This engagement with the sacred, within and without, and sharing it with like-minded beings, is *The Living Nemeton*. It is the sacredness to be found in the everyday, and in every day, if you have the eyes to see it.

The Song of the Eastern Sea

Status; currently active. Central Coast New South Wales. OBOD Seed Group

Chris Parker

TOWARDS THE END OF 2016, *The Song of the Eastern Sea* OBOD Seed Group was formed. It is situated on the Central Coast of NSW and meets eight times a year to celebrate the Wheel of the Year. The group was formed so that members of OBOD can get together and perform the Group Ceremonies that are provided as part of the OBOD course.

We are an OBOD Seed Group, but we are open and welcome anyone with an interest in Druidry to join us at our gatherings. Our members are mainly from around the Central Coast, but we also have some travelling from further afield, in Sydney and Newcastle areas.

In August 2017, *The Song of the Eastern Sea Seed Group* hosted the 16th Southern Hemisphere OBOD Assembly in Pennant Hills in Sydney. At that point our membership was at its greatest, and we had a wonderful time being hosts to such a wonderful gathering.

Since then our membership has varied, but we continue to meet at different locations around the Central Coast, usually somewhere where we can be one with Nature, and can participate in the ceremonies in relative privacy. Some of the locations have become quite special, and so we return to them again each year.

During the first couple of years we performed the OBOD Group Ceremonies as they are written, but now we are developing our own style of ceremony. One that works more in the inner world, and also one that is inclusive to all, with very little need to work from notes, and to read from a script. We are really enjoying this new stage of our development and are very keen to keep moving forward, celebrating the turning of the wheel, and developing a small community of like-minded people on similar paths.

The Urban Druid

Status; currently active. Sydney surrounds.

Ben Hopkinson

IN EARLY 2017 A DESIRE to explore my personal relationship with the urban environment arose. I had recently finished reading *The Circle of Eight* by Jane Meredith and her story spoke to me very deeply. The places she talked about were familiar, her experiences while different, were familiar. And I began to see my own story emerge in the landscape around. Until that time, my Druidry was met with a desire to escape to the forest to connect with the spirit of the land, my Druidry, and my own story.

However, what became more apparent over the coming months was that an important thread of my story was urban. It was buried underneath the pavements I walked along every day. Because beneath them was a network of stories, and superhighways of mystery that awaited anyone patient enough to listen out for them. The urban landscape carries the memories of the old and the new, so the stories emerging were very modern and personal.

I needed to apply my training as a Druid, and a witch to my circumstances to develop a deeper understanding of what these stories were, and how they worked through me and my spiritual practice.

With the assistance of other urban Druids, we established *The Urban Druid* upon returning from a pilgrimage to the UK, and in November of 2017, *The Urban Druid* was born. The intention had been set:

> *The Urban Druid aims to bring together Sydney-based Druids who wish to deepen their relationship with the sacred within their urban environment. We'll be doing this by organising regular events to discuss, experience and engage with the seasonal changes throughout the greater Sydney landscape.*

The intention was always to complement personal or other group work undertaken by participants. To support this, events were organised in advance of the eight primary fire and cross quarter celebrations. By engaging with the land around us, we hoped we could anchor ourselves in 'our' urban place, heal ourselves, nurture and support each other, and develop a meaningful practice that brought together anyone who sought a connection with their urban landscape.

Walking the wheel started with midsummer, Alban Hefin, in a reserve north of the heart of the Sydney basin, and continued for a full cycle in each direction, following the sun, and ended with a searing walk along Sydney's north eastern coastline and ocean.

The practice is still in my heart and something I work at on a spiritual and magical level. Most events are now incorporated with the practices of my community, the Seed Group *Song of the Eastern Seas*. However, from time to time *The Urban Druid* hosts events when the need arises, or when the land calls out for our acknowledgement, love, and our support in those urban places that can sometimes be neglected, and their magic forgotten.

Wollemi Seed Group

Status; currently active. Mid New South Wales. OBOD Seed Group.

ROLLICK STARTED THE *Wollemi Seed Group* in 2015. He commenced the OBOD Course in 2009 and was inspired to start a Seed Group after attending the Assembly held at Port Lincoln in 2011. After putting an advertisement in the Imbolc 2015 edition of *SerpentStar*, the first meeting was held at a local park under some mighty fig trees. *Wollemi Seed Group* brought people from the Hunter and Central Coast together for the first time.

The name Wollemi came from the ancient Wollemi Pines which grow in the area. Although members come and go, there is a strong core of people who meet monthly and on ceremonial holidays.

SOUTH AUSTRALIAN DRUID GROUPS

Adelaide Seed Group, Wind Harp Seed Group and Druidry in South Australia

Adelaide Seed Group: inactive
Wind Harp Seed Group: active, OBOD Seed Group

Sarah Marshall

MY NAME IS SARAH MARSHALL and I moved to Adelaide from New Zealand in 2008. This is my experience of Druidry in Adelaide.

Having joined *The Order of the Bards, Ovates and Druids* (OBOD) in February 2011, I spent several months looking in Adelaide for a Druid community to join but was unable to find one. I attended a Pagan event in the city because I had heard Damh the Bard would be there and I was aware he was the Pendragon of OBOD. During that event he asked who, amongst the attendees, was a member of OBOD – two people put their hands up and one of them was me!

Knowing his attendance in Adelaide might prompt others to join OBOD and wanting to meet more like-minded people, I decided to put out feelers to see if people were interested in meeting up to talk about Druidry. The response was encouraging and at the first meeting five of us gathered. It was good to learn that two others were already OBOD members.

This initial meeting was held at the Governor Hindmarsh Hotel. From there we moved to holding meetings at the Hackney Hotel every couple of months roughly, and the group grew – some OBOD members, others not. The *Adelaide Seed Group* was formed and what an eclectic and enthusiastic, albeit small, bunch of Druids we were. People came from all over Adelaide, and even further when they were able, to gather together at the pub and discuss Druidry; what our understanding of it was, how we incorporated Druidry into our daily lives, how we worked with differences of the Southern Hemisphere when most of the teachings were focused on the Northern Hemisphere. We did rituals in a small secluded park next to the hotel. Our numbers fluctuated, there was often between five and occasionally as many as twelve attendees, but sometimes as few as only two of us.

Eventually, due to lack of attendance, the *Adelaide Seed Group* folded but some great things had come from its small and humble start. The most important of this was the connections and friendships made by people in and around Adelaide and South Australia who had identified as Druids, as well as those who wanted to learn about Druidry and perhaps become a Druid. *The Golden Wattle Seed Group* was started by people who came together at the *Adelaide Seed Group*. It is based in the more southern part of Adelaide and is an open group which celebrates the Wheel of the Year and holds rituals for peace and healing. They facilitated the 2018 OBOD camp held at Glenhaven Park, Stockport, South Australia.

The Wind Harp Seed Group also became formalised in 2017 as a result of the networks that grew from the *Adelaide Seed Group*. Again, from meeting like-minded people at the *Adelaide Seed Group* and forming relationships and developing and strengthening friendships with each other. Prior to becoming *The Wind Harp Seed Group* this was an established group of like-minded individuals and friends who came from both Wiccan and Druid traditions and met regularly to celebrate the Wheel of the Year. I felt honoured to be asked to join them.

The name was born from a weekend at Terry Allen's property, which he generously opens to the wider Pagan community, *The Green Man Grove*, with Druid elder Bev Lane who had been invited by our group to spend the weekend teaching about local plants and herbs. Wind Harps are another name for the Casuarina or She Oak trees which are native trees of Australia and make a harp-like sound when the wind blows through them.

Since then *The Wind Harp Seed Group* has been active in supporting the Druid community, honouring the Wheel of the Year with ritual and celebration, including holding open rituals for the wider community to attend and most recently organising and facilitating a Druid camp with special international guests Damh the Bard, Pendragon of OBOD and musician, his wife Cerri Lee, artist, writer and Druid, and Kristoffer Hughes, author and head of the *Anglesey Druid Order* in Wales. People came from all over Australia and New Zealand and even from the United Kingdom to participate in this 2019 camp.

The significant and tireless efforts of Adrienne Piggott, lead singer of the band *Spiral Dance*, must also be acknowledged in *any* conversation about Druidry in South Australia. She regularly fundraises within the generous South Australian Pagan and wider communities to bring Damh the Bard and his wife Cerri Lee to Adelaide from the United Kingdom. They have visited Adelaide several times and whilst here, Damh holds concerts - solo events and with *Spiral Dance*. Both he and Cerri hold workshops focused on a wide range of Druid related topics and have participated in previous camps hosted by members of the Adelaide Pagan community. This has had a direct influence on the rise of OBOD membership and interest in Druidry in South Australia.

Adrienne is also instrumental in organising a yearly Wassail which is held in South Australia's beautiful Barossa Valley, as well as *The English Ale*, which is an annual seasonal festive event held in the Adelaide hills. This festival celebrates the end of summer and the greening of the land with Morris dancing, singing, music, mummers play, a parade with giants, hobby horses, music, more dancing by the Morris dancers and culminating in a large and well attended community ritual for peace and the burning of a wicker man. It is a whole day event and begins with *The Druids of Oz* presentation which is a morning of education dedicated to topics related to being a Druid. *The Druids of Oz* presentation is dedicated to the memory of Lynne Sinclair Wood (30/11/1950 – 12/01/2011) who is lovingly remembered by those who knew her as a Druid elder, artist, teacher, author and activist.

Whilst there have been Druids and people following this path in this area for many more years than I have been a member of OBOD, for various reasons many of these individuals kept to themselves and groups were not always easily accessed or open to everyone. Over time this has significantly changed and there is now a vibrant and active Druid community in Adelaide and South Australia open to all.

Green Man Grove based at Rosedale, South Australia

Photo credit: Sarah Marshall

Image adopted by Wind Harp Seed Group

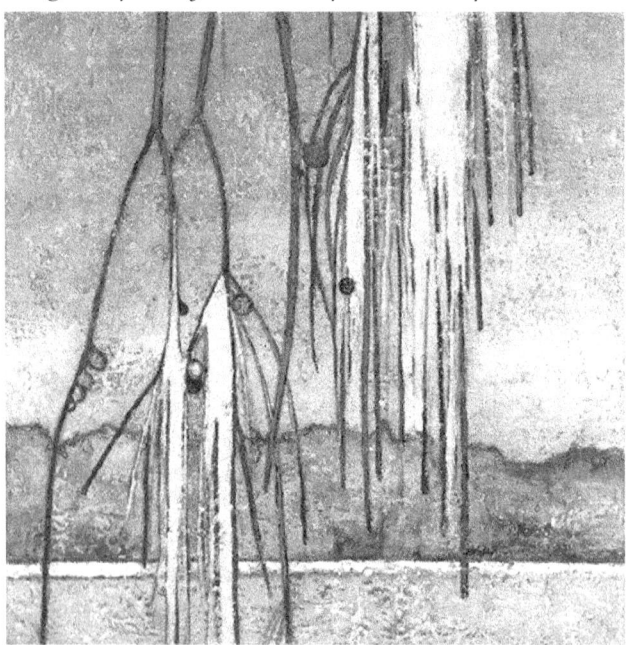

Artwork by Karyn Fendley – Australian Landscape Artist
Image provided by Adrienne Piggot

Cooringal Grove

Status; currently active. Port Lincoln, South Australia. OBOD Grove.

Rafayard

I JOINED OBOD IN 1989 when I was living in England. I returned to Australia in 1992 and came to live on the property Cooringal with my husband Dean. *Cooringal Grove* came into being during that year. We spent the following years having children, re-vegetating the land and developing the Bardic, Ovate and Druid Groves. Later came the men's and women's groves.

For near on thirty years we have been holding rituals and festivals with Druids and the local community. We hosted the National Southern Hemisphere OBOD Assemblies in 1999, 2006 and 2011. These were times when the Order in Australia was small, so it was possible to open up our home and farm at this time. We were few but our connection to each other strong and we paved the way for the future of Druidry in Australia. We wrote our own rituals and pondered life under the southern stars and what it meant to be connected to our great southern land with our European heritage. Beer and whiskey flowed and sharing good organic food and music was very much a feature! We also held groves in special places along our beautiful wild, west coast. A lovely memory was when we made a healing salve while singing our hearts out to Merlin's Black Dog!

I tutored within the Order in the Bardic and Ovate grades for many years and started a music school in town in Dean's family home. *The House of Creative Learning* was blessed and my intentions witnessed before the Druid Grove at the Assembly in Kingaroy in Queensland. That was fifteen years ago and the business is still going strong as a centre for helping people find their creativity through the arts.

Today, within the chaos of running a school, we live quietly, still honouring the Wheel of the Year and enjoying the rich peace and beauty that Cooringal has to offer. Here is a verse from the 2011 Assembly which sums up the call to gather together.

I shall laugh at the folly of hilarity
I shall weep at the tenderness of love
I shall sing to the heavens of eternity
And fly to the stars up above
I'll surrender to the spirit of Awen
Be uplifted, renewed and inspired
I will be all I possibly can be
And sleep soundly in knowing I tried
I have answered the calling to be here
And I offer my friendship to all
as I dance in delight in the moonlight
Let the spirits of wisdom be called
(by Rafayard)

The stone circle at Cooringal Grove, during the third Assembly in 1999

Photo credit: Sandra Greenhalgh

Druids of OZ and The English Ale

Background information and image provided by Adrienne Piggott

The next image is from a 2010 *Silverwheel Men* publication. It explains how Druidry became a part of *The English Ale* celebration.

Lynne Sinclair-Wood was a Druid elder in the South Australian Pagan community. After seeing a growth in interest in Druidry after Damh the Bard's visit to Adelaide in 2009, Lynn approached Adrienne with the idea of including a Druidic aspect to *The English Ale. Druids of Oz* was born!

The English Ale is South Australia's yearly Pagan Winter gathering, described as *"a seasonal gathering to celebrate the customs and ritual traditions from the British Isles that still survive today."*
Information sourced September 2019 from https://www.theenglishale.org/mainpages/about.html

Druids of Oz image

Calling Druids of Oz

- Lynne Sinclair-Wood

This year in May, once again our local Adelaide Pagan community honours our moving into winter in southern hemisphere with '*The English Ale*' at Mylor in the Adelaide Hills. Always a great event, I have felt over past few years that there was perhaps a need to include a simple ritual before the burning of the 'Wicker Man'. I have also been thinking that some Druid input into this event would be interesting, so after a conversation with Adrienne from 'Spiral Dance', I have been given the opportunity this year to work a ritual with some Druidic content as part of the 'English Ale'. Then, I thought, what a great opportunity for a gathering of Druids here in Adelaide leading into this ritual as part of the evening event of the '*English Ale*'.

After the fiasco of the 'Druid Dreaming' event last year and then the inspiration of **Damh the Bard** and his music at the concert in McLaren Vale, I was inspired to bring together all those working on the Druid path in Adelaide, South Australia and Australia in general to sit down together and talk about being a Druid in Australia, bringing the spirit of our ancestors into the sacred place of another living spiritual tradition.

I believe that the time right now is a significant time of change, a time for laying down new patterns based on elements of the old, with those of all spiritual traditions coming together. It has been rare for Druids in Australia to come out from the trees and stones and talk with each other about our life and practice here in Australia with respect for the indigenous culture.

Of course such a gathering would take a great degree of organization but for this year I suggest we start with a '**Gathering of Druids of Oz**' now in 2010, for anyone out there on Druid path or interested in learning. I suggest an afternoon session (3-4 hours) on **Saturday, 15th May**, leading into the evening event of 'English Ale', with those involved in the Druid Gathering to create a simple ritual on Druid principles for the evening event around the 'Wicker Man'.

This would be a Gathering of Druids of all persuasions: those who have studied with OBOD or Emma Restall-Orr or other British Druid groups; those who have worked with individual teachers or mentors or from family lineage; those who work in groups or those who are solitary in their practice. I am asking for Druids in Adelaide and South Australia for now but also any from interstate who may also be interested in this inaugural Gathering.

I envisage that from next year in 2011 we call a full day '**Gathering of the Druids of Oz**' from all over Australia to sit together, hopefully with some indigenous people as well, to talk about our work here in Australia and how we can work together with respect for the ancestors of our own spiritual and blood lineage and the ancestors, guardians and spirit beings of this land.

Personally I have followed a spiritual path through Druid wisdom and Celtic culture for over 30 years. I originally worked with Colin Murray and the *Golden Section Order of Druids* in London (while OBOD was in recess) in early 1980s and have since worked with individual teachers and mentors in UK, Ireland and here in Australia in the indigenous community. In 1999 I published a book with Capall Bann publishers in UK on Women in Celtic Myth titled "Creating Form from the Mist". For many years I have run courses and workshops on Celtic Culture and Spirituality.

I run tours on mythic themes, taking people with Celtic or British ancestry back to sacred sites in UK and Ireland. In 2010 the tour is '*The Goddess and Green Man*' in September/October where we will celebrate Full Moon at Autumn Equinox at Callanish Stones in the Scottish Hebridean Islands, along with other adventures at sacred places in UK and Ireland for period of 25 days.

Images credit: Adrienne Piggott

Exerts from the above publication:

"*I believe that the time right now is a significant time of change, a time for laying down new patterns based on elements of the old, with those of all spiritual traditions coming together. It has been rare for Druids in Australia to come out from the trees and stones and talk with each other about our life and practice here in Australia with respect for the indigenous culture.*

*Of course such a gathering would take a great degree of organization but for this year I suggest we start with a '***Gathering of Druids of Oz***' now in 2010, for anyone out there on Druid path or interested in learning. I suggest an afternoon session (3-4 hours) on* **Saturday, 15 May**, *leading into the evening event of 'English Ale', with those involved in the Druid Gathering to create a simple ritual on Druid principles for the evening event around the 'Wicker Man'.*

This would be a Gathering of Druids of all persuasions: those who have studied with OBOD or Emma Restall-Orr or other British Druid groups; those who have worked with individual teachers or mentors or from family lineage; those who work in groups or those who are solitary in their practice. I am asking for Druids in Adelaide and South Australia for now but also from interstate who may also be interested in this inaugural Gathering."

Golden Wattle Seed Group

Status; currently active. Adelaide surrounds. OBOD Seed Group.

Kacey Stephensen

THE *GOLDEN WATTLE SEED GROUP* came about in 2014 when a fellow Druid ('Richard') and I attended Binna Burra (Lamington National Park) in Queensland for the 14th OBOD Assembly, which was also the 50th Anniversary of the Order's founding. Inspired by the magic and community, I proposed forming a Seed Group and within a few weeks of returning to Adelaide, Richard and I planted the first seeds of this new fledgling group.

We started working regular ceremonies and invited interested people and other OBOD members along. A name was shortly decided upon, in respect of *Acacia pycnantha* - The Golden Wattle as it is commonly known in South Australia.

I've always had a strong affinity with wattle, its yellow flowers like clusters of little suns and their calming scent in early spring, the first flower buds beginning to open just a week or two after Alban Arthan and heading towards Imbolc. We spent a while contemplating what to call the little Seed Group but, in the end, *The Golden Wattle* was chosen for its name.

The wattle brings the light of the Mabon (the Child of Light) and rebirth at mid-winter through tree root, trunk and leaf from deep in the belly of the southernmost point, through the Imbolc South/East gateway and around sunwise, progressively but organically to the heart of the East, where Alban Eilir sings the song once more of spring; the blossoming of illumination from the unconscious, into the conscious and back again; one cycle - the flower and the circle.

On the 30th - 31st of August 2014 *The Golden Wattle Seed Group* planted a little grove in the back garden of the house I grew up in, working with the Order's Grove Planting Ceremony. Within this magical space and time, we planted the circle that we had marked out and prepared prior to ceremony. All of this a sacred process, spending considerable time connecting with the land, feeling the different areas and nuances of time and place; listening to what the spirits of place were telling us, building those relationships, giving offerings, and so on.

Within the centre, Richard carefully chose and placed four stones at the cardinal directions around the central fire pit, underneath which we buried offerings of mistletoe and wattle flowers and leaves. In the main part of the ceremony we had pre-dug the holes for the trees and placed next to them water and compost to be ritually planted. We planted some ogham trees and local indigenous trees and various herbs around the circumference of the circle. Over time, further trees have been planted, including an English Oak that I nurtured from a seedling and planted in the northern quarter for Earth Day, the following Imbolc season.

Many a ceremony was had in this grove and many campfires for the first few years. We went through dormant periods and then very active periods, celebrating the eight-fold wheel, also working magical rites for environmental courses and full moon peace ceremonies and meditations, bush walks and casual picnics as well.

Over the past few years, we have connected with other sacred places around the Adelaide hills, the Mallee, the Adelaide Botanical Gardens/Botanic Park, the southern and northern coastal beaches and members' houses.

One particular place we've been building a relationship with regularly, is a grove of big Sequoia (California Redwood) trees in the Adelaide Hills. This grove offers great shelter and a temperate micro-climate, even in 40 degrees! It is a really nice place for observing the seasons, meditation and Grade-relevant workings.

We are currently catching up to celebrate the wheel and to do inner group work, nurturing the collective mind of the group and learning from the land where we connect and work together.

For Imbolc 2018 we hosted the 17th OBOD Assembly here in South Australia, which was a big turning point for our group and really brought us closer together. While we have had our challenges like any group might have, we continue on and focus on nurturing the group as we evolve, adapt and change to the needs, seasons and cycles of our lives, collectively and individually.

The little yellow suns that are born from the wattle mother are the lantern lights of peace and the creative force of nature - Awen which wattle expresses and dispenses forth into the world and which is gifted to life by the Goddess of Moon and Earth and all living cycles, Ceridwen. It is the golden hair of Lleu Llaw Gyffes (the Lion headed youth with the steady hand) or the transformed Taliesin with the bright blossom from his brow, or Angus Mac Og. He is the flower and Brighid is the quickening Nwyfre through earth, that nurtures his returning love for her, reflected in his father - Og the (Sun) and all trees teach us this wisdom: as above, so below from earth to sun the axis mundi is made whole again.

We look forward to a bright future in our little group, both inwardly and outwardly; to serve, heal and to nurture each other and the earth. We know not what the forest path will bring further down the way, but wherever the wattle is flowering, inspiring and guiding people with her inner sight, wattle will continue to bloom at the turning point between winter and summer, between and within the unconscious and the conscious, the winter cave and the Beltane meadow, the memory of this ancient sacred land and the memory of our own ancestry.

Triad of a wattle:
Three things which enrich the wattle's heart:
1. Compassion for each other and the planet, because her flowering is gentle in existence,
2. Nurturing joy and friendship because life is a gift that joy fulfils and celebration enlivens,
3. Meditation to support the blossoming sun-flower within us all that is born from the depths of earth and which grows into the light of day, both within and without.

Golden Wattle Seed Group pendant

Photo credit: Kacey Stephensen

QUEENSLAND DRUID GROUPS

Australian College of Druidry (ACOD)

Status: not currently active. Was previously based in Queensland.

Corin Thistlewood

The Founding of ACOD
I feel very privileged to be asked by Sandra Greenhalgh of *Macadamia Grove* to do a write up about the *Australian College of Druidry* (ACOD) for the anthology *A History of Druidry in Australia*. Many people have told me that ACOD was quite instrumental in those early days. But as founder of ACOD, I think a little background about myself and the conditions that led to the founding would be useful.

Born in Liverpool of Irish and Welsh descendants, it was perhaps not surprising that as a child I was quite psychic. Spirit guides talked to me and helped me with my schoolwork, but only maths and science. My English was very poor which lead me to believe the guide was Irish.

In my early teens I used to dismantle and repair electronic equipment - much to the dismay of my parents who knew nothing of this, and I wasn't taught this at school. They eventually asked me how I was able to do this, and I told them it was the man in my head telling me how to do it. They were clearly horrified and said I shouldn't tell this to anyone! I took to a career in electronics with gusto and eventually became an Aerospace Engineer working for the Ministry of Defence.

However, I was also passionately interested in the supernatural and read extensively about it thoughout my teens and twenties. Eventually, in a bid to try and meet others who had similar interests, I enrolled in many different personal development courses. These I very much enjoyed but I came to realise there were not many people in these circles with my supernatural gifts or interests. In those days there was no internet, emails or chat rooms, so it was very difficult to find like-minded people.

Anyway, after many years of searching I was eventually admitted to a coven. I had to drive thirty miles to attend but it was well worth it as, at last, I was mixing with like-minded people who knew about the supernatural. My teachers were wonderful, and I soaked up the knowledge eagerly. It was a Gardnerian coven and so taught in a degree system. I went through my first and second degree very happily. It was much harder work than I thought but loved it.

There is too much to say for this short piece so I will be brief, but I had been reading up about history of UK Wicca and magic and going back to before the romans to the early Celts. The Celts fascinated me, and the early Celtic Druids interested me. I could see in those early times they were more like medicine men or shamans. I loved the idea of working outdoors in nature, with the sacred sites and megaliths.

One day while talking to a priestess, who was third degree, about how I felt, she agreed with me and said she was originally from Anglesey where there are many old sacred sites that are virtually unknown and rarely visited. And what an ideal place these would be to work my third degree which was coming up soon. I felt quite an affinity to this very wise older woman and wondered about this.

Anyway, to be brief, she talked privately to my high priest and priestess, and everyone agreed that, if I was willing, I could work my third degree with this priestess at one of those sacred sites. When I heard this, I wasn't so sure, as all our rituals had been indoors in a purpose built temple. It felt like a really big step. But she said that she would rewrite the ritual and adapt it for outdoors at a sacred site, an old long barrow that wasn't locked up and hardly anyone went there; I was hooked.

Afterwards I felt incredibly empowered and went on to work at sacred sites regularly. This is what started me on the shamanic path. Our rituals became more and more shamanic. We eventually set up our own coven and worked this way for many years. I still ran workshops looking for people who might want to join our coven. And in time, with Julian and Cat Vayne, we started regular Pagan meetings in the back room of a local pub, called The Gathering. This grew enormous and people from radio and television came to interview us often.

However, I grew to be very disturbed by the way western society abused and polluted the natural world. I wanted to 'walk my talk' and live off the land. In time I moved to the west coast of Ireland, and set up a smallholding there trying to live as self-sufficiently as I could. I set up *Tree-Wheel Crafts* making wooden staffs and wands, many other magical tools to order including Ogham sets. We got quite a name for ourselves for this in Ireland, UK and America. People there started to call me a Druid and so I felt that that was what I probably was.

Over the years I met and worked with the many Druids I found there and learnt so much about the old ways and Druidry and their affinity with the trees and the system of Ogham and so much more. We set up the *Grove of Sinnan* and ran many workshops for people who were interested in the old ways and Paganism. I was editor to Ireland's first Pagan magazine *Sheela-Na-Gig*. This reached many people in the most remote parts of Ireland; networking with them and enabling them to see they were not alone, there were many others there who were part of the growing Celtic Pagan revival.

Meanwhile I joined OBOD doing their correspondence course for several years. One of my fellow Druids and I went to visit Olivia Robertson at Huntington castle. We presented to her one of our bog oak wands which she treasured. Consequently, we were invited to many rituals at the castle, one of which I attended was filmed for a BBC TV program. Through this also the *Grove of Sinnan* became affiliated with the *Fellowship of Isis*. It was during my time in Ireland that I drafted what later became ACOD's Celtic Shaman correspondence course.

The Gods move in mysterious ways, I feel my life has been fated, in many ways I feel I often don't have control of my direction; I am here to serve the Goddess and where she sends me. And so what started off as a short traveling trip to Australia, ended with me marrying my lovely partner Naomi and staying there for many years.

In about 2001 I settled in the mountains behind the Gold Coast and found what seemed like a gift, this amazing house twelve-sided yurt made of wood with plenty of land to run workshops. I also wanted to link up with other Druids but there I drew a blank. It seemed that the Druid revival that was happening in the UK and which we had helped rekindle in Ireland, hadn't reached this corner of Australia yet.

I started going to any psychic fairs I could find, selling craft work and doing rune readings using the Ogham which most people were intrigued by. Then I found there were Pagans here, and went to the many Pagan gatherings, I talked to many people asking about other Druid groups and again drew a blank till some people said why don't you start your own, I'm sure people here would be interested, which seeded the idea and it grew from there.

So, I started running workshops, and hosting groves in my lovely garden in the mountains. They became very popular, I dug out my notes that I had drafted in Ireland and turned them into a small booklet called *Introduction to the Celtic Shaman*. Sales of this encouraged me so I started to write out the Celtic Shaman correspondence course. At the time the Celtic culture was undergoing a huge revival. Though at that time, generally what we had was two main paths or cults - the solar cult and the lunar cult, with adherents tending to stick firmly to their prescribed path, i.e. Wicca or Druid.

Enter ACOD. Over the years the two paths of the Solar cult and the Lunar cult have undergone a multitude of changes and revivals. Having been educated in both Wicca and Druidry and as the founding principal of the *Australian College of Druidry* it is my firm belief that these two paths were originally part of the same Druid college curriculum and if so, would give students a more balanced magical and esoteric education. So, this is how I went about creating the correspondence course - blending Wicca and Druidry. And to suit the modern educated student, I brought in some of the New Physics that was emerging then at that time - a mystical and esoteric self-development program, based on Celtic spirituality.

The courses proved to be very popular with people from all over Australia enrolling. We even had members from the UK and Europe. However, I also felt it very important to create a sense of local Pagan community, so wanted to involve local people face to face. The website *CelticDruid* helped with this. On there we had pictures and information about the hand-fastings (Celtic weddings) we did and also the many naming ceremonies for young babies born into the Pagan community. This included our own son Oliver who was dubbed the accolade 'the littlest Druid'. We also ran regular Grove meetings at all the eight festivals throughout the year. These were well attended, with people traveling many miles to be there.

We bought a tepee big enough to hold weekend retreats, involving people cooking on the open fire and sleeping in the round, feet towards the fire. I loved these retreats - I think they were my favourite. As previously mentioned, we ran many workshops in the grounds of our house (called the *Celtic Druid Grove*). These workshops included construction of a labyrinth, working with Celtic knots, talisman making and the ever-popular drum making workshops. This venue was also used by other people who ran their own workshops including our friends from Ireland Janet Farrar and Gavin Bone.

Back in Ireland the Pagan movement continued to grow and ACOD became affiliated with HOOD (*Hibernian Order of Druids*). Through this, the summer solstice gatherings at Tara (Ireland's sacred heart) began. I was invited to officially attend, representing the Druids of Australia. All the amazing photos of the wonderful costumes and ceremonies went on to the ACOD website and were viewed by the many Pagans who were part of the growing Pagan movement in Australia.

I would just like to point out that, although we charged for the courses and workshops, we ran the whole of ACOD as a not for profit organisation. All proceeds went back into covering costs or to expanding and buying things like the tepee, workshop materials etc..

As can be seen, ACOD had a very rich and varied foundation and I feel we, at ACOD, had a very positive effect on our local community and also Australia in general. We showed people who didn't know anything about Pagans how very human we were and that we were not to be feared. In fact, I feel very much that part of Druidry's popularity is that it is just that - a very human approach to honouring our connection to the natural world.

Macadamia Grove

Status: currently active. Based in Queensland. OBOD Grove.

Sandra Greenhalgh

THE ORIGINS OF MACADAMIA Grove (an OBOD Grove) arose from the inaugural Australian OBOD Assembly in 1997. At this Assembly I met Tuan, who was also from the Brisbane area, and we were inspired to create a new Brisbane Seed Group.

Our first ritual (in 1998) to inaugurate *Macadamia Seed Group* occurred on acreage which was owned by a friend at Ellen Grove. Tuan and I walked down the paddock together, and finally identified the 'right' spot for our Grove to be situated. As there were already two different witchcraft circles located on the property, we respectfully kept clear of those areas.

We came down to two choices for the name of our nascent Seed Group, both of which were based on local flora. I originally liked the idea of 'Moreton', as this was the English name for the bay and beautiful island east of Brisbane. It was also the common name for the majestic *Ficus macrophylla*, otherwise known as the Moreton Bay Fig Tree.

The other name option we both considered was Macadamia. Macadamia trees are local to north east New South Wales, and south east and central Queensland. These hardy trees grow the famous macadamia (or bauple) nut, which have a tough shell under a thick outside cover and need to be cracked open to reveal the delicious white nut within. Apart from childhood memories – Queensland children often spent many happy hours bashing the hard nuts with a hammer – we liked the Oghamic links between the macadamia nut and the mythology and lore associated with the hazelnut. As Tuan had already brought along a packet of macadamia nuts to celebrate our new Seed Group, the rest, as they say, is history.

As an aside, the name of our Grove has inadvertently caused much mirth to Australian OBODies over the years. At the Mt Hyland Assembly in 2015, the four original members of the rebirthed *Macadamia Seed Group* were housed in the same dwelling. When we expressed our joy at discovering this, we were told "yes, we put all of the Macadamias together." Somehow that changed to "ha, the Macadamia Nuts are in one place" and then the conversation further deteriorated (perhaps in a gently derogatory manner) to calling our temporary dwelling "the nut hut." However, the Macadamians rallied in our usual manner, finding this terminology a vast source of amusement. We now often call ourselves "the Nuts" … as we know the secret sweetness, nourishment and myth-wisdom that can be found beneath the hard shell of a bauple nut. Later, at SHOBODA in New Zealand in 2019, we also developed the Grove cry of *"Macca macca nut nut,"* with the valued assistance of Trudy Richards.

But that is in the future; and I must first continue to recount the past events prior to that time.

At some stage around 2000, Tuan moved away from Brisbane, and I began birthing and raising my children. Although *Macadamia Seed Group* existed in the OBOD communications, and I would receive the rare email from other members, the Seed Group lay dormant for many years. During this time (from early 2000 through to 2014), I continued to be involved in local south east Queensland earth-based spirituality gatherings as much as I could be, by attending events such as those run by the *Australian College of Druidry* (ACOD). However, with the challenges of raising two young children, attending any OBOD Assembly was not possible for many years.

Facebook is a great way to network, and on the 5 March 2011, I created a new Facebook group called *OBOD Macadamia Grove Seed Group*. On 27 August 2013, Mandy Gibson joined the Facebook group and on 21 October 2013, Linda Marson was added. These women, along with Carmen Holloway, would later become the foundation members of *Macadamia Grove*.

I didn't properly engage in-person with Australian OBODies again until January 2014, when I went to the 'Golden Anniversary' Southern Hemisphere OBOD Assembly, which was attended by Philip and Stephanie (the Chosen Chief and the Scribe of OBOD). It was in my own backyard, after-all - less than two hours' drive away. Nevertheless, it was a difficult decision to make, as it meant precariously leaving my children and husband together for a couple of nights as well as spending time with a group of people who were relative strangers.

But Elkie organised things – as she so efficiently does! - and pulled me into the fray. Before I knew it, I was sent a shopping list for breakfast and was the designated driver for Philip, Stephanie and Mandy.

At Binna Burra I spent time with Mandy, Linda, Carmen and Murray – who all lived within an hour or so from Brisbane. To represent Queensland during the main ritual, we added macadamia nuts, seedlings and a sunny orange and yellow scarf (donated by Mandy) to the tableau at centre of the ritual. It was a wonderful weekend, and we Queenslanders (plus Linda from just over the New South Wales border) found that we shared a sense of fun as well as a love of things Druidical.

Carmen and I also bonded as we both identified as being introverts, which somehow meant that we often seemed to find ourselves being introverted together away from the crowd.

We all agreed to meet up after the Binna Burra Assembly. From our first meeting, under the Moreton Bay Fig trees at the base of Mt Coot-tha, *Macadamia Seed Group* was reborn. We formally became *Macadamia Grove* in 2015 when a second Druid Grade member (Keri) agreed to participate in the Grove's activities.

In the early days from 2014 to the beginning of 2015, we only had about four people attending, but this small start formed a strong foundation. As a group, we have minimal emphasis on teaching, as we feel that the OBOD course provides the structure and material for everyone to work through at their own speed and style. Therefore, our activities are focused around celebrating together at the Equinoxes, Solstices and four Fire Festivals, with the occasional social 'coffee catch up' in between.

Due to this approach, we find that when members come together, we experience a sense of companionship, sharing of significant aspects of life (highs and lows) and lots of joy. Although we take our spiritual practices very seriously, we also enjoy having a great time together. There is usually mead to share after our ritual, regardless of the season. In our hot Queensland summers, we find it best to store our mead chilled in an 'Esky' or icebox.

As of mid-2019, we have nearly thirty active members, and most rituals involve ten to fifteen attendees. Our members travel from Pottsville in Northern New South Wales, hail from as far north as Hervey Bay, and as far west as Toowoomba. To facilitate travel requirements, most of our events are held in the middle of the day, on a Sunday. We find that this timing works best to enable maximum attendance and member availability.

In accordance with feedback from existing *Macadamia Grove* members, we prefer to keep the majority of our events limited to OBOD members only. We feel there are other opportunities available for people interested in generic earth-based spirituality. That way, when we celebrate together, we all share the same ethos and spiritual foundation, and this feels remarkably harmonious.

Our regular events include celebrating the eight seasonal celebrations and undertaking initiations. We keep the opening and closing components of rituals in the usual OBOD format, although we do sometimes modify the ritual within. Usually we try and include a bardic circle, however the majority of Grove members seem to be craftspeople rather than talented musicians. However, we don't let that stop us, and regardless of our perceived skill level, Mac-Grovers will join in to quote a poem or sing a song. Often images from Macadamia Grove rituals – or artefacts associated with our rituals – are included in *SerpentStar* by Mandy Gibson, who is currently the editor.

Finding our grove
Most of our rituals and events are hosted on Mt Coot-ha, which is a 3,700-acre tract of bushland, located twenty minutes' drive from Brisbane's central business district. Coot-tha means 'place of the honeybee.' For many years, Mt Coot-tha has been informally considered 'neutral territory' for those following an earth-based spirituality path in south east Queensland, and many rituals and gatherings have been celebrated under the gum trees in different locations. As *Macadamia Grove* members hail from a few hours north, south and west of Brisbane, it seemed the obvious space to seek a secluded place for us to celebrate our rituals.

On the day I sought our Grove location, I drove around Mt Coot-ha for about an hour, checking out different places. However, none of them seemed completely right; either too far away from car parking (which disadvantaged people with physical limitations), or too public, or just didn't have the right 'vibe.' Finally, in despair, I asked that the area to "*show me your secrets*" and within a few minutes I found the perfect site.

Our Grove location is an abandoned picnic area, boasting a dismantled stone table (which was previously used for a BBQ) located in the east. We use this structure as an altar as well as a handy storage area for bags and special items. Although the ground is stony, with shards of glass sometimes appearing from the earth after heavy rain, the grove is sheltered within a nest of trees, including a beautiful green-skinned gum to the West. The space feels protected and safe, although it is only a short walk away from the road. I do regret that bare feet are not possible for safety reasons, but that is my only criticism of this space where we gather to celebrate.

On the next terrace level down from our Grove were pre-cut, huge tree stumps, and over time we hauled these up and placed these in a circle. These stumps help shape the space as well as being very handy to sit on after the ritual. Sometimes these stumps are rearranged by other people sharing this space when we aren't present, but we diligently drag them back into the correct placement when that occurs.

Over time, we as a group have created shared stories and customs, such as the particular role of the Mabon (who is the youngest person in the Grove); consistently placing a heavy cast iron cauldron – which contains a cornucopia of candles, rocks, seeds and ritual items - at the centre-place of our rituals; the story of an inadvertent meeting with hair and candle; pronunciation of equipoise… or is that equi-porpoise?; spending a few moments quietly meditating in the bush before Carmen calls us back with the singing bowl; the gathering around after ritual, sitting on camp chair or stump; and the creation of the Grove banner.

Our Grove banner features four Australian creatures relating to the elemental energies we invite and later farewell during ritual. The bold and strong kangaroo stands in the north, place of summery warmth. In the east is the yellow tailed black cockatoo, as these magnificent birds with their consciousness-changing calls have visited us in the Grove during ritual. The red-bellied black snake is to the south, with the earthy-related energies of that direction. In the west, place of the mountain creeks and streams, is the unique and mysterious platypus. The banner was created in 2015, and during one of Linda's many visits to England, she arranged for our banner to be hung in Glastonbury Town Hall at the Summer Gathering, alongside other Grove banners from around the world.

Macadamia Grove – special mentions

While our members are each noteworthy in their own way, bringing many amazing skills and a wide range of knowledge to the Grove, here are some key (and favourite) shared group activities:

- We became an OBOD Grove in 2015.
- Facilitated over twenty Bardic Initiations and three Ovate initiations for members.
- Plans are in progress for *Macadamia Grove* to host the 2021 Southern Hemisphere Assembly.
- Held a couple of overnight *Macadamia Grove* Camps. The first camp included the group creating a three-metre-tall wicker man which was ceremoniously burnt in ritual. Shawn's safety demonstration of "safe" and "not safe" positions for burning torches made us all laugh. Both camp rituals included an enormous bonfire from dead trees and branches which needed to be burnt for fire-safety reasons.
- Held stalls at various local weekend markets.
- *Macadamia Grove* was the first Australian group to change the Ovate ritual format to a more shamanic-style option. This format has now been adopted across Australia and New Zealand at Assemblies.

- Miscellaneous rituals and gatherings of note include John Jordan's edible planet lesson; fiery enhancements courtesy of Valkyrie's and Jeremy Runnall's pyrotechnical and engineering skills; the dramatized Lughnasadh ritual we enact each year; a visit by the *Druid Pilgrim Grove*; sociable trips to Bribie Island.
- The 2015 Assembly at Mt Hyland was attended by four *Macadamia Grove* members; Linda, Mandy, Carmen, and me. We arrived at the venue after driving south through torrential rain. Linda nearly didn't make it to the venue that night, as the creek which crossed the access road was so high. However, she fortunately made it safely across before the road was cut off. At this Assembly, Mandy facilitated the Women's Circle, and I organised the Samhuin Ritual. We also put in our bid to host the next Assembly in Queensland.
- The 2016 Assembly was hosted by *Macadamia Grove* on Bribie Island. There were about twenty Grove members in attendance at different times over the weekend, with approximately forty people attending. Features of this Assembly included:
    o Each person brought a stone from their home area, which was placed into a cauldron of sea water. At the end of the Assembly, we each chose a new stone, with the extra stones being left on the earth. We later found that there are no local stones on Bribie, and it was a practice of Aboriginal people to bring their own stones with them when they visited here.
    o We invited a Gubbi Gubbi (the Australian Aboriginal people who are the traditional custodians of the island) person to tell us the local stories of this place. He entertained us with his passion about making rope.
    o Challenges included 'dessert-gate' and the unseasonable chilly weather, which made swimming in the nearby ocean less enticing than usual.
    o A stronger focus on presentations and workshops, including introducing Grade-specific workshops and the regular Men's and Women's Circles.
    o A designated time for markets and divination sessions.
    o The most amazing Beltane ritual, which included a triple spiral as well as a fire arch which was created by Valkyrie Blacksmith. A

YouTube video (created by Linda Marson) can be found online by searching 'Firearch Beltane OBOD'.
- o Inaugural Academia in Druid scholarly presentations session.
- The 2017 Assembly near Sydney was attended by thirteen Macadamia Grove members. This Assembly started in the usual magical fashion of greeting old friends and making new ones. One highlight (for me) was hearing how many people identified as being a member of *Macadamia Grove*, as we spoke our names and locations via the Talking Stick session. Unfortunately, my time was cut suddenly short, as I had to leave on Saturday morning due to sudden family ill health. I was devastated to miss participating in all the activities planned, including initiations, but particularly the Bardic Eisteddfod, and the Imbolc ritual, which featured many of the amazingly talented folk from *Macadamia Grove*. Fortunately, there were videos of the Eisteddfod, and I was delighted to be able to watch these afterwards.
- The 2018 Assembly in South Australia was attended by six Macadamia Grove members; Liz, Sam, Mandy, John, Carmen and myself. The MacGrovers were thrilled to be sharing a cabin together again, and there may have been a photo taken which featured us smiling with lolly teeth [Australian sweet shaped like oversized teeth and gums]. This event was such a wonderful opportunity to meet with OBODies from Western Australia, and my memories include the amazing indoor Ovate initiation (where it was cosy warm, unlike outside), and the wonderful Spring Equinox ritual (where it was chillingly icy in the enormous tin shed) which featured the rebirth of the Goddess. The South Australian Assembly was slightly smaller than the previous Druid events I had attended, but this was advantageous as it allowed a strong feeling of community and connection.
- The 2019 Assembly in New Zealand was attended by seven *Macadamia Grove* members; Mandy, Cecily, Rebekah Carr, Liz, Nina Saxton, Carmen, Linda and myself. Experiencing Druidry with embedded Maori cultural influences (and language) was an eye-opener for us Australian visitors, who are used to being scrupulously cautious and guarded against any cultural appropriation practices in our Druidry. We were also delighted to be able to spend time with Philip and Stephanie Carr-Gomm, as well as the incoming Chosen Chief, Eimear.

Finally, I shall leave you with a song. I crafted the words as a contribution to the Bardic Circle at the inaugural *Macadamia Grove* Samhain Camp. It is best experienced while sitting in front of a fire, surrounded by people who are dear to you, and sung to the tune of *The Wild Colonial Boy*.

Macadamia Grove Mighty Druids song

There was a Grove of OBODies
To one thing they did aspire;
They left their comfy homes and hearth
To build a bloody big fire.

They gathered at the Binghams
To fulfil their sacred quest
Bringing cane and stories and lots of mead
They worked hard with little rest

CHORUS
We'll wander over mountains
And we'll hug a lot of trees
For we are mighty Druids
And we like to drink our mead
(*Alternative: And we drink a lot of mead.*)

This bunch of mighty Druids,
Well they planned a Samhuin rite.
A wickerman, they did build,
To burn that April night.

In it and around it,
They wove spells of magic lore,
And far off in the distance…
The Ravens began to caw.

CHORUS

The flames leapt high,
Their spirits rose –
The wheel would spin again.
The old year it was burned away…
And nothing was the same.

By Oak and Ash and Yew and Thorne,
We'll burn away the dross,
By sacrifice, we'll be reborn,
And celebrate the Dawn!

Macadamia Grove banner design

Image credit: Sandra Greenhalgh

The Chair of Caer Witrin

Status: inactive. Based in Melbourne, groups in Queensland, Red Druidry

ACCORDING TO AN ARTICLE *What is Druidry?* Robin Fletcher (previously known as Timothy Ryan) names himself the Chief Druid of the *Red Druidic Chair of Caer Witrin*, the first formally constituted Red Druidic chair in the Southern Hemisphere, which he founded in 1985.

Above information sourced August 2019 from https://theslugfile.files.wordpress .com/2017/03/what-is-Druidism.pdf

Fletcher is not considered as representative of Druidry either historically, or in contemporary practices and he is excluded from Australian Druidry for valid reasons that are on public record, so further information is not provided within this volume.

For historical accuracy it is noted that a Queensland branch of *The Chair of Caer Witrin* began in Brisbane in 1991, utilising a range of written materials available to members. It closed in approximately 2000. This branch was separate to the Melbourne branch.

Queensland *Caer Witrin* members held public events and ran market stalls, including producing and selling a range of carefully researched and crafted items, such as Tawlbwrdd and Brandubh gaming boards (these are precursors to chess) drawing upon Welsh and Irish historical records.

Information regarding *The Chair of Caer Witrin* in Melbourne was not available and therefore has not been included.

[NOTE: The Editors, contributors and Australian Druidic communities do not condone or support any illicit or harmful actions undertaken by Fletcher. Abuses of power hold no place in Druidic philosophies and practices.]

VICTORIAN DRUID GROUPS

The Melbourne Grove (TMG)
Status: currently active. Based in Victoria. OBOD Grove

Elkie White

OUR GROVE BEGAN AT THE Spring Equinox in the year 1998, when three members of OBOD met and decided to form a Seed Group for Melbourne members of the Order. We agreed to meet eight times a year to celebrate the solar points, marked by the solstices and equinoxes, and the lunar gateways in between. We conducted our first ceremony at Beltane of that year with some of our friends. Gradually we established a small harmonious group of people who enjoyed each other's company. A circle of trees was planted to contain the energy and this would grow and become our Mother Grove.

It wasn't long before we began the task of adapting the traditional Northern Hemisphere ceremonies to their Southern Hemisphere correspondences. Intrinsic to the process, we adopted a policy of each person working with one particular role for 'a year and a day', before moving on to another. In 2002, Mike began creating diaries to match each role so that we could keep a record of our findings.

Between each ceremony we held a planning meeting to discuss the celebration that was coming up next. These evolved into a time to do practical work, pass the Touch Stone and share our personal development. Sometimes we attuned at deeper levels through meditation and always we listened respectfully to each other.

On the eclipse night of August 11 1999, we conducted our first Vision Quest. Consequently, we now have a site known as "Merlin's Chair". On December 1st of the same year, a group of women who had been working together spiritually for several years, decided to unite as an 'Elder Grove', providing further strength for TMG. Its function was (and still is) to offer healing, and to help younger members, as requested, and also to support and nurture the supporters and nurturers.

On January 26, 2000 we formally adopted the name *The Melbourne Grove*. The name 'Melbourne' can be literally translated as 'mill-stream', but also contains the mysticism of being 'born by the mill'. In the year 2000 we also conducted our first Naming Rite and commenced Bardic Groves, the first being held near the Ferntree Gully National Park. In September 2000, the fourth OBOD Southern Hemisphere Assembly was conducted in Albany, W. A. Prior to that, Assemblies had been conducted near Wiseman's Ferry near Sydney, 1997 and 1998, and at *Cooringal Grove*, Port Lincoln, 1999.

In 2001 Ann created a business called *Ancient Sacred Sites Tours* for people interested in visiting the ceremonial sites of our ancestors in Britain and Ireland. These would run for well over a decade. Very much closer to home, we started our Seasonal Observations booklet around this time (although informal work had been going on since our founding). At the time of writing, this little booklet has grown to over forty pages! The Assembly was held at Yulara that year in two cabins at the Caravan Park. We conducted an evening Winter Solstice Celebration at the lookout in the Park, after visiting Uluru and Kata Tjuta during the day.

2002 was a landmark year for Druid activities in Melbourne, quite literally, as the Guardians of the Mountain began revealing to us some very ancient, very sacred places. In response, we began to align our ceremonies with these sites. By aligning our southern hemisphere cycle of ceremonies with these places, we discovered the sacred geometry that has always existed around Mounts Dandenong and Corhanwarrabul. This work has a 'once and future' feel about it. These sites are so ancient they predate the Aboriginal peoples, although their ancestral presence feels strong and supportive.

Concurrently, we began to align these sacred places with the sacred times on the Druid calendar, so that spring equinox was celebrated at sunrise and autumn equinox at sunset. We celebrate summer solstice at noon but we don't wait until midnight for our winter solstice celebration because we have found any time after dark equally effective. Beltane is thus celebrated mid-morning at what we call "The Green Man's Spring", Lughnasadh mid-afternoon at "Lugh's Tor", Samhuin begins at dusk on the "Cailleach's Tor" and Imbolc, pre-dawn at our "Bridget's Well".

But back then, in 2002, before the above fell into place, we held Samhuin in Research and Spring Equinox near the Olinda Falls.

The Grove highlight of 2003 was the presence of two young Wurundjeri people at our Beltane Ceremony, and they planted a tree to mark the occasion. This was the year that Elkie's Naming Rite was conducted. The Assembly that year was hosted by Wyverne and Nellie in Punyelroo, SA, from November 22-24, and three of us were able to attend. A feature was the presence of Susan Jones, Tutor Coordinator, and the first Tutor's Meeting in Australia was held in the orchard on hay bales.

The first OBOD Tutors meeting in Australia

Image credit: Elkie White
Australian OBOD Tutors/Mentors with Susan, the Tutor Coordinator: Keith, Susan, Elkie, Rafayard, and Wyverne.

Southern Echoes, a collection of writings by Australian Druids, edited by Murray Barton, was launched at this Assembly. TMG's Bardic Groves were hosted by various members on the second or third Friday of the month, throughout 2003.

TMG conducted its first Marriage Ceremony at the beginning of 2004, and a lovely Joining of Hands Rite at Beltane. We also inaugurated a Stone Temple at

Flinders, thus linking Mountain and Sea. Another highlight of 2004 was linking up with the *EarthSoulScience* cooperative, from which several mutually rewarding friendships developed. The Assembly was held in Kingaroy, Qld, that year; hosted by Cherry and Denis Carroll. Our play – the story of Taliesin, adapted by Keira Lyons as a part of TMG's Lughnasadh Celebration – was a feature of this Assembly.

The year 2005 brought another important connection, this time with Caerleon, a local healing centre. On March 13, seven of our members created a seven-tier labyrinth at Naomh. It was also the year that four of our members – Marigold, Nicola, Amanda and Mike - created our Grove Banner. Made in May, it would arrive in Glastonbury for the Summer OBOD Gathering and hang proudly alongside the banners of other OBOD Groves from around the world in the Glastonbury Town Hall. A special copy of our beautiful Grove Book (Volume I) accompanied our banner to Britain. It records our earliest Southern Hemisphere rituals, enriched with artwork and Eisteddfod by various members.

That year, Samhuin was conducted on the Cailleach's Tor for the first time and Amanda and Mike hosted the Winter Solstice at a site in Ferny Creek. The Assembly was held on the south coast of NSW from October 28-30, hosted by Carole Nielsen and Wayne Clarke.

2006 was quite dramatic. Mike undertook a Vision Quest on what we would thenceforth call "Visioning Hill" above Ferntree Gully Cemetery. The Assembly returned to Cooringal the spring of that year, and an opening ceremony was conducted for a Men's Circle. Five years later, Men's and Women's Circles became a regular part of the Assemblies for a while. On September 3, Elkie announced that she was withdrawing from active participation in TMG for a while so that she could focus on the Ogam. At Beltane, as participants celebrated eight years of successful gatherings, they were blessed with the presence of a lyrebird at the site. Seasonal celebrations continued as before until the Autumn Equinox of 2007.

In the winter of 2007, some of us went to Gariwerd (Halls Gap) and participated in a cultural event there. Amanda told the story of Taliesin, and Elkie organized a winter solstice event with the blessing of the Indigenous custodians. Upon our return we swung straight into helping Clare organize a winter solstice in Belgrave as a part of the Lantern Parade celebrations.

During the winter months of 2007, *The Melbourne Grove* lay dormant and re-visioned itself. During this time, Elkie launched her website for *Pans Script*, which included a journal of her progress through the Ogam. Then on September 16, her preparatory work on the Ogam complete, Elkie recalled the Grove and presented a vision that correlates with an ancient myth from Ireland. It is an ancient story about a Central Pool with Five Tributaries. We correlated these 5 Streams with the 5 ways that *The Melbourne Grove* expresses itself, the main one being seasonal and public celebrations such as namings, weddings, house, and land blessings. No longer restricted to one part of Melbourne, these rituals were conducted in or around this great city. As before, Grove members invited their friends to these rituals but now with a clearer understanding that they are responsible for their friends.

The second stream we called 'extended activities', this part of the vision serving to extend our understanding of what it means to be a Bard, Ovate, and Druid, in today's world. Individual members of TMG are involved in a number of independent activities and, where these reflect activities in keeping with Druidic philosophies; they are embraced and supported by TMG. Thus members may be involved in groups and projects that support the community, the environment, or social justice. Other activities enjoyed by members enable bardic expression, such as music, story writing and performance. Members may also be engaged in healing practices such as shamanism. Furthermore, and in addition to our own celebrations, TMG sometimes joins up with other community groups in and around Melbourne that honour the land and celebrate the seasons.

We specified 'going solo' as another strand within TMG because every Druid needs to be able to connect with their inner guides, guardians and groves and conduct their own ceremonies. Working on your own for a cycle of celebrations helps you to attune in a totally personal and inward way to the land, the guides, and the meaning of the rituals.

Another strand at that time was called 'affiliated groups.' These were independent groups whose practices and philosophies complemented those of TMG. This included *The Elder Grove* facilitated by Elkie, the *Grove of the Diving Kestrel* run by Amanda and Mike, the *Pan-Corhanwarrabul Grove* conducted by Elkie, *Cú in Cockatoo* run by Lady Cú, and the *Grove of the White Cockatoo* run by Trudy in Kyneton.

Specializations of OBOD supplied the fifth strand. Complementing TMG's seasonal rituals are more private rites. These are for members of OBOD only and include the Initiation Rites into the Bardic, Ovate, and Druid Grades. The Southern Hemisphere OBOD Assemblies also belong to this Stream as we actively participate in these.

Mike and Amanda hosted a Summer Solstice Vigil from their home near Flinders, in 2007. Then, after a brief rest, our regular cycle of seasonal celebrations resumed at the Winter Solstice of 2008. They now comprised twenty parts aligned with the magic of the Ogam. TMG's 10th anniversary was marked by a very special event that brought most of us together. On September 21, 2008 we conducted a Marriage Celebration Ceremony for Mike and Amanda at their outdoor temple at Flinders. It was a day blessed by good weather, good company, and a whole lot of love!

Samhuin 2009 was special because it was conducted in the newly-created Ogam Spiral at Heartswood in the Strathbogie Ranges. It was also TMG's first weekend retreat and it gave us time to not only conduct the ceremony but also to review the document you are reading, and to discuss the progress of our plans for an Assembly in April 2010. Another highlight of that weekend was that during the Samhuin Eisteddfod, Jowen presented each of us with a booklet entitled *The Melbourne Grove: Songs for Ceremony*. In it are all the songs that Jowen and others had created over the past two and a half years. These beautiful songs remind us of our intimate connection with the elements, the seasons, the land, and those that guide us. They are easy to sing yet quite profound. At time of writing, Jowen is still adding to these.

Another highlight of 2009 was an impromptu walk Elkie and another member undertook in response to a vision of Pan. This led to the discovery of what we would call "Pan's Sanctuary": an oak grove in the midst of Lysterfield Lake Park!

Between 2009 and 2016 – for a full nine-year cycle – we had a Central Pool of TMG members to keep things running smoothly. Members of the CP were members of OBOD who had shown an ongoing commitment to TMG. The first Central Pool was held on July 25, 2009. This was the team that steered us to, and through, the 10th Southern Hemisphere OBOD Assembly conducted in Cockatoo, from April 23 to 26, 2010.

The Assembly was definitely the highlight of 2010. Hosted at Cú by Lady Cú, her husband, and their three hounds, and with over thirty other people in attendance, it witnessed Reilly's Bardic Initiation in the Birch Grove, MV's Druid Initiation in the Oak Grove ("Pan's Sanctuary"), and Cherry Carroll's Croning in the Yew Grove. This was the first time a group ritual had been conducted by us in any of these places. In our mind's eye, our sacred centre – the William Rickett's Sanctuary - is now peopled with Druids from all over the place. The best eisteddfod we have ever experienced brought the theme of the Assembly – Pan – to a crescendo, which was then further developed in the Play the next day.

Written by Keira Lyons and directed by Mike, masked characters danced the circle as they played their part in honouring this magical deity. At this Assembly Ngatina launched the druidryaustralia.org website; currently moderated by Chris Parker.

Samhuin was conducted at our Flinders Site directly after the Assembly, with one of our guests staying on in order to experience it with us. Prior to that, Autumn Equinox had been conducted at the 'She Oak Site' in Montrose. Spring Equinox was conducted in Cockatoo at the same place as the Assembly, and Beltane was conducted at Trudy's place in Kyneton.

As we approached our 12th Anniversary, we considered the question: "what would we like TMG to look like at the end of the next twelve years?" We recognized that this was a difficult question to answer, for the Grove is an organic and evolving entity, and unforeseen change can come quite suddenly. We were happy with the progress of the Grove and the Assembly had brought forth much inspiration and energy towards our perceptions of TMG and our hopes for its future. We felt that rather than the business model of 'end product', we preferred the magic of casting a ray of light into the future with the best of our intentions and seeing what happens; placing us in harmony with the dynamics of the Grove and leading us to deeper places within ourselves and within our relationships with each other. We wanted to spend more time with our 'Druid family' developing trust and understanding both within the grove itself and with Assembly participants. We were inclined to extend our seasonal celebrations, so that they included an overnight stay near to our places of ceremony, giving us time to explore each site and season more deeply together.

In 2010 we experienced joy and sorrow, in equal measure. Three beloved people and three beloved pets winged their way to the Summerlands during the latter part of the year, and Elkie conducted her first Memorial Service on behalf of a friend during this period.

Given the ferocity of the storm that interrupted our Summer Solstice Celebration, one could be forgiven for thinking it was the Spirit of Melbourne's attempt to wash all the sadness away. Yet we will remember this occasion equally for the special guests who attended it with us. With two of our Assembly friends (Reilly from Sydney and Murray from Brisbane) and the two who missed the Assembly (Wyverne from South Australia and Nigel from North Wales) present, it gave the gathering the feeling of a mini-Assembly. Nigel is co-founder of *Druidic Dawn* and Elkie was its Southern Hemisphere representative, this occasion giving them the opportunity to liaise. To say it was a big year is a gross understatement.

Everything irrevocably changed in 2010 and left us in awe of what 2011 might bring.

We were not disappointed! 2011 began with much movement of people to be followed by the movement of ideas. The year began for some of us with a trip to Sydney to participate in the marriage of a friend we made at the Assembly. Then Jowen moved to Queensland for a year while Mike and Amanda took care of her home. Before leaving, we acknowledged Jowen's naming of her home as the *Grove of the Mountain Ash* (GMA) and for the coming year GMA and the *Grove of the Diving Kestrel* became as one. *Monday Night Druidry* (MND) began there shortly afterwards. This offered us the opportunity to meet weekly and meditate together. We worked on our personal creative projects during this time. We also listened to each other's music and discussed books that have influenced us. In 2012 MND participated in the *Global Art Project* with a painting we had all contributed to. MND activities would also lead to Volume 1 of *The Druid's Fireside Book of Tales*, comprising original works by members, and edited by Jowen.

The other exciting thing *The Melbourne Grove* did in 2011 was host Damh the Bard's inaugural concert at Bar 303 in Northcote. Ten of us put in $40 each to cover the fares from Adelaide to Melbourne. *Spiral Dance* sponsors Damh's concerts in Australia and we were treated to a concert that included them both. They flew into Melbourne on Friday May 19 and we picked Damh and Cerri up from the airport. We took them to Ceres for a look around and then onto a restaurant with lots of seating just a few doors down from 303. After the concert we drove to Kyneton where Trudy had prepared a comfortable bed for our special guests. We enjoyed their company over brunch and then Lady Cú drove Damh and Cerri to the airport in time for their Sydney concert on Saturday night.

In 2011 Lughnasadh was hosted by Trudy at the *Grove of the White Cockatoo* in Kyneton, and Mike and Amanda hosted Autumn Equinox at Seawinds, Arthur's Seat. Mike also hosted 'Imbolc-Unscripted' at our regular site. A very pregnant Julie Mills (Brett) was visiting us from Sydney at the time and she, with Matt Brett, joined in the celebration with us.

On September 11, we returned to Heartswood in the Strathbogie Ranges and there conducted a very special Spring Equinox Ceremony, with the *EarthSoulScience* mob and some of the locals. The preparatory work done, we stayed overnight at Heartswood and conducted a ritual when the full moon was setting in the west while the sun was rising in the east. Steve's harp stood to the west and seemed to play of its own accord at significant moments, like when the babies in the centre spontaneously joined hands during the Blessing of the Children.

In October 2011, the Assembly returned to *Cooringal Grove* in South Australia, and, as a direct result of the Melbourne gathering, Rafayard extended the number of days to five. (Note, as of 2018, this pattern for Assemblies continues: Friday for arriving, Saturday for Bardic Grove, Saturday for Ovate Grove, Monday for Druid Grove and Tuesday for departing. This structure still works for us.)

TMG's Beltane was hosted by Marigold that year, in her home, because it was pouring outside. Masks were a distinct feature. For Summer Solstice we returned to the *Grove of the White Cockatoo* in Kyneton and included an overnight vigil in our celebrations.

2012 was a creative year, during which the idea of the host deciding how the ceremony will be organized took hold. It brought us into line with the way that the Australian OBOD Assemblies have always been run.

The special task of the third CP was to oversee the birth of TMG on the world-wide web. Initiated by M. C. as his Bardic gift to TMG, he explained his concept to us the day after our Winter Solstice Ceremony in Kyneton. The response was passionate and by Samhuin 2012 we had a fully functioning and beautiful website, complete with an Intro to Druidry, an audio track, blog, events calendar, member's corner, and affiliated groves section; Mike working tirelessly as our 'chief executive'. At Autumn Equinox 2012 we began a section called the 8-fold year, the idea being to take the traditional themes of each Seasonal Celebration and illustrate ways in which they relate to us here in Melbourne.

The *Grove of the White Cockatoo* hosted two ceremonies in 2012: Samhuin and the Spring Equinox. Damh the Bard, Cerri Lee, and *Spiral Dance* returned for a second Melbourne concert in May. During that year Jowen contributed articles about us in *The Druid Network's Groups and Groves* Newsletter.

On April 14, 2012, Bardic Groves resumed after a period of dormancy. Instead of the emphasis being on the gwersi as it was for the initial gatherings, it was now on Eisteddfod. On July 14 Reilly McCarron took this to the stage with an original piece of work: *Sleeping Kingdom, Waking Beauty*. Then in September we moved sunwise from east to north with Holly hosting.

The 2012 Assembly was hosted by Ngatina Sylvanius in Beltana, and from October 25 to 29 we were treated to visiting sites in the Flinders Ranges, South Australia. There was a film being shot there at the time – *Tracks* – but that didn't impact much on us. Highlights included separate Men's and Women's Circles – each at their own special site – on separate days. When the men returned from their Circle, it was to lunch prepared for them by the women, and likewise, when the women returned from their Circle, it was to lunch prepared for them by the men. Another highlight was Ngatina showing us each plant of her Flinders Ranges Ogam. The labyrinth that served as our Opening and Closing 'circles', was another feature. At that Assembly we honoured the Morrigan and dressed in her honour at the Eisteddfod.

On January 6, 2013 Initiations were the focus of Bardic Grove and we initiated six bards. Elkie knew that it was unnecessary to carry the load all by herself and so she introduced the idea of 'Helpers'. Five people—Amanda, Mike, Jowen, Debra and Lady Cú —initiated at earlier Bardic Groves - became Helpers for the six new ones. This idea would catch on at Assemblies, which invariably conduct multiple initiations. The Eisteddfod presented by the new bard at our 2013 Initiations, as their gift-of-appreciation, was another highlight of this ceremony. (This is yet to catch on at Assemblies but maybe we can get it going at our next one).

In 2013, Autumn Equinox was hosted by Trudy in Kyneton, and Samhuin by Lady Cú in Cockatoo. Elkie missed those celebrations because she was in the UK but Lady Cú kindly hosted a second Samhuin for us the following year.

At Winter Solstice and Imbolc we conducted our traditional ceremonies at our traditional sites and we felt truly blessed. Each of those sites revealed much to us either during or after the ceremony. We know now that there are actually two groves at Singleton's Reserve: our traditional circle, now with its own gateway, and the Guardian's Circle to the south-east. Bridget's Well revealed caves beneath our feet. Thanks to the insight of several Grove members, much of it gained during the meditations we conduct as a part of our seasonal celebrations, we are aware that we are living and working on a land populated by beings of multiple dimensions, many of whom are supportive of us.

Jowen hosted Spring Equinox from her home in both 2013 and 2014, including the option of an overnight stay so that we could begin before sunrise.

2014 began with an Assembly in Queensland, which several TMG members attended. Philip and Stephanie joined us as did OBOD members from Queensland, South Australia, New South Wales and the ACT. We celebrated OBOD's 50th Anniversary with 50 beeswax candles and into the Circle we created with them, Elkie told the story of the Australian Assemblies since their beginning in 1997. Sandra Greenhalgh and Elkie were both at that first Assembly but after about three years the *Macadamia Seed Group* went into dormancy. At this Golden Anniversary of OBOD, Sandra met other enthusiastic Brisbane members and the

Macadamia Grove exploded into action. Also at this Assembly, we started a fund, initially to support Philip and Stephanie's visit, but then gifted by them for future Assemblies. Cherry Carroll looks after this for us and it is used to pay deposits.

Shortly after the Binna Burra Assembly, TMG gained three new members, all beginning at the *Grove of the Black Swan* in Williamstown. Khe-Ra hosts these events for us and appropriately they are conducted down by the water at Autumn Equinox, at sunset. We include a Prayer for the Healing of the Waters in these rituals. On a clear day we can see Mounts Dandenong and Corhanwarrabul to the east of where we stand, which means that this site aligns with our sacred geography.

Imbolc was special that year too. We conducted it at our regular site but this time we were treated to breakfast at Deb's place, which is in walking distance of Bridget's Well. We didn't walk because rain was threatening, but thankfully it didn't break until our ritual was complete. At Beltane we were treated to a site that Trudy found for us near Daylesford – Woolnough's Crossing – fulfilling a delightful weekend experience.

In 2015 all of the seasonal celebrations were conducted at our traditional sites. As well as these, Jowen and Barb hosted Yule by the Winter Fireside at Barb's house in Kallista. It was a joyous event with feasting, music and story-telling. The Wassail Bowl was passed around, candles were lit by each person to represent a wish for the year ahead, and a Yule Log was lit. Jowen would later shift these events to her place and introduce the Kissing Ball, made mostly but not exclusively of mistletoe. These Yule celebrations would ultimately lead to Volume II of *The Druid's Fireside Book of Tales*.

The team effort that has been a feature of Assemblies since our hosting in 2010, continued with the one near Dorrigo, hosted by M. V. From April 24-28, 2015, we, including five TMG members, stayed at a special place in Mt Hyland, NSW. There, we honoured Samhuin and conducted our first Peace Ritual at the time of the full moon.

On September 20, TMG conducted its Spring Equinox Ritual in the Hamer Arboretum, Olinda.

By 2016 our Calendar of Events had a different host for each of the seasonal celebrations, each host presenting their preferred form of ceremony and interpretation of the event. As before, some members opt to host a particular event for more than one season and thus develop their ideas. Christina Davidson began hosting Imbolc, still at Bridget's Well, and Narine began hosting Spring Equinox by the Yarra River. Fiona Songbird hosted Summer Solstice that year. It was clear that the Central Pool was no longer needed and so on February 6, 2016, we closed it. At Spring Equinox that same year it was decided to open a private Facebook page for *The Melbourne Grove*. We stopped collating Grove Books at that point because much of what used to go into them was now covered by our Facebook page.

On June 23, Trudy and Elkie met in the Druid's Café in the city and undertook a thorough inspection of the entire Druid's Building in Swanston Street. Originally home to the UAOD, they were disappointed to find little evidence of this.

In October 2016, the Assembly was conducted at Bribie Island near Brisbane and hosted by the burgeoning *Macadamia Grove*. We were each gifted with an 'Awen bag' made by Cherry Carroll and were also given gifts that represent *Macadamia Grove*. Five TMG members attended, including Fiona, for whom we conducted a Druid Grade Initiation there (with Cherry). The idea of 'workshops' was initiated by the *Macadamia Grove*. These gave OBOD members an opportunity to talk about a topic of interest to them. To date this idea has proved popular. Also at this Assembly the idea of scholarships was introduced. As they booked into the Assembly, participants were given the opportunity of making a donation towards a fund that would support members who wanted to come but needed financial support. To date this is working well and Cherry Carroll is looking after the scholarship fund for us. Another initiative at this Assembly was the early morning meditations. Led by Jeremy Runnalls and Mandy Gibson at Bribie Island, others would carry this forward at future Assemblies.

For ten years Elkie offered a *Course in Druid Mysticism*, based on the work she was doing with the Ogham, and a number of TMG members participated. On November 26, 2016, the final session was conducted at our Flinders Site in honour of Mór, the Sea.

One remarkable insight that emerged from the course was that our rituals could be backed by the structure of the Ogham, adding thus to their efficacy and power. With only a very slight adjustment, the OBOD seasonal celebrations can be given twenty roles (plus one for the Mabon). Each role can then have a corresponding Ogam (plus the mistletoe). None of the beauty of the OBOD rituals is lost in this, indeed the adjustment is so slight that one has to wonder if, in the larger scheme of things, this structure has been inherently there all along.

For Lughnasadh, 2017, we visited a sacred site in Werribee: Cobbledick's Ford. Hosted by Khe-Ra, it was a hot day and we enjoyed a dip in the river afterwards.

In August 2017, seven TMG members attended the Assembly in Pennant Hills, Sydney, hosted by Chris and Glenda Parker and the *Song of the Eastern Sea Seed Group*. At a Welcoming Ritual on the evening of 'Arrival Day', we were each ceremonially gifted a blue bag with a whale picture on it and a token gift inside from each member of the seed-group by way of introducing themselves. This was the first Assembly that celebrated Imbolc and over fifty people attended. We've honoured Bridget before – at the 2011 Cooringal Assembly and the 2014 Binna Burra Assembly – but this was the first time we honoured her exclusively at what is rightly her celebration. At this Assembly, the program was changed so that workshops were held in the morning and initiations in the afternoon, and it worked well. This was when Elkie launched the *History of Druidry in Australia* project. Eleven people applied for Bardic Initiation at this Assembly and thus this became the first time that we split the initiates into two groups. By now there were sufficient Druid Grade members to be able to do that. (In future when this happens, I would like the two groups to come together at the end for a combined celebratory Bardic Grove).

Also, in August, Elkie was invited to join the *Pagan Collective of Victoria* (PCV) as a representative of OBOD. This she did and has since been able to assist with articles for the *Wild Hunt*, which the PCV President contributes to.

On September 6, five of us visited Seven Acre Rock for the first time. And then on November 26, eleven of us visited Wurdi Youang for the second time; (the first being in December 2015). These very sacred sites directly relate to the sacred geography work that *The Melbourne Grove* has undertaken the past nineteen years.

At Summer Solstice 2017, *SerpentStar* celebrated its 20th Anniversary. *SerpentStar* is the newsletter for Southern Hemisphere members of OBOD. Created at the first Assembly by Carole Nielsen, it has had a succession of brilliant editors, the current one being Mandy Gibson. She decided to offer a special Summer Solstice edition to mark the occasion, inviting subscribers to write about their first encounter with Druidry in the Southern Hemisphere. Summer Solstice in Melbourne was a big event that year too, with a record 19 people in attendance at our traditional site on the mountain.

On January 7, 2018, Fiona, Trudy, Jowen, Khe-Ra, Narine and Elkie initiated five new members into the Bardic Grade in a ceremony as delightful as its predecessor in 2013. This time we were also honoured to have newlyweds Debs and Bracken in attendance. Marriage Equality became law in Australia on

December 7, 2017, and although Debs and Bracken had married earlier than that in England, we were still delighted to celebrate this wonderful event with them.

From March 2 - 5, 2018, Julie Brett hosted the inaugural *Druids Down Under National Gathering* (DDUNG) in Sydney. Most members of TMG are also members of the *Druids Down Under* Facebook page, which has been operating since 2007. Elkie felt fortunate to be able to attend the DDUNG and invited to talk about OBOD and the work we have been doing here in Melbourne. She called her talk *OBOD, Awen, and Communing with the Land*. Several other Druids presented workshops as well and many were recorded. At the DDUNG, members of OBOD, ADF, and the BDO combined to produce rituals that featured key elements of each of these Druid teaching organizations. *Spiral Dance* entertained us on Saturday evening and Eisteddfod was improvised on the other evenings. We all got on really well and are looking forward to doing it again.

On June 10, Bardic Groves resumed within TMG, this time at the Burvale Hotel; the location chosen to be fair to members from all four 'corners' of Melbourne. We held them once a month until September.

From August 10-14, the 17th Southern Hemisphere OBOD Assembly was held at Stockport in South Australia, and hosted by *The Golden Wattle Seed Group*. This was the first Assembly to honour the Cailleach and she certainly made her presence felt in the freezing cold weather! The Seasonal Celebration cleverly marked the transition from winter under the Cailleach to spring and the awakening of Bridget. Ritual drama can be so effective when it is lovingly done!

Twenty years since our founding, our anniversary became a triple celebration: Beltane, at the usual time and place, an overnight gathering at Gilwell Park with a Bardic Initiation, and our first public ritual for Summer Solstice on behalf of the PCV.

In January 2019 the 18th SHOBODA (as the *Grove of the Summer Stars* folks called it) was held in New Zealand. A total of 70 people attended this Assembly, including Philip, Stephanie, and Eimear. Three members of TMG were among those 70 attendees – Trudy, Narine, and Elkie – and as our gathering drew to a close, we were given the Assembly Candle to bring home with us.

We are looking forward to hosting our second Assembly in 2020. This one will be in Gembrook, not far from where we hosted the first. To this end we've opened a *Friends of The Melbourne Grove* Facebook page. We are hoping that the *History Project Book* will be ready to launch at this event.

The Melbourne Grove banner

Photo credit: Elkie White

Silver Birch Grove

Status: active. The author is based in Victoria. Ár nDraíocht Féin: A Druid Fellowship (ADF) is an international group.

Shaz Cairns

Please describe where you live:
Lalor, northern suburbs of Melbourne, Victoria, Australia.

When did you join ADF?
I Joined ADF in January 2007. A friend of mine, Rob, was running a Pagan youth group and I had been giving him a hand with that. We had taken some of the group to Mount Franklin, both for the experience of a public rite and to teach them a few camping and life skills. I had already identified as a Druid at that point and hadn't had any luck finding groups with that focus. I was solitary, but not by choice.

Then we became aware of some of the problems that were occurring in the community (I refuse to write his name) and Rob and I were looking for online resources to help keep these kids safe. Rob found ADF and the *Cult Danger Evaluation Framework*. It's a checklist to ask you whether or not the group you have found is a cult. Rob joined ADF in late 2006 for the study program and suggested I check it out because he knew of my situation.

I joined in January 2007 and was overjoyed with the amount of information, the study program and that there were actually other Druids I could correspond with. There weren't many Australian members at that point, but I was able to start getting to know other Druids in the USA. I began some small ADF rites as a Solitary and began enjoying writing my own rites using ADF's Core Order of Ritual. Rob was amused, given I had said how much I enjoyed my simple rites at home.

I could see what other ADF Groves were achieving in the States. We had a look at what was required to start an ADF Grove here in Melbourne. It seemed straightforward, so after deliberating on a name, I chose *Silver Birch*, for a number of reasons, but mostly because we were the first Grove in Australia and because Birch is the first letter, Beith, in the Ogham alphabet. We became an ADF Protogrove on 31/7/2007.

I was still struggling, being so far away from the main body of ADF. I began to correspond with Kirk Thomas who was Vice ArchDruid at the time and he was incredibly supportive. The Grove by this time included Rob, his partner Rose, my sister Ang and one other.

Rob Lewis, the then ADF Secretary came to visit us at our Grove's Nemeton in 2009. Even though there was only a handful of us, he still sat with us and presented an ADF 101 workshop. It was so reassuring to feel that what we were doing mattered. With Rob Lewis and Kirk's encouragement, we decided to apply for full Charter in 2010. To do that we needed three paid up members of ADF, character references and a document to notarise Rob's, Rose's and my signatures as the three first officers of the Grove. The three of us went to Epping police station to get it done. The very friendly officer asked, "What did I just sign?" Rob replied, "You just helped to found a Church". The look on her face was priceless. So, in March 2010, we became a Chartered Grove of ADF.

Ang and I went to our very first *Wellspring* in May 2010. *Wellspring* was then held at Brushwood, Sherman, New York. Ang and I were the first Australians to make it to the festival which is also ADF's Annual General Meeting. We were so well taken care of. Rob Lewis was our host, he showed us around New York and then took us to the campsite. Karen Clark in particular made sure we had everything we would need before we had even arrived.

Kirk was elevated as Arch Druid at this time and I was asked to call on the Earth Mother during the evening Sumbel. It was a wonderful experience and certainly helped Ang and I to see full ADF rites for the first time in person.

We went again in 2011 and Rob and Rose joined us there. We made our own way there and were a bit more relaxed and really enjoyed renewing the friendships we had made the previous year.

ADF is split into Regions and each Region has a Regional Druid that looks after its members and Groves. Australia was part of one of the Regions in the States and New Zealand was part of Europe. Drum had become Vice ArchDruid and we went through a process to form a new region, Asia Pacific, which included most areas of the world who followed a Southern Hemisphere practice.

On 1st September 2011 the new Region was formed and I became Regional Druid for the Asia Pacific. Drum and Kirk were now making sure that ADF called itself an international organisation.

In 2015, Drum came to visit us in Australia as Vice ArchDruid. *Silver Birch Grove* was hosting the main rite at the Mount Franklin Pagan festival. Drum thought that it was a great excuse to visit Australia and he came and camped with us, ran some wonderful workshops and discussions and made us all members of RDNA.

It was my pleasure to be included in the rite when Ang and I returned to *Wellspring* in 2016 to be part of Drum's elevation as ArchDruid. Drum is planning to return to Mount Franklin for the 40th anniversary of Mount Franklin.

More recently I was made Deputy Regional Druid. So now ADF is truly international, with members and Groves all over the Southern Hemisphere

Why did you join? Why not some other Druid group? What do you like about ADF?
The internet was a little different to the way it is now, just 10 years on. I had done some online searches for Druid groups and couldn't find anyone local. I am aware now that the OBOD *Melbourne Grove* existed, but I didn't then.

I had looked at some other online groups and was a member of a couple. They weren't really my cup of tea, mostly because I was interested in comparative mythology and they seemed to, well basically, make a lot of stuff up.

When did you realise you were a 'Druid'? And how did that feel?
It's hard to pinpoint one specific incident. I had started to question my place as a member of the Anglican Church. It was all about the pine trees and snow to be honest. I wanted to understand how they fitted into the Christmas narrative. I had also been drawn to Druids in popular culture and was playing a number of online games and would always choose to be a Druid character. I began reading comparative mythology and it just resonated. I would make small offerings at the solstices and equinoxes and it just felt right

When did you first meet another Druid or member of ADF? Describe that encounter.
I think the most significant first meeting would have to have been when Rob Lewis came to visit. It was a wonderful feeling, just to have someone else there who spoke the same language with regard to Druidry

Are you involved in any other groups (related to your Druidry or spirituality)?
I belong to some genealogy groups. It helps me to connect with my Ancestors. I do belong to a number of environmental groups as I feel it is my duty as a Druid to protect the Earth Mother in all her forms.

Do you see any link between the Druidry that you practise today and the Druidry that was practised by the United Ancient Order of Druids in the early years of European settlement?
They cared for their community.

Why do you think Druidry is becoming more popular in Australia? What do you think people are looking for? Has this changed over the years?
I really am not sure why the change. We certainly have a lot more people attending our rites and meet ups. People often tell me that they find our group to be more relaxed and laid back and that it makes it more accessible.

I think the internet has changed too and it is now easier to find groups online. When I was starting on my path, I had a number of friends who were witches and wiccans and I just wasn't interested in joining a coven. I had been invited to a number of rites which I attended with them, however it just didn't resonate with me. There were plenty of groups online, but very few Druidic groups and they were all overseas.

What do you think is distinctly '*Australian*' with regard to Druidry?
The Earth Mother is everywhere. Travelling overseas has only made that feeling stronger for me. We follow and honour the seasons as they are occurring around us and I feel that supports an Australian practice.

Silver Birch Grove banner detail

Image credit: Shaz Cairns

Silver Birch Grove Banner

Image credit: Shaz Cairns

WESTERN AUSTRALIA DRUID GROUPS

Druid Journey
Tyna King

BACK IN 1988 WHEN I was 20, I read a couple of novels which sparked my curiosity. I'd heard of witches but not too much about Druids (they seemed rather mythical back then, ahaha).

I moved from Sydney to Western Australia by myself in 1990 when I was 22. I spent a few years looking for a Coven to join but none were grabbing me. Meanwhile I just kept reading more and more stuff.

Then in 1997, the local community centre (Minnawarra House in Armadale) bulletin board had a notice for a six week Druidry Today an Introduction course. Well this got my curiosity dancing. I phoned, spoke to a woman about the course and signed up. Originally it was to be held at the community centre but because there were only three people interested, they decided to hold it in their backyard grove.

The first time I stepped into the grove it was like a 'coming-home' feeling. By the end of the six weeks I found I didn't want to leave; I wanted to know what I had to do to stay. So, on 27/12/1997, I was initiated into the Bardic Grade. The grove in 1997 was called *Sgiath an Fhithich* or *Ravenswing*; it was an OBOD Seed-Grove. I signed up to OBOD so I could learn from the gwersi.

During 1998 and 1999, having changed from a Seed-Grove to a Grove due to Ceit and Ruiseart becoming OBOD Druid graduates, the Grove morphed from being English speaking to Scottish Gaelic, falling in line with the family lineage of Ceit and Ruiseart who headed the Grove. Their group originally started in December 1989. I graduated Bard 29/10/1999 and was initiated as Ovate 10/11/1999 (heavily pregnant).

At Summer Solstice 1999 Ceit and Ruiseart formed their own Order, the Gaelic Druid Order of the Southern Cross, with blessings from Philip Carr-Gomm of OBOD and Emma Restall Orr and Philip Shallcrass of BDO. At Samhain 2000, Ceit and Ruiseart conducted the Naming Day for my daughter. I graduated Ovate and initiated Druid on 24/03/2004. I left the Grove a month later due to differing visions.

In 2007, the Order changed its name to the Gaelic Druid Order, with Ceit and Ruiseart moving to Scotland 09/04/2008. The Order closed December 2016 but Sgiath an Fhithich still continues as an independent Grove and is still affiliated with OBOD and BDO.

I was fortunate enough to meet Philip Carr-Gomm from OBOD in September 1998 when Ganieda Grove bought him out to Australia. And then to meet Emma Restall Orr, aka Bobcat, from BDO in March 2000 when Ceit and Ruiseart brought her out to Australia.

During 2005 and 2006 I joined Murray's Bloodwood Grove, which was OBOD associated. This was a Grove that gathered at festival times.

Through the guise of a monthly book club, before I knew it, I was in SoLuna, Tamara Lampard's group, from 05/02/2012 to 03/02/2013, offering the support of a friend in her first year. The original intention of the group was to be a mix of Druid and Craft with lessons.

I was re-introduced on 26/02/2016 to the Gaelic Druid Order, through The Ashby Grove, which was led by Eamonn and Robyn O'Treasaigh. The Ashby Grove was seen as the daughter-grove to Sgiath an Fhithich, commencing 2007 and closed December 2016. Eamonn continues to be a distant support, mentor and teacher for me.

In January 2006, I re-signed with OBOD but had to start back at the beginning. I worked through my Bardic gwersi completing them in December 2012. I commenced my Ovate gwersi January 2013 but due to both parent-in-laws, my parents, grandmother, aunty, business-mentor and a couple of friends all crossing the veil between November 2013 and June 2018, plus being a mum, wife and working, my Ovate studies took a slide. I have recently picked them back up. My intention is to continue and eventually complete the Druid gwersi.

Even though my Druid journey has had its ups and downs with meanders in and out of different groves, I am very happy on the Druid path, liking that it is nature based, encourages self-growth and is more a spiritual path rather than a religion. At the moment, I would be classed as walking the path in a fairly solitary capacity.

Dreaming Tree Grove

Status: currently inactive. Affiliated with the British Druid Order.

DREAMING TREE GROVE BEGAN ON the Summer Solstice of 2012 under the name of *The Perth Hills Druid Grove*. The Grove changed its name in 2014 due to a move of location from the Perth Hills to property located in the Perth Southern suburb of Treeby.

The following information was sourced October 2019 from https:/www.Druidry.co.uk/getting-involved/bdo-groves

> "Based in Perth – Western Australia, Dreaming Tree Grove has evolved into a collective for those who wish to come together to explore the surrounding landscape and its changing seasons as we each journey our way around the wheel of the year.
>
> While our practices may be informed by nature based philosophies, such as modern Druidry, we are open to all those who wish to explore their spiritual connection to Nature and Self regardless of spiritual tradition and background. Dreaming Tree Grove is affiliated with The British Druid Order but it's through these lands of Australia that we explore our spiritual path."

Gaelic Druid Order

Status: currently inactive. Group was based in Western Australia.

The following information (assistance provided by Lili), was sourced July 2019 from:
https://web.archive.org/web/20090528031917/http://www.geocities.com/gdosc/

> *"The Gaelic Druid Order is focused along traditional lines by founders and Joint-Chiefs Ruiseart and Ceit Alcorn and currently has two groves. The Mother Grove (Sgiath an Fhithich) is based in the little village of Newtonmore, situated in the Cairngorm National Park in the heart of the Scottish Highlands and our Daughter Grove (The Ashby Grove) is in Western Australia.*
>
> *Our aim is to help develop the spiritual potential of the individual whilst working with the energies of Nature, via the traditional groves of Bard (poet, story-teller), Ovate (seer, prophet) and Druid (philosopher, priest, magician).*
>
> *Also, it is our belief that a connection to one's ancestry is very important and for this reason the study of the Gaelic language and culture forms an integral part of Bardic studies. This connection is not to be confused with living in the past; the intention is to provide a foundation for the future, both individually and as a group. People of all backgrounds are welcome. Those of Gaelic descent can find a connection to their heritage, whilst "non" Gaels can use the Order as a platform from which they can discover their own roots."*

Ganieda Grove

Status: not currently identifying as Druidic.

GANIEDA GROVE WAS FOUNDED IN 1993, according to the 1998 Alban Arthan edition of *SerpentStar*, sourced August 2019 http://*SerpentStar*.Druidryaustralia.org/wpcontent/uploads/2015/06/SerpentStar-Alban-Arthan-1998.pdf

The following information was sourced August 2019 from https://www.drkennan.com/2018/06/22/about-ganieda-guild

> *Following over a decade-long association with Jung's work, academically and as a practising analyst, I felt a compelling need to connect with my heritage. As an expatriate Englishman now living permanently in Australia, I wanted to explore this more deeply and understand how this may relate with, and connect to the deep spirituality that I was experiencing living here (at that time being Albany, in Western Australia's Great Southern).*
>
> *To do this, I undertook a correspondence course in Druidry. This was with a British-based Druid organisation, called The Order of Bards, Ovates and Druids (OBOD). The course was internationally disseminated and I found it a great foundation for my explorations. I subsequently completed the course and became an initiated Druid within OBOD in 1997. During this period, I developed a 12-acre property near Albany, calling it Ganieda Sanctuary. Ganieda (pronounced Gan-Yay-Dah) is the legendary sister of Merlin the magician, according to the twelfth century chronicler and priest, Geoffrey of Monmouth.*
>
> *I was profoundly drawn to Merlin, or maybe the Myrrdin of history. In spite of my association and now friendship with the Chosen Chief of OBOD, including an Australian Druid Conference at Ganieda in 2000, hosted by him, and the delivery of an online 2-year Diploma course (Traditional Medicine Ways) through OBOD, I found Druidry too revivalist, being mainly of the last few hundred years duration.*
>
> *My deeper drawing to the Ovate grade, being more magical and shamanic, I found not to be well covered in OBOD. So, I gradually drifted away from my association with the Order becoming instead what could be referred to as a Hedge Druid, or solitary practitioner.*

Silver Eyes Seed Group

Status: currently active. Based in Western Australia. OBOD Seed Group.

Tina Merrybard

THE *SILVEREYES SEED GROUP* BEGAN with myself and my husband and sister, who were sharing my Bardic course, and her oldest daughter who was a teen at the time and would join in if the whimsy took her!

We chose the name *Silvereyes* because, while the little bird of that name is not specific to our region alone, we really loved its cheerfulness, socialness, courage and adaptability. I took photos of the ones that come to feed in our grapevine outside the window of our cottage, then used them and a local Jarrah tree frond as a reference for a water colour painting, and my hubby added lettering and made a logo for us.

We began with monthly meetings and would generally discuss what we were seeing in the beautiful natural environment around where we live in the Perth Hills. We read poetry to each other, did meditations together, made corn dollies and Brigid's crosses at Imbolc, had a bonfire at Alban Arthan (a tradition we have continued) and generally did very low-key celebrations at the festivals.

In one session we four sat down around the table and my sister's husband joined in, and we came up with local animals and correspondences for the season here that fitted the northern one. Then I made up a chart for us.

Then, my sister got very busy with work and young children, and the monthly meetings began to slip by unmet, and then the festivals too, and before we knew it, *Silvereyes Seed Group* was not happening at all. We let OBOD know that we were in recession, and it stayed that way for some years. I kept going with my studies, but my sister dropped out of Bardic and hubby made it to Ovate then stalled. I was alone in a physical way, but always had online OBOD friends to help me keep my connection and motivation.

It was only when I met Frances via the *Druids Down Under* Facebook page that things began to come back to life. We had a way, via Facebook, to contact other interested people, so we began to set up meetings for Western Australian (WA) Druids at cafes, then we set up the Druids of WA page. We now have an inner circle of OBOD members, and a wider circle of interested people. We have yet to have a purely inner circle meetup, but we have begun to have online video chats because our members are far flung across this vast State.

The wider circle meets at cafés still, but also for picnics at places of natural beauty, and for bushwalks, and we host the Midwinter bonfire here at our property. One year we even made a wicker man, which was a major undertaking! We particularly enjoy the company of the people we have met through these get-togethers. It is lovely to be able to talk freely of all the things Druids love to talk about!

Frances moved to the Eastern States this year, and we miss her, but with the help of others in the group we have kept the momentum going and we're sure the *Silvereyes* will be alive well into the future. Now we just need one more Druid to make us a Grove!

The Silvereyes Seed Group logo

Image credit: Tina Merrybard

Western Australia Druidry
Tiki Swain

A few of us were practising Druidry solo in Perth in the late 90s and early 2000s. Some couldn't get to Ruiseart and Ceit's grove in Armadale, for others it wasn't their thing. We met together to do rituals when we could organise it.

One was hosted by David, a lovely elderly gentleman living up Lesmurdie-way with a fondness for strong tea. Another was hosted by M., also up in the hills. We met often enough that M. began talking seriously about starting a proper Seed Group or Grove, something David had been trying to build but much more gently. Our first meeting though was a disaster – M. turned up with a long list of conditions and statements that we all had to agree to, that he'd worked out himself, and to his honest surprise we all said "No". We'd been a fairly communally-oriented bunch, willing to work together as individuals, and that was a bit full-on. Not long after that, he told us he was 'closing' the Grove he'd opened.

The rest of us - mostly Marnie, Peter, Leon, Rick and me - continued to meet for rituals, usually following the relaxed, earth-oriented script from the OBOD pamphlets rather than the full-Arthurian version. One was held at a bushland area I'd been protecting, Hillview Terrace in East Vic Park. Others were at someone's house.

We performed Leon's Ovate initiation in the sportsgrounds of Curtin University. He was the only person we did an initiation for amongst us, I think, the others were all solo. I've been told by senior Druids since that we shouldn't have been able to do that since I was the only other Ovate and the others were still Bardic grade, but I beg to differ. The Bards amongst us spent a bit of time in preparation working out how to challenge Leon to leave their nice safe space, and when he did, I walked away with him for the rest of the ritual. It was the only real option for a group initiation that we had, and each of us at some point had wished we could have one.

Over time, the five of us drifted apart (West Australia's a big State) and couldn't continue our erratic meetings anymore. Somebody had set up a YahooGroup for Perth Druids, which had solo Druids, people from the BDO, newbies wanting to know about Druidry and more using it. So, a lot of people stayed in touch by email through that (such as Robyn G., who spent a year or more living in Gove in the remote Northern Territory and trying to adapt to the seasons there. Her stories were amazing.) The excitement when Juliet Marillier released a new book!

I administered that email group for a couple of years until I left for Melbourne in 2005, and it was starting to fall into disuse around then. We did use it though to organise a few meetups, such as a gathering on the coast somewhere north of Fremantle to watch the sun set on the day of the autumn equinox.

Silvereyes Seed Group's Wheel of the Year

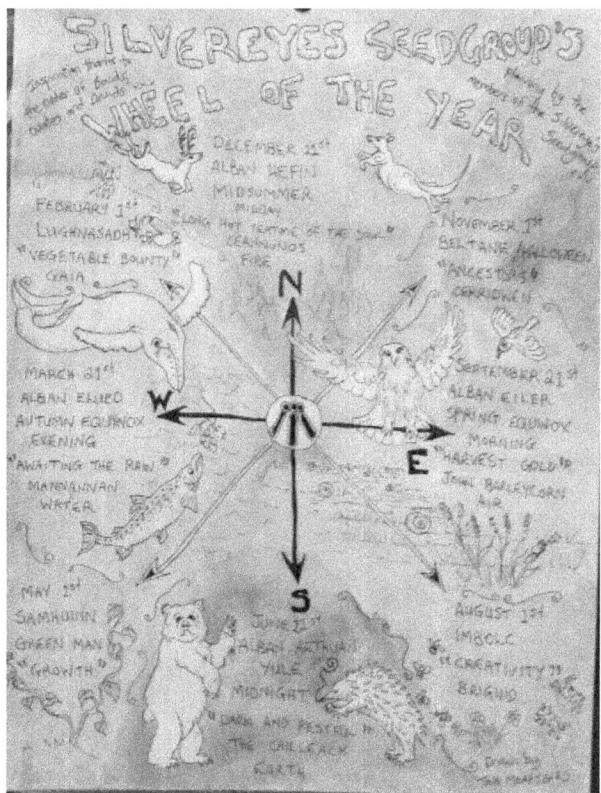

Image credit: Tina Merrybard

The ritual to celebrate the 50 year OBOD anniversary at the 2014 Assembly

Image credit: Sandra Greenhalgh

Part III

THE AUSTRALIAN DRUID HISTORY PROJECT

PREFERRED TERMINOLOGY AND IS DRUIDRY DISTINCT FROM OTHER PAGAN GROUPS

Preferences regarding terminology

AS DISCUSSED EARLIER, ELKIE White designed a questionnaire which was made available to OBOD members practising Druidry in Australia. The form included a section asking whether people had preferences regarding terminology relating to Druidry:

> *"As members of OBOD we are not asked to be anything other than that. However, some people attach the following words or phrases to Druidry, hence the question: how comfortable are you with the following words? Please rate each from 0-10, with 0 being the least comfortable and 10 the most comfortable."*

Seventeen OBOD members returned questionnaires. Answers and scores have been de-identified and listed in a randomised manner.

Due to the limited number of responses, it is not possible to form an accurate and representative view of the beliefs of Australian Druids with regards to preferred terminology. However, the questionnaire results showed that the word 'Druid' had the highest average score of 9.4/10. The least preferred term was 'religion,' with the lowest average result of 3.4/10.

Table: Preferred terminology results

Word choice																Average score
Druid	10	10	10	7	10	10	10	7	10	10	10	5	10	10	10	9.4
"nature-based spirituality"	0	9	10	10	8	10	10	10	10	10	10	8	9	8	10	8.9
Pagan	3	8	7	8	10	10	10	10	0	9	2	5	4	8	0	6.5
eclectic (Druidry)	0	7	5	5	0	8	5	10	10	10	8.5	2	1	6	5	5.7
home-grown (Druidry)	0	7	2	5	2	8	8	10	5	9	1	2	1	4	5	4.8
the word 'religion'	3	7	5	1	0	9	8	8	2	7	0	0	4	0	0	3.4

Comments regarding preferred terminology

Some respondents chose to include comments with their scores, and their feedback has been collated below with the associated word/s.

Druid

- I preferred "following a Druidic path." When I was at the Bardic and Ovate grades I felt that describing myself as a Druid was presumptuous.
- Other people call me this. I don't call myself it so much.
- I use it as it helps others understand my practice, I prefer option 5.
- Basic recognition of attitude.

Pagan

- To me this is a very broad umbrella term and I feel that all forms of nature-based spirituality, including Druidry, fall under this. Members of my family and close friends "get it" when I say Pagan weekend or Pagan meeting.
- Only because of the "????" society's misunderstanding of term and likely so evil of Satanism.
- The term 'Pagan' has become associated with a lot of groups and practices which I don't particularly identify with, for example, many use it to identify as not or even anti-Christian which to me is the opposite of what Druidry is about.
- Pride of practice.

Eclectic (Druidry)

- The gwersi constantly remind us to take what we need or what sits well with us. In that respect we are creating our own eclectic practice. But, on the other

hand, this is the nature and character of the OBOD courses. So we could say that we are adhering to OBOD Druidry.
- In this context, I think eclectic generally means "confused" and I say that as a practising Druid and a practising Buddhist [smiley face image]. To an extent, it is all made up and so I wouldn't set myself up to be the judge of someone else's practice. However, in my experience a lot of people who blend and adopt practices haven't taken the time to develop a deep grounding and connection to the Druid tradition and don't have an understanding of the spiritual consequences (if you accept that Spirituality is transformative) of what they are doing or how one thing goes with another. If you sew on enough bits of other animals when does it stop being a horse? For the record, I don't practise Druidry and Buddhism at the same time; I do one or the other. I do draw on both indiscriminately to navigate the vagaries of life but I don't think of it as Buddhist Druidry or Druid Buddhism. While my altar has images and icons from both traditions, I work with them separately. But maybe I am just deluding myself too!
- Mere words.

Home-grown (Druidry)
- Again, there is a dichotomy. I am studying a northern hemisphere spirituality while experiencing my own natural surroundings. Quarters are different, deosil is different, and the creatures we honour in ritual are different. This allows for an understanding and appreciation for the roots of our traditions while allowing for the local environment to speak to us personally.
- I think this downplays the complexity.
- Spirituality outside of a tradition is unlikely to be transformative (you can't solve a problem with the same mind that created it) and hence more likely to be self-serving. See above [smiley face image].
- Mere words- vague – just your own view.

"nature-based spirituality"
- I like this, it is a term I use a lot.
- The core belief.

The word 'religion' (in regard to Druidry)
- The word religion is too strongly associated with the major, revealed faiths. To me it carries strong connotations of dogma and power and control.
- In a non-dogma or no organised way.
- I am a bit anti religion, although I appreciate it can offer monetary savings.
- I don't consider myself religious, but I am more comfortable with religious than Pagan these days!
- Religion = concrete attitude.

Is Druidry distinct from other Pagan groups?

The questionnaire also requested respondents to reply to the following question:

"Related to the above, do you think that Druidry is worth seeing as distinct to other Pagan groups?"

Not all respondents replied to this question. The fourteen qualitative responses have been provided below in a numbered, randomised order.

1. Yes, Druidry has some specific differences to other groups and should be defined as such.
2. Absolutely. Druidry has a particular kind of focus that includes:
    - magic as inspiration through Awen
    - an interest in Celtic/British mythology, music and folklore over any other cultural influence
    - a history in many other people through history who have imagined the Druids
    - a connection to certain sacred sites and pilgrimage places in Britain.

   Additionally, Australian Druidry would also have an interest in:
    - comparing Celtic/British folkloric culture with that of local Indigenous culture
    - the land that we stand on because of an interest in nature
    - the ancestors of a place that we visit because of an interest in ancestors
    - creative arts because of the idea of Awen/Imbas.
3. Yes! For many reasons. An important point is that Modern Druidry is grounded in over 300 years of evolution; to its present day flourishing and

continued development with its own plethora of traditions, cosmologies and mysteries. Its history and development are different to that of the wider Pagan movement.
4. Absolutely.
5. Yes, each is different and offers what the individual needs.
6. Absolutely. While many Druids are part of other traditions and religions that are under the umbrella of Paganism, I feel that the practice of Druidry is quite distinct. We are following a path that is indelibly linked to our ancestors, and to me this makes Druidry a living history, and one which I feel should be seen as distinct from other forms of Paganism.
7. Each form of Paganism can and should be seen as a separate entity and in this way maintain their own distinction.
8. Yes, I believe it is distinct from other Pagan groups and paths… however some Pagan groups are practising elements/ concepts of Druidry, but do not call it that, which helps to blur the lines somewhat.
9. I firmly do not believe that if you 'call yourself a Druid, you are one.' That annoys me. I believe there are specific traits and practices of contemporary Druidry, which make it distinct as a spirituality. Unless you follow or undertake some of those practices, I'm not sure how – or why – you would identify as a Druid.
10. I'm not sure as I'm not very familiar with other Pagan groups.
11. Well yes, I don't identify as a Pagan. [smiley face image]
12. Yes, but with strong overlap.
13. Yes, it is a bit different.
14. Yes, each has a distinct flavour of its own. It is acceptance which has power. Diversification. I believe we are all one, just as sky is same as earth, so power comes. It is not demanded.

HISTORY PROJECT QUESTIONNAIRE RESPONSES

This section includes completed Australian Druid History Project questionnaire responses, which have been sorted into alphabetical order according to the first name or initial of the author. Some responses have been de-identified to preserve anonymity, or have not been included in accordance with the author's request.

For purposes of clarity the following changes have been made:
- Unanswered questions, and some single word responses have been removed
- In some cases, the wording of questions has been modified from the original. For example, *'Generally speaking, do you support the idea of writing a history of Druidry in Australia? What value might it have?'* was modified into *'What value might writing a history of Druidry in Australia have and what should it include?'*
- Responses to the preferred word/s and belief as to whether Druidry should be considered distinct from Pagan groups are included in the previous section, commencing on page 136.
- The paragraph regarding the 20th Anniversary of *SerpentStar* has been removed.

Cherry Carroll

Please describe where you live.
Kingaroy QLD Town bushland volcanic land.

What is your local Indigenous language group/cultural tribe?
Gubbi.

Do you have any contact with them?
Some.

What value might a written history have and what should it include?
I feel it is important to record the history for future reference. As the Druid family in Australia grows, opinions, ideas and protocol may come into dispute and the structure needs roots for reference even if change is inevitable. There needs to be a firm basis and guidelines on which to grow. The heritage of Druidry needs to be protected.

It may be interesting to include projects which have been initiated and executed by Druid groups for the benefit of the general community.

Aims, beliefs, growth, progression.

When did you join OBOD?
2002.

How far along the course are you?
Just completing Druid Grade.

When did you join OBOD and why?
I had been searching for some time to find a path which suited my beliefs.

On a trip from our home in Qld to Tasmania in 1998 our car broke down and we ended up in a back street in Footscray for repairs. I wandered down the road in search of food and came across Akimbo's bookshop and of course had to explore this. I bought one book *The Druid Source Book* by John Matthews. This book held everything that I was seeking. It rested on my shelf for four years before I opened it again and discovered in the back a reference to OBOD in the list of Major Druid Orders. The rest is history and I joined the Order in January 2002. Nothing happens without a purpose – even car breakdowns. I was firmly led to join OBOD and felt that I had come home.

I appreciate the freedom allowed in the course – being able to proceed at one's own pace. The gwersi are well written, deceivingly simple to follow but hold a wealth of knowledge and are gently challenging. It is comforting to have a tutor to contact when the need arises but nice not to be pressured to continually present work. The Grades build gradually and at each new stage entwine to create a deeper understanding of Druidry and the capacity that we as individuals have. The power of nature, power of the mind and power of Spirit are revealed as we continue our journey, which is never finished.

What was your first OBOD experience? When did you first meet another Druid?
My first OBOD experience was at the November 2003 Assembly at Wyeuro South Australia, hosted by Wyverne.

It was the first time I had travelled so far on my own and also the first time I had met another Druid. So many "firsts"! I met Elkie at Melbourne airport after flying in from Brisbane. I have no idea what I was expecting a Druid to be like but it was such a relief to see a friendly face and I felt that I was reuniting with a long lost Sister. We then flew on to Adelaide and shared a hire car to Wyeuro.

Wyeuro is wild desert country and the primordial spirit of the land is palpable. I was fortunate to be taken by Wyverne, who is so in tune with that spirit, to a naturally cleared area which had once been an ancient ocean bed. Standing in the centre of that sacred space I closed my eyes and was buffeted by its energy. I wrote in my journal later.

> *Moving into the centre I was buffeted by a powerful force and could not get my balance. Wyverne was standing on the edge of the area and called out for me to move back further which I did and I immediately experienced a huge surge of energy which became as a whirlpool of water sweeping around and over me, filling me with invigorating radiance.*

Wyverne told me that she had seen waves crashing over me as I stood motionless.

This was a magical time of exploring the raw warmth of Mother Earth, meeting trees of power which held images of dragons, goblins, horse heads and other creatures. Sandalwood, pepper tree and Mallee called to me as I passed and faerie folk watched with curiosity this strange human who crept past, fearing to disturb them. One sitting on a tree root allowed me a fleeting glimpse before chuckling and disappearing from view and others teased me as they flitted in and around the pepper tree.

Down by the Murray River I meditated with a huge Old Man Willow. His craggy face and gnarled limbs became obvious as he invited me to sit with him. He was full of wisdom and has remained with me as a mentor on my inner plane ever since that first meeting.

I celebrated my group Bardic initiation during the Assembly, which was a profound experience, being drawn deep into the Earth and held safely in the arms of the Mother. The feeling of all-encompassing love within the circle was overwhelming. Sharing rituals, music, laughter and companionship for the first time with fellow members was beautiful. Complete strangers had become family.

This first experience of an OBOD Assembly lives forever in my heart and will always be my favourite Assembly. Not because it was my first Assembly but rather because of the blissful simplicity of merely sharing and absorbing the vast energy of wild places, feeling the endless connection with it and experiencing the utter joy that this brings.

When did you realise you were a Druid? And how did that feel?
From 8 years old onwards. Fascinated by Arthurian literature and all mention of Druidry.

It felt like coming home. Always was a Druid but didn't know the title!

What do you know about the history of Druidry in Australia?
Only know the history of English Druidry (or rather UK generally).

Are you involved in any other groups (related to your Druidry or spirituality)?
Bob Irwin Wildlife and conservation.

Do you see any link between the Druidry that you practise today and the Druidry that was practised by *The United Ancient Order of Druids* **in the early years of European settlement?**
A common thread of compassion for all creation.

Why do you think Druidry is becoming more popular in Australia? What do you think people are looking for? Has this changed over the years?
Probably becoming more popular as people realise there has to be a change of mind set and approach to both environment and all fellow beings if we are to survive.

What do you think is distinctly Australian in regard to Druidry?
Mateship – helping others when the chips are down.

Where do you see Druidry in the future of Australia? Or, what do you vision for us in the future? Where would you like it to go? Can you relate your ideas to what Druidry in Australia has been in the past?
Healing and conservation education. Druid colleges were once respected and sought after.

If someone asked you to specify what a Druid is in three sentences, what would your three sentences be?
1. A Druid Respects and nurtures mother earth and all thereon.
2. A Druid has integrity and can be trusted implicitly.
3. A Druid has compassion for all creatures.

What is a Druid?
1. A Druid is one who learns through the wisdom of ancient ways to uphold justice, hurt none and protect all of nature.
2. A Druid develops and explores the flow of energy within him and connects to the energies of the Universe in many ways to recognise the connection of all things and become one with them.
3. A Druid humbly gives service wherever and however he is able.

Chris Parker

Please describe where you live.
Gorokan / Central Coast / NSW / coastal region with salt water lakes, beaches, bush.

What is your local Indigenous language group/cultural tribe?
Darkinjung.

Do you have any contact with them?
Not really.

What value might a written history have and what should it include?
It will give new people coming to Druidry an idea of how it has developed in Australia. As I am the one to receive contact emails from *druidryaustralia.org* I get quite a few emails where people are looking for information about their ancestors who were Druids. Most of the time these are members of the United Ancient Order of Druid (UAOD) or Ancient Order of Druids (AOD). A comprehensive history may help these people get a better understanding.

Every detail of Druidry in Australia that can be mapped into a timeline. It would also be good if some of the archives of the earlier Orders be uncovered. I believe they exist and it would be good to gather them together before they become lost.

When did you join OBOD?
2014.

How far along the course are you?
Nearing the end of the Bardic Grade.

Why did you join? Why not some other Druid group? What do you like about OBOD?
I was rediscovering spirituality for myself and was a bit lost until someone mentioned OBOD. I read the first few pages of the website and felt like I had been there before. It was like a homecoming and I was excited. I looked at one other Druid group and it didn't make me feel at home as much. OBOD was for

me. I love the structure of the OBOD gwersi. I personally needed to be grounded with the depth of knowledge that we cover in the Bardic gwersi. Following them, my life has changed for the better.

When did you realise you were a Druid? And how did that feel?
When I first read about OBOD on the website, I felt like I was looking back at a life I had previously lived. I felt like I was home and it was very exciting.

When did you first meet another Druid or member of OBOD? Describe that encounter.
Apart from my personal experiences working through the gwersi, my first real OBOD experience was when my wife and I decided to attend the 14th Southern Hemisphere OBOD Assembly in Mt. Hyland.

We had never met any OBOD members before and we were very nervous about travelling into a reasonably remote part of Northern NSW to spend five days with a group of strangers. I had also put my name down to be initiated into the Bardic Grade. After travelling up into Mt Hyland we pulled up at the venue and were met by Michael. He was the first Druid we had ever met.

Over the next few hours most of the others arrived and we were made to feel very welcome. We soon realised that OBOD members came from all walks of life and were all very happy to be gathering amongst other members who were following the same spiritual path. We felt so comfortable getting to know everyone and we were made to feel very welcome within our new family.

For my Bardic Initiation I knew there would be a time where I would be asked to say something. For this I wrote my first ever poem and I spent a long time memorising it. I was rather nervous reciting it, I almost chickened out, but in the end, I was so glad I did. The response from those present made it all worthwhile.

We left the Assembly totally inspired by the wisdom, creativity, talent and awesomeness of the people we met there.

What do you know about the history of Druidry in Australia?
Unfortunately, I know very little about the history of Druidry in Australia, apart from what I have heard about at the OBOD Assemblies, and that the AOD and

UAOD existed in Australia from around the mid 1800s up until the mid 1900s I think. The AOD continues to exist today as the *NobleOak Insurance* company as can be seen here https:/www.nobleoak.com.au/about.

As far as OBOD Druidry in Australia, or any other Order existing here, I know very little. The Assemblies have been going on for 20 years. Beyond this I know nothing.

Are you involved in any other groups (related to your Druidry or spirituality – including historical societies, other spiritual groups, environmental groups, and social justice groups)?
I visit and meet with other similar minded people in my local area. It began with a visit to *Pagans in the Park*, which has now changed to the *Magickal Tribe Picnic*. We meet more as friends than being part of a named group.

As part of my own Druidry, and from being inspired by my OBOD gwersi, I volunteer with a local Landcare group and plan to become more involved in my local community.

Do you see any link between the Druidry that you practise today and the Druidry that was practised by *The United Ancient Order of Druids* in the early years of European settlement?
The main link is obviously in the use of the word Druid. The AOD and UAOD have almost no similarities with my own Druidry apart from them being very community minded and having similar morals. They also refer back to the Druids of prehistory and believe that they are continuing the tradition. Interestingly as can be seen on http:/www.neoPagan.net/UAODbooklet they also talk about Bards, Ovates and Druids, but place the Ovate as the beginning grade, followed by the Bard and then the Druid. So I think the main similarity is the support of community that both Orders uphold.

Why do you think Druidry is becoming more popular in Australia? What do you think people are looking for? Has this changed over the years?
I think that Druidry is becoming more popular today for a number of reasons. It is partially as a response to environmental issues. Most of us can see nature around us being slowly damaged, if not destroyed and any caring person knows this has to change. Druidry can connect us with Nature and inspires us to do

something positive for the environment. At the same time, we are also seeing the result of large corporations forcing small businesses to close, which has the roll-on effect of damaging local communities.

Without a sense of community more and more people become lost and have need to find something to belong to. A place for them to feel welcome and needed. And people are also seeking some form of spirituality but are becoming more disillusioned with mainstream religions. Even new age spirituality is become more and more dilute as more and more people become involved and there seems to be an ever-expanding selection of spiritual paths to follow. Druidry is in danger of the same dilution, but Orders like OBOD give it a very stable base.

So, based on those points, I believe people are attracted to Druidry due to it being based around a love of Nature and the Earth. It builds a sense of community where people can feel that they belong. It teaches us ways of developing our own spirituality and spiritual connections. But it also holds a sense of mystery due to the history of Druidry going back to prehistoric times, and at the same time has a very tangible belief system. And probably one of the main reasons Druidry is becoming more popular in Australia is that people can learn from Druidry at the same time as following other religions or paths.

What do you think is distinctly Australian in regards to Druidry?
In the beginning, I felt a need to find local variations on what I was learning from OBOD. But after visiting the UK recently I feel that this is much harder than I thought. And for now, I am very happy to work with what I am being taught. At the moment I can't really name anything I think is distinctly Australian in Druidry. I do think that our Indigenous people and the ancient Druids certainly would have a lot in common in their beliefs and way of life.

Where do you see Druidry in the future of Australia? Or, what do you vision for us in the future? Where would you like it to go? Can you relate your ideas to what Druidry in Australia has been in the past?
I see Druidry as a growing spirituality in Australia. More and more people are driven to help the environment and connect with Nature as well as seeking a spirituality they can relate to. I think the more people hear what Druidry is about, the more people will be attracted to it.

Chris Pingel

Please describe where you live.
North Ipswich, Queensland. About 20 minutes SW of Brisbane. Bushland.

What is your local Indigenous language group/cultural tribe?
Jagera people.

Do you have any contact with them?
No.

What value might a written history have and what should it include?
First appearance, timeline, significant events, notable individuals, personal anecdotes, traditions followed (ADF, OBOD, solitary, etc).

When did you join OBOD?
2013 as I recall.

How far along the course are you?
Part way into Druid grade.

Why did you join? Why not some other Druid group? What do you like about OBOD?
I had read several of Philip's books and was aware of OBOD's well respected correspondence courses.

When did you realise you were a Druid? And how did that feel?
About 15 or 16 years ago my wife and I were introduced to Paganism. She was able to join a women-only coven and I pursued a more solitary path with reading, study and personal practice.

During that time I read a lot about Druidry from many different authors and was strongly drawn to it. Reading *DruidCraft* was a real turning point for me. I was able to join a coven and have reached second degree witchcraft but with Druidry I feel as though I have really "come home".

What was your first OBOD experience? When did you first meet another Druid?
I met Sandra around 15 years ago when my wife became involved with the coven she leads. My wife and I became heavily involved in the witchcraft/Pagan scene in SE Queensland. We helped to organise a number of Pagan weekends and even ran an Australian Wiccan Conference. It was at one of these events when I discovered that Sandra was also studying Druidry with OBOD. This led me on the path to OBOD many years later.

I remember at one of these weekends a Druid [Editor's comment: this was Corin Thistlewood of ACOD] was invited to speak. He took us outside and led us through an exercise where we could sense/feel the energy auras of trees. I was truly amazed with the sensations I felt. This sold me.

I was always reticent to commit so much money to a correspondence course. My wife eventually insisted I do it. It was one of the best decisions of my life. Number one was, of course, marrying such a wonderful woman.

What do you know about the history of Druidry in Australia?
Nothing I'm afraid Elkie.

Are you involved in any other groups (related to your Druidry or spirituality – including historical societies, other spiritual groups, environmental groups, social justice groups)?
No

Do you see any link between the Druidry that you practise today and the Druidry that was practised by *The United Ancient Order of Druids* **in the early years of European settlement?**
I have no idea how they practised in Australia.

Why do you think Druidry is becoming more popular in Australia? What do you think people are looking for? Has this changed over the years?
I think people are increasingly disillusioned with so many aspects of our society. Politics, major religions, dogma everywhere we look. We are manipulated in so many ways and life is becoming more insular and superficial. People want to

believe and relate to something real. They want to reconnect with what is really important.

Druidry's emphasis on personal creativity, connecting with the natural world, environmentalism and the ability to create a personally meaningful spiritual practice all speaks to people. They are able to take back some semblance of control in their lives, lead more meaningful lives and enjoy the whole process.

I think this is why so many people are happy to stay in the Bardic Grade for so long (or forever). They can immerse themselves in experiential joy and personal fulfilment.

What do you think is distinctly Australian in regard to Druidry?
Our natural surroundings vary so much (it's a big island!!) as opposed to the mother Druidry of the British Isles. Our country's spiritual history is vastly different too. On the one hand we are a very young country still, but the spirit of the land and its Indigenous peoples go way back before the time of the proto-Druids and the Celts. In a sense we are younger and older than the spirituality of the British Isles. I think we just see things quite differently.

Where do you see Druidry in the future of Australia? Or, what do you vision for us in the future? Where would you like it to go? Can you relate your ideas to what Druidry in Australia has been in the past?
I think we need to be careful that it doesn't grow too big too quickly… or at least that our planning doesn't keep up with the growth. More regional activities may fragment the beautiful national inclusiveness that we have at the moment. Last year's Assembly had 30 or so people attend, this year was 54 (I think). Can you imagine an Assembly, possibly in not too many years, where well over a hundred people might want to attend? Individuals start to get lost in the crowd.

If someone asked you to specify what a Druid is in three sentences, what would your three sentences be?
1. It is a nature-based spirituality that recognises the existence of a divine masculine and a divine feminine.
2. It cultivates personal wellbeing through the creative arts.
3. It honours the relationship we have with the world and it can be a vehicle for self-reflection and self-actualisation.

Janine Hartley

Please describe where you live.
Victor Harbor – South Australia is a coastal city 1.5 hours south of Adelaide.

What is your local Indigenous language group/cultural tribe?
Ramindjeri and Ngarrindjeri - the boundary runs through Victor Harbor area. Ramindjeri are Cape Jervois/Kangaroo Island and Ngarrindjeri Coorong/River people.

Do you have any contact with them?
Yes

What value might a written history have?
For new members to understand the lineage of Druidry it is important to them as this creates a connection to the land, structure and foundation. To have a historical record available to new Australian members could avoid that sense of isolation can that occur for new people and give them a sense of connection.

What should it include?
All Druid Groups – not only a history of OBOD. Significant milestones and names of people involved that have been influential in the bringing together of an Australian Druidry. Places that have been significant in the practice of Australian Druidry.

When did you join OBOD?
2008.

How far along the course are you?
Druid – initiated in New Zealand in 2019

Why did you join? Why not some other Druid group? What do you like about OBOD?
The flexibility of learning – no rules – take what you want, leave what you will. Support if desired but not necessary. I love the diversity of people and the wealth of experience, talents and skills so readily shared.

What was your first OBOD experience in the Southern Hemisphere?
A sense of synchronicity with the environment and a sense of purpose coming here. I struggled with the material and ritual for quite some time as, to me, it felt like a continuation of the spiritual colonisation that the Aboriginal people have endured since we arrived to bring in yet another spiritual practice into the land. It wasn't until an experience with Aboriginal Ancestors during a cave painting tour that I was able to come to peace with Druid ritual in this land.

When did you first meet another Druid or member of OBOD? Describe that encounter.
My first reaction was amazement that there were others in South Australia! It took nine years for me to attend the first Assembly and what a fantastic experience it was to find my tribe. It was so good to talk openly about my experience of Druidry and my struggles!

When did you realise you were a Druid? And how did that feel?
I think I have always been a Druid but finding OBOD helped me with direction and depth.

Having been born in England with Welsh and Irish Ancestry it was important to me to know my spiritual roots but, as above, it felt out of place. In a way it still does as most books and material are written only noting the Northern Hemisphere experience.

Would you be willing to research the history of Druidry in your local area for this project?
Yes but very unlikely there is a history - very conservative town.

Are you involved in any other groups (related to your Druidry or spirituality – including historical societies, other spiritual groups, environmental groups, and social justice groups)?
I am very involved in social justice issues and issues related to protection of the environment. I write about the experience of colonisation and have had a few articles published. Mainly Tibet and Palestine. I belong to a few social justice groups.

Do you see any link between the Druidry that you practise today and the Druidry that was practised by *The United Ancient Order of Druids* **in the early years of European settlement?**
There may be similarities, but does it really matter? Meaningful spirituality evolves to meet current needs. I don't know anything about UAOD but it would be interesting to know how the practitioners related to the Aboriginal inhabitants and how they adapted (if they did) to the Australian environment.

Why do you think Druidry is becoming more popular in Australia? What do you think people are looking for? Has this changed over the years?
I think the current system of politics and religion is not working for many people, especially the young, and we are seeking a new paradigm and writing our own myths. People are looking for a spirituality that protects the cultural heritage of the land and the environment. I think this has changed significantly over the years as we move from the good old protestant work ethic and materialism back toward community and sustainability.

What do you think is distinctly Australian in regard to Druidry?
Adapting the cycle of the seasons. Recognising native animals and respecting the spirit of the land (Aboriginal). Understanding and respecting native plants and what they offer.

Where do you see Druidry in the future of Australia? Or, what do you vision for us in the future? Where would you like it to go? Can you relate your ideas to what Druidry in Australia has been in the past?
It is evolving. It is inclusive of new ideas so I just want to see that continue and not get bogged down with committees but to remain a group where spirit can move freely. Talking to people that come into my shop they want a spirituality that includes the environment, social justice issues and respects their personal experience without trying to explain or control. I enjoy the freedom that Druidry offers the way it currently is in Australia and I hope it stays that way. I would like to see more Druid trained people in positions of decision making with a strong support group behind them.

John Jordan

Please describe where you live.
Brisbane, Queensland, sub / semi tropical.

What is your local Indigenous language group/cultural tribe?
Turubul, Yugambeh and related dialects, including Gugingin, Bullongin, Kombumerri, Mingunburri, and Birinburra.

Do you have any contact with them?
No.

What value might writing a history of Druidry in Australia have and what should it inclulde?
A record, cultural memory, collected historical learning and reference work, inspiring history and research to be undertaken and identity around shared history to be formed, and shared roots of inspiration for future Druids.

Everything! - names, dates, activities, personal experiences, journal entries, creative input, stories, poems, issues of *SerpentStar* and other records, dates and times of changes of season as observed by the Druid groups, records of keeping of seeds and bees and tending of the garden of nature, preserving habitat of endangered species, preserving biodiversity, records of numbers of attendees at events, supports for local councils on advice regarding nature in the area, blogs, newsletters, emails, pictures, stories, jokes and cartoons, records of rituals and their effects on nature and the people, inspirations and ideas that come from the meetings and Assemblies, plans and initiatives to promote membership and the aims of the Order, records of adaptations of ancient Celtic history to the modern Australian culture and land, interviews with local Aboriginal elders and people, preserving their knowledge before it's too late.

When did you join OBOD?
March 2016.

How far along the course are you?
Ovate Grade.

Why did you join? Why not some other Druid group? What do you like about OBOD?
For fellowship, learning, to create lasting beauty, to make love grow for all beings, animals and plants, to be of service to others, to discover the natural world, to help preserve life on earth. OBOD was the most obviously active and offered structured learning, I like the fun and fellowship of the OBOD and the gwersi to learn, and the activity level of my local *Macadamia Grove*.

When did you realise you were a Druid? And how did that feel?
Only realised this year that I was doing Druidic things all my life, appreciating and revering local nature, planting gardens in the spaces between the cracks in the city and concrete, creating music and recording songs and poems, talking to birds, recording seasons and appreciating the actual wheel of the year, collecting seeds, keeping a garden, exploring with a Druid eye the local ley lines and song lines of parks and wildlands, learning about elements of nature, meditating on natural beauty, etc. It felt great to find a place to share my journey with others.

As a possible starting point to the above: when did you first meet another Druid or member of OBOD? Describe that encounter.
I first met Sandra Greenhalgh at Mary Ryan's café in Brisbane after I had joined the OBOD course and contacted *Macadamia Grove* on email. We met for coffee and she explained the group and its history and chatted for a long time about the culture and history of Druids and the paths that you may take through the forest. We arranged an initiation time for me to come and join the group formally. It was a lovely long relaxed chat with much clear insight about the nature of the path and people in the group. She offered me a contact to also talk to who became my helper into the grove, and I met Chris and Sarah who later became close friends. I met them for coffee, and they explained again the individuality of the path and how people learn and progress in Druidry.

What do you know about the history of Druidry in Australia?
I don't know much about it except local history since March 2017.

Are you involved in any other groups (related to your Druidry or spirituality)?
No.

Do you see any link between the Druidry that you practise today and the Druidry that was practised by *The United Ancient Order of Druids* **in the early years of European settlement?**
Yes, similarities and differences, yet Druidry teaches to look for similarities rather than differences, and in spirit and essence, even though it is in a different area with different history the aims and goals are the same, just translated for local people and conditions and updated for the modern era.

Why do you think Druidry is becoming more popular in Australia? What do you think people are looking for? Has this changed over the years?
It is an accepting non-denominational nature based Celtic/Shamanistic spirituality that does not dictate doctrine or dogma and does not have strong base of codes or book of rules to follow but is very accepting of diversity and encourages creativity. People are looking for love and belonging to a group that gives meaning to an increasingly consumerist world which is obviously not sustainable, and an outlet for reverence for the world that feeds us and the spirits that represent those facets even if from other lands and times Celtic/prehistory.

It offers an alternative to a structured dictated 'dead revealed God outside our reach mediated by others', more like an 'immanently living direct-experienced self-mediated internally sensed Spirit' that is obvious in the natural world around us (which we are trying to cover with concrete and steel, because we are afraid of it being naked).

I am not sure how it has changed over the years, I have been in it only since March 2017.

What do you think is distinctly Australian in regard to Druidry?
The land, the climate, the seasons, the earth (desert sand), air (cyclones to droughts), water (large surrounding oceans) and fire (bushfires and summer heat) of Australia, the flora and fauna, the culture, the people, the value dimensions of masculinity/femininity, low power distance, high collectivism, mateship and a fair go, uncertainty avoidance, high indulgence (versus restraint) and the irreverent social attitudes to colonial history.

Where do you see Druidry in the future of Australia? Or, what do you vision for us in the future? Where would you like it to go? Can you relate your ideas to what Druidry in Australia has been in the past?
Druidry will grow and further integrate into Australian Pagan culture and it will reach out and try to adapt to the native Aboriginal culture of land and knowing of the flora and fauna in a more intimate way. I envision a renaissance of a seasoned approach to knowledge of Celtic cultural history and mythology adapted and meshed with local culture and story for the benefit of all who live in this wide brown land. It will be a non-'religious' support for spirituality that offers a welcome alternative to those seeking a more nature/mythic or Pagan path.

If someone asked you to specify what a Druid is in three sentences, what would your three sentences be?
1. A follower of an ancient Celtic/shamanistic nature-based spirituality based around a renovated 'wheel of the year'.
2. A Pagan-oriented lay earth-and-nature-priest who draws their inspiration from a variously lost Brythonic tradition of myths and rituals, reviving it through various traditions originating in Britain and Brittany.
3. A person who likes to dress up in robes and perform rituals in circles on seasonal occasions and sing, tell stories, play music and drink mead around a fire.

What further questions would you like to see included in a questionnaire about the history of Druidry in Australia?
- What percentage of your time would you estimate you spend on Druidry related activities, e.g. rituals, learning, meditation, preparation, communication, etc (not just hobby/craft related activities)?
- Do your friends, family, workmates know you are following a Druid path?
- Do you consider yourself a solo or group practitioner of Druidry?
- Have you been to a national gathering of any Pagan or Druid group? How many times?
- What would you say are your particular Druidic talents? (e.g. herbs, song, story, divination, memory keeping, nature law, healing, myths and lore, seeing signs, readings and so on)
- Have you been to visit any ancient historical Druidic sites, e.g., overseas? Which ones? How did the visit affect your understanding of the path?

- How are you progressing in your studies of the gwersi?
- Do you identify with a totem animal or plant? Which one?

[Editor's comment: Some of the excellent questions from this list have been touched on in this book but not all. Perhaps the next edition will provide further information, with more people providing their feedback]

Julie Brett

Please describe where you live.
I grew up on the Northern Beaches of Sydney region and have lived now in the Blue Mountains since 2016.

What is your local Indigenous language group/cultural tribe?
Guringai where I grew up, and now Darug and Gundungurra.

Do you have any contact with them?
I did volunteer work for the Aboriginal Heritage office in Sydney in 2008. This involved site monitoring of some carving sites in Cromer Heights. There were also yarn nights at the office that the public could attend. This helped me to meet some of the community there. I also made friends with some people who were Aboriginal who came to the circles I ran for *Druids Down Under*.

In the Blue Mountains I have mainly met people who are from the neighbouring Wiradjuri country. I have attended dance classes and workshops. This has been a wonderful learning experience and I hope to learn more about this area and about Aboriginal culture as there is a lot being offered here.

What value might writing a history of Druidry in Australia have?
Knowing where we have come from and how Druidry in Australia has developed is important to understand. It helps us define ourselves, but also helps us see where we are headed in the future. I also think Australian Druidry has a unique story to tell that is separate from the history of Druidry as a whole.

What should it include?
I would love to know our origin story. All the who, what, when, where, how and whys. How Druidry arrived in Australia and how communities developed and changed. Who was involved and where did events happen? I would love to hear about our personal stories of discovery. I would also love to see statistical data and names and dates of important people and events as I know how important it can be for academic research and history.

When did you join OBOD?
2009.

How far along the course are you?
I finished Bardic in 2018 and then began the Ovate course.

Why did you join? Why not some other Druid group? What do you like about OBOD?
My initial introduction to Druidry was in 2007 through the *Gorsedd of the Bards of Caer Abiri* at Avebury in England, and through my friend Morgan Rhys Adams who was the public face of the Gorsedd. Morgan was a member of the *British Druid Order* (BDO) and the Gorsedd was associated with them too. I mainly learned one on one with her and through books like *Living Druidry* by Emma Restall Orr, and *The Bardic Handbook* by Kevan Manwaring for the first few years.

I had heard of OBOD, but it was not initially within my budget to become a member. I saw Damh the Bard play at Chalice Well in 2007 and when I spoke to him he mentioned it to me.

When I got home to Australia, I missed learning about Druidry and wanted to find others. There were no Seed Groups in Sydney at the time, but a friend and I decided to start the course together anyway. One of my main motivations for joining was that I wanted more chances to meet others and OBOD was the most well-known.

I have, however, also looked at the *British Druid Order* coursework and plan to do that too one day and have friends who have also studied with ADF. OBOD is certainly the most influential in the country and the course is highly regarded. I also enjoyed the introductory materials and did these before I began the course.

When did you realise you were a Druid? And how did that feel?
This is a difficult question. When pressed, I used to say I don't refer to myself as a Druid. Instead I would say "I study Druidry", that I am a Pagan, but prefer to see the idea of the Druid as something to continually strive for. The Druids lived in the past, and Druidry is a spiritual path that is inspired by them. I wasn't sure I was deserving of the title. But more recently I have been becoming more comfortable with the term for myself perhaps as I take on more responsibility

and feel more confident in my knowledge. I feel it's not something you just decide to be. It's something you become fairly slowly and it's a title not to be taken lightly.

On the flipside, however, I have always used the term in a light way to differentiate myself from other Pagans, or to refer to a group of us getting together. It's a useful term to use, but I think there is a more serious side to our understanding of it too.

That said, I realised Druidry was a good fit for me when I was in the UK studying it there. The focus on nature and creativity was very appealing to me. I had worked in the creative arts but had lost my inspiration and through Druidry I found a way to reignite it once again. I have also always been drawn to Celtic mythology and art and loved that Druidry had such a Celtic and British focus. I also loved the combination of personal experience and academic interest that seemed to be nicely balanced within the path.

As a possible starting point to the above: when did you first meet another Druid or member of OBOD? Describe that encounter.
I met Morgan Rhys Adams who became my mentor in England at a Spiritual Pub Meet in Glastonbury. We were sitting in the beer garden. I had been living there a month or so and was looking for a teacher to help me better understand the Wheel of the Year in its homeland. Morgan was working with the *British Druid Order* (BDO) rather than OBOD, though she was a member of OBOD, she preferred the more shamanic and Pagan approach that the BDO offered at the time. I was identifying as a witch when we met, but she explained the similarities with Druidry particularly in the Wheel of the Year and agreed to teach me. As I learned more from her over endless cups of tea and drives around the countryside, I realised how much this path really suited me. The focus on nature, Awen and the ancestors was most important to me.

What do you know about the history of Druidry in Australia?
This is very difficult to know for sure. I have been told some stories, but I don't remember the details. This is one of the reasons I am very keen to have a copy of our history. I can tell you about the history of the *Druids Down Under* group though.

OBOD in Australia…

At Imbolc in 2011 I went to visit *The Melbourne Grove*. I was hoping to collect information myself on the history of Australian Druidry and interviewed Elkie White and Vicki Minahan. These are some of the notes I made of what they told me at that time:

- Elkie's home is called Naomh. She's been there 30 years.
- She planted a grove there for rituals. It was where they held the first ritual of *The Melbourne Grove* when she started the group.
- The second location they used they call Brigid's Well. While I was there, we went to that location to do an Imbolc dawn ritual.
- Elkie joined OBOD in 1995 and started *The Melbourne Grove* in 1998.
- She met other Druids at Wiseman's Ferry and was inspired to start the group.
- Her three reasons to do so were 1) Personal spirituality, 2) It's good for the Earth, and 3) For community/social aspects.
- Vicki held the 2010 OBOD Assembly at her home. There were 44 people there.
- She and Elkie had been family friends but met again in 2007 through OBOD.
- Both found out about OBOD from the *Druid Animal Oracle Cards* published by Philip and Stephanie Carr-Gomm.
- Vicki grew up surrounded by bush and folklore. She was taught to read the signs of nature. They lived off the land a lot, but felt frustrated at not knowing more about bush foods and how to prepare them.
- When *The Melbourne Grove* began, they agreed to practise their rituals in a Southern Hemisphere format switching the seasonal timing by six months to suit the Australian seasons.
- They also switched the north and south elemental correspondences to reflect the Southern Hemisphere, where the equator is to the North and therefore the place of Heat/Summer/Fire, and Antarctica to the South and thus the place of Cold/Winter/Earth. They also maintained the concept that Druidry is solar-based and thus East is the place of sunrise, West the place of sunset, North where the outer-sun is at its peak, and South when the inner-sun radiates its light, by polarity.
- They began mapping sites that they used regularly for seasonal celebrations and Elkie has developed a theory behind the sacred geometry of this layout.
- They explained that putting Druidry in Australia makes you question why you do something. Not just follow along. It has to make sense.

- They associated certain deities with the seasons: Brigid for Imbolc, Lugh for Lughnasadh, The Cailleach for Samhain, and the Green Man for Beltane.
- They noted the need to be careful though as there are other spirits here in Australia. You need to respect the spirits of place.

As it turned out, this small attempt of mine to discover more about the history of Druidry simply showed me how enormous a task it was and how much information there would be to uncover. Though I was grateful to have learned so much from Elkie and Vicki, I realised it was not within my abilities to fully tackle this project. Especially not with a baby on the way. I was 33 weeks pregnant when we took this trip. As such, I'm very grateful that this book is being created.

While I was there, I went with them for the Imbolc ceremony at Brigid's Well. It was my first ritual with a group of OBOD Druids. I had been holding Druidry rituals in Sydney, but they were not OBOD focused. I was touched by their Australian inclusions of native animals at the directions, and the reverence held for the lyre bird and its connection to the William Ricketts Sanctuary that was close by. He seemed to be a guardian spirit of sorts for them and was clearly a Bard and a very spiritual man in his own right. The connection they had with that land was very special and it was inspiring to be a part of it. I loved that they also saw the symbolism of the Bard in the lyrebird.

Assemblies I have attended:
Sydney 2017
I started attending Assemblies in 2017 when one was held in Sydney by the *Song of the Eastern Sea Seed Group*, hosted by Chris Parker. I had been unable to attend any earlier, in the beginning because I was at university with exams, and then for the next few years because I had a small child and travelling interstate wasn't possible. This event was not far off for me. It was held at the Baden Powell Scout Centre in Pennant Hills in Sydney. It's a site that has been used for many more general Pagan events over the years but as far as I know this was the first OBOD one there. I had my Bardic initiation then and though it was nine years since I began my OBOD journey, and I was very close to finishing my Bardic course, it felt very significant to me. It was a real coming home and welcoming into the OBOD community in my heart.

It was also at this event that Elkie's idea to go further with the *Australian Druidry History Project* was shared. I had recently published by book *Australian Druidry* for which I had hoped the history could have been included, but realising it was outside my abilities to do, I had let Elkie know I couldn't include it in my book. I was ever so happy to hear that the project was going to be managed by the elders of our community who could piece it together.

At this event I also made a lot of great personal connections that would only grow over the years.

Adelaide 2018
I completed my Bardic course with OBOD at the end of 2017 and so was able to have my Ovate initiation at this Assembly. It was moving and I am currently thoroughly immersed in the Ovate work. I was also able to share a workshop there on plant symbolism. We went out into the gardens of the site and talked about the symbolism of the plants, as a group identifying quite a few key features and symbols. This site would later be used for other camps and it is a place we are getting to know better as a community.

New Zealand 2019 'SHOBODA'
I was ever so pleased to be able to attend this Assembly. It was the first time I got to meet Philip and Stephanie Carr-Gomm, and also Eimear Burke, as well as many of the New Zealand Druids I had not yet met. It was an incredible experience to see how they combined their knowledge of Maori culture with their Druid practice, and it has encouraged me to work harder on finding a better understanding of Australian Aboriginal culture and political issues. Their cultural interrelationship is aspirational. After meeting Philip there he asked me to host some of the *Tea with a Druid* videos for the OBOD Facebook page. I am very pleased to have been able to make that connection and help the stories of Australian Druidry to be shared around the world. I also interviewed Philip and Eimear about their experiences at SHOBODA (Southern Hemisphere OBOD Assembly) for my podcast *Forest Spirituality*.

Are you involved in any other groups (related to your Druidry or spirituality)?
I started and administer a number of Facebook groups: *Druids Down Under*, *DDU Bardic Circle*, *Druids for Peace and Justice*, and *Australian Nature Spirituality*. I'm a

member of PAN. I have helped run events with *Gliding Seal Events*. I regularly run workshops for the *Australian Wiccan Conference*. I have attended the Mount Franklin Pagan Gathering in Victoria. I have attended Druid Camp and the English Ale in Adelaide. I help with PAN and Applegrove events in Sydney. I have also been to *Cloud Catcher Witch Camp* in the Reclaiming tradition and go to the Reclaiming witchcraft circles in Katoomba. I am also involved with *Red Tent Australia*, helping run a circle in Katoomba and offering workshops at their events.

Do you see any link between the Druidry that you practise today and the Druidry that was practised by *The United Ancient Order of Druids* in the early years of European settlement?

Perhaps. I think the joining element is the practice of imagining the ancient Druids in a positive light as good role models for ourselves in the present. We may have seen them in different ways, but the idea that we had noble, wise, spiritual, creative, nature loving, music loving ancestors was certainly something that we shared and their visions of who the Druids were have inevitably been a part of our own history in imagining them, even if our outlook might have changed somewhat, particularly in terms of their relationship to Christianity.

Why do you think Druidry is becoming more popular in Australia? What do you think people are looking for? Has this changed over the years?

There are many reasons. I can really only speak for myself, but what I tend to share with others in Druidry is our love of the old stories and nature, our love of creativity, wonder and magic, our concerns for the environment, our appreciation that Druidry is inclusive of different kinds of beliefs (some Druids are atheists, polytheists, animists, Christian, Buddhist, etc.) but we can all work together. Druidry also doesn't have the gender politics we can sometimes find in spiritualities like Wicca. There's no focus on a heteronormative divine couple as a creative force in Druidry. Instead there is more focus on Awen in this regard. This makes it more appealing in its inclusivity to many people I have spoken to. It encourages empowerment through creativity, which is really tangible and real and the creative output of the community is really inspiring and beautiful.

I think people may also be drawn to it out of a desire not to appropriate other cultures too. It's an ancestral tradition not out of exclusivism, but out of a sense of honour to our cultural inheritance. Rather than taking from other cultures, instead we recognise the significance and wisdom of our own. I think the main reason is the way it benefits our lives. It brings in a lot of good, and it helps us to connect with other people who are doing the same thing. It's the community that strengthens it.

What do you think is distinctly Australian in regard to Druidry?
Our interest in the local environment – animals, plants, seasons, directions, sacred sites, Indigenous culture and history. Also, perhaps our sense of the foreignness of ourselves, our deities, and our sacred animals, plants and celebrations. We have a unique path in negotiating how to make Druidry "work" here.

Druidry is a tradition of nature, ancestors and sacred sites. We work with what is here with us, so many adapt their practice to the land. We also have a diaspora relationship with Britain. Many people take pilgrimages to the 'mother-land' to visit the origins of our tradition. This gives us a unique relationship with both places.

I think we are distinct from other parts of the world in this in that we are in a state of discovery. Nothing is set in stone. Nothing can be wholly attributed to tradition. There will always be negotiations here to make stories, practices or correspondences make sense. We are in a stage of doing a lot of discovery work and I think that makes us quite unique.

Where do you see Druidry in the future of Australia? Or, what do you vision for us in the future? Where would you like it to go? Can you relate your ideas to what Druidry in Australia has been in the past?
I'd like to see a more integrated approach to Druidry here continue to be developed. I'd like to see the native plants, animals, seasonal changes and connections with Aboriginal culture be more important in our rituals. And I am seeing this more and more. For me, Druidry has been a path of finding ever more connection with the land around me, and though we are working on this gradually, I think we have a lot of work to do in learning about the messages in the land here. The stories of the plants and animals speak directly to us, but there is also much we can learn and share in friendship with people of the Indigenous cultures. It's a slow process though.

It will happen over time as individuals work on projects such as understanding native plants or animal symbols, or we gather more from our inspirations. It's a slow process of cultural change. We come as a foreign culture and slowly over time, we become more like the culture of the place we are in because of our interactions with that environment and the people we interact with too. We learn from each other and change occurs. I think that right from the beginning of OBOD there was this interest in incorporating Australian plants and animals, however this is bigger than just OBOD. This is also about Australian cultural change as a whole and our practices within OBOD will reflect that too.

I would also like to see us work towards a wonderful relationship with Australian Aboriginal culture and communities as the New Zealand Druids have achieved with Maori people. But this doesn't just happen through Druidry. It's a societal change that needs to occur. It's a part of a bigger picture, but our own changes in these regards in Druidry can help make that difference. It happens one step at a time through compassion, curiosity, good relationship and really taking time to listen.

If someone asked you to specify what a Druid is in three sentences, what would your three sentences be?

A triad: Three things that define a Druid: a love of the ancestors, a love of nature, and a love of the flow of Awen.

1. A love of ancestors: A Druid feels a deep connection with the ancestral spiritual traditions of the British Isles and any land they stand on.
2. A love of nature: A Druid seeks the wisdom of the trees; the wisdom of nature; the messages of spirit in the flight of a bird, the budding of a flower, the movement of water, or the stories in the turning of the seasons.
3. A love of the flow of Awen: A Druid understands the flow of Awen within themselves, in others and in the world as the blissful state of peace and creativity that turns action into art.

Kacey Stephensen

Where I live:
Adelaide South Australia. Temperate Mediterranean climate - grassy scrubland, mixed introduced and indigenous plants and animals.

Local Indigenous people:
Kaurna people. I can learn about and get in contact with Kaurna elders at *The Kaurna Living Centre* in Marion.

What value might a written history have and what should it include?
To understand Druidry's influence on Australian Paganism and how Druidry has changed within Australia. To get a good scope of the different Druid traditions within Australia and a history of OBOD Druidry within Australia.

History of OBOD, ADF, BDO and other traditions. The history of fraternal Druidry in Australia, personal experiences of Druidry within Australia, how has Druidry changed and adapted overtime to the environment here?

When did I join OBOD?
In 2013.

How far along the course am I?
Ovate grade.

Why did I join OBOD? Why not some other Druid tradition?
I spent a great deal of time researching OBOD, BDO and ADF and Ireland's *Druid School* to try and grasp how they were different and similar. ADF being the most different from the British Orders. I was most attracted to OBOD in the end because I met OBOD members and experienced OBOD ceremony. The OBOD approach appealed to me too because of its focus on nature spirituality, mysticism, meditation and self discovery within a Celtic Pagan context.

I was also looking for an overall structure and foundation to work with, I found it in joining an Order which gave me a grounding in modern Druidry.

When did I realise I was a Druid? And how did that feel?
Like the ignition of flame, the feeling of, wow... this is what I've been looking for. That was the initial feeling and then with time it grew on me in many different ways. There wasn't a specific moment where I thought I am a Druid. It feels rather like something you - become, something that you work towards and develop - as a life style choice, as a way of life. Yes, in spirit I was always a Druid but I realised what that was when I found it and began working with the ways deeply. I believe we embody Druidry by living and working with it, seeing beyond the label into what Druidry feels like, what it is in practice.

When did you first meet another Druid or member of OBOD? Describe that encounter.
I met a few OBOD members and Damh the Bard who is the Pendragon of OBOD. It wasn't until I met a dear friend 'Richard' whose commitment and enthusiasm for Druidry in a very esoteric, philosophical, down to earth way inspired me to make the decision and take the leap into starting the Bardic course in OBOD.

What do I know of the history of Druidry in Australia?
I know that the fraternal Orders have been here since the 19th century and locally, Revival Druids planted Druids Avenue near their lodge in Stirling back in the early 1900s. I know that OBOD Druidry has been in Australia since the early 90s and possibly the late 80s always with a rather small number of initiates.

In the last few years however, at Assemblies we have experienced an exponential increase in members. The Melbourne OBOD Grove has been going since the late 1990s. Mostly, the history of OBOD members in Australia has been a story of solitary folk searching for other people in the same tradition! That is no longer such a difficult enterprise. The OBOD Assembly has been going for 16 years with the 17th to be held in South Australia.

Am I involved in any other spiritual groups?
Currently the OBOD community and the local Pagan community are the groups I am active in.

Do you see any connection between the Druidry you practise today and the Druidry that was practised by *The United Ancient Order of Druids* **in the early years of European settlement?**
Apart from the inspiration of the Druids as a starting point, no. OBOD grew out of an esoteric Order of fraternal Druids who go by a similar name to the united Order but are different with different origins: - The Ancient Order of Druids (AOD) which came about in 1909.

AOD themselves claim history back to 1717 founded by John Tolland but there's only evidence from George Watson Macgregor Reid onwards. George Watson Macgregor Reid along with others created the original name of this same group - *The Universal Bond of Druids* and continued by his son Robert Macgregor Reid. They are active to this day and we still share elements in common with them. Ceremonial structure and cosmologies which Ross Nichols refined and continued to grow and develop within OBOD when he split off from AOD to form *The Order of Bards, Ovates and Druids*. There could potentially be direct influences of UAOD on OBOD but it's mainly The Ancient Order of Druids.

Why do you think Druidry is becoming more popular in Australia, what do you think people are looking for? Has this changed over the years?
I think it has a lot to do with socio-political and philosophical changes. People are responding to the human neglect on the environment which is connected with human issues. This comes back to a deeper human preoccupation, for meaning and connection to place and cosmos.

Modern Druidry from the beginning has always been concerned with wellbeing in all its forms; especially preoccupied with the health of humanity's spiritual connection with Nature and the Divine. Within Australia we are seeing devastation of The Great Barrier Reef, old growth forest logging in Tasmania and the general destruction of and disinterest in nature within our cities and social circles.

Many people sensitive to it are affected in their core by the pain caused by Western invasion of this land 200 years ago. They are looking for something which reconciles that pain, which connects them to a positive healing of their ancestry with the land they live on today. People want to connect and have respectful relationships with the spirit of this land, Druidry offers that approach.

Their calling often arises from seeing their culture's disconnection or disassociation from nature in a deep spiritual sense. More and more people are coming to Druidry - ADF, OBOD, BDO etc because they feel the calling of the land; they feel the spirits of the land calling them to connect, to connect with their ancestors and with the gods of their ancestors.

The fundamental reason is this; Druidry offers a natural, contemplative Paganism or spiritual way that stresses the importance of the embodied world and a 'back to nature' approach to magick and esotericism. In Australia it strives to heal our sense of disconnection from our ancestral homelands and a need to reconnect with the spirit of those lands, the folklore, culture and customs. In saying that, people are drawn to Druidry because not only does it embrace ancestry, but it simultaneously calls us to connect with the spirit of the land we find ourselves living with here and now; and all the new inspiration that arises from that. You could say, people who are drawn to modern Druidry, particularly within the context of OBOD, are looking for a spiritual philosophy rooted in their Pagan ancestry.

Druidry also seems to attract people who are more nature and philosophy-focused than magick and craft-focused even though these elements can be present in Druid work. Focus tends to be towards spiritual states of being in the world over magic work in the sense of Witchcraft. People are drawn to the emphasis on sacred creativity and life force; the divine flow of Awen and the fundamental primal force that flows within all things: Nwyfre.

What do you think is distinctly Australian in regard to Druidry?
For starters, the interest in adapting the traditional European (Druid) wheel of the year to that of Australian climates and ecology or in creating completely new seasonal observances. These things are unique to individual Druids and their relationship with the land here. There are wonderful attempts too by individual Druids to create Australian oghams, using the spiritual meanings of the European trees and meeting tree spirits here which have the same qualities as their European counterparts. Some creating a completely new tree alphabet system for Australian plants and trees.

The 'Spirit of place' as a concept is not unique to OBOD. All Druid groups are about connecting with and adapting to the spirits, deities and beings of a specific place and time. Being within Australia, this basic Druidic idea naturally ends up reflecting the local environment. What we see within Australian Druidry is a need, on the one hand, to understand and study our ancestors and pre-Christian/medieval European culture; to better develop our traditions, but at the same time, a need to align those traditions and practices to the places we find ourselves attuning to now and all the environmental and ethical issues we face in the process. On the one hand, there is memory of culture and then, there is culture inspired by the past but rooted in place and time which is an ancestral gift for the future of tomorrow's Druidry.

Where do you see Druidry in the future of Australia? What do you vision for us in the future? Where would you like to see it go? Can you relate your ideas back to what Druidry in Australia has been in the past?
I see different Druid groups and traditions coming together and discussing ideas on a regular basis; sharing knowledge and wisdom like they would have done thousands of years ago. With gatherings like the *Druids Down Under* gathering [DDUNG] coming up this year, we will see representatives of many different types of Druids. Overall, I see Druidic concepts becoming more mainstream in eclectic Paganism. Where in the past, eclectic Pagans were mostly inspired by Wiccan cosmology, they will also be heavily influenced by concepts like Awen and triplicities of forces - land, sea and sky for example. Animistic focuses will seep more into the general Pagan community and a fascination with ancestor reverence.

For people studying particular Druidry lore within Australia, we will all continue to grow in our own traditions and adapt and evolve different things to the ecologies and landscapes of Australia. We will continue to listen to the ancient wisdom of this land that sings to us. There will be more and more people who are versed in more than one Druid approach within Australia as communication and interest between different Druid traditions grow.

Druids will also have a bigger impact on the Pagan community. Druidic ideas will become more common place like that of Wiccan concepts in Pagan communities. Many more people will incorporate basic ideas of Druidry into their lives; using bits here and there.

If someone asked you to specify what a Druid is in three sentences, what would your three sentences be?
A Druid in modern times is someone who practises a nature spirituality that is inspired by the ancient Druids. The word Druid is made up of two root words Dru and Id - Dru for Tree and Id for wisdom or knowledge i.e. Knowledge or wisdom of the trees.

A Druid is someone who wants to form harmonious relationships with nature and themselves in a magical and spiritual way that connects them to their ancient ancestors and has a love of the arts, poetry and culture. Within OBOD Druidry we use the scheme of Bard, Ovate and Druid, the system that Strabo talked about in his Geographica.

> *"Among all the Gallic peoples, generally speaking, there are three sets of men who are held in exceptional honour; the Bards, the Vates and the Druids. The Bards are singers and poets; the Vates, diviners and natural philosophers; while the Druids, in addition to natural philosophy, study also moral philosophy."*
> (Book IV Chapter 4 Geographica - Loeb Classical Library Edition 1923).

What further questions would you like to see included in a questionnaire about the history of Druidry in Australia?
- Druidry's historical relationship with other spiritual and Pagan groups in Australia - Wicca, Witchcraft, Buddhism, spiritualist and occult communities.
- Druids who have been involved in Australian politics, environmental campaigns and community service work in Australia's history - including *United Ancient Order of Druids*.
- The history of different Druid traditions communicating within Australia
- Were OBOD Druids aware of any other traditions in the 80s or 90s around Australia?

Marigold

Please describe where you live.
Dandenong Ranges, Victoria. – temperate rainforest with villages.

What is your local indigenous language group/cultural tribe?
Wurundjeri tribe.

Do you have any contact with them?
No.

What value might writing a history of Druidry in Australia have?
Reference material for future Australian Druids.

What should it include?
Groves and activities.

When did you join OBOD?
2003?

How far along the course are you?
Studying Ovate.

Why did you join? Why not some other Druid group? What do you like about OBOD?
Only one I knew about at the time.

When did you realise you were a Druid? And how did that feel?
Still not sure exactly what it means! It felt like coming home, though…

My first OBOD experience in the Southern Hemisphere
It was a ceremony not far from where I live now. The leaves were falling from tall gum trees, and I was very excited to be sharing ritual with people I thought were of like-mind.

When did you first meet another Druid or member of OBOD? Describe that encounter.
I think in 2003, I contacted someone, who was a Grove chief – it turned out I already knew them, but not as a Druid… I was delighted to have someone I knew as the person who would introduce me to Druidry and OBOD.

What do you know about the history of Druidry in Australia?
Not much.

Do you see any link between the Druidry that you practise today and the Druidry that was practised by *The United Ancient Order of Druids* **in the early years of European settlement?**
Only the new environment – not climate – also, probably not women, but I don't know…

Why do you think Druidry is becoming more popular in Australia? What do you think people are looking for? Has this changed over the years?
Paganism generally is more acceptable. It has changed.

What do you think is distinctly Australian in regard to Druidry?
Replacing British trees and animals with Australian ones in ceremony. We don't have the same traditional food and drink either.

Where do you see Druidry in the future of Australia? Or, what do you vision for us in the future? Where would you like it to go? Can you relate your ideas to what Druidry in Australia has been in the past?
I think it will become increasingly environmentally focused and hope it will become more politically aware. Also, that it may develop into a new form, which encompasses new traditions, and seasonal changes, rather than following the Celtic Wheel of the year.

If someone asked you to specify what a Druid is in three sentences, what would your three sentences be?
1. A Druid reveres Nature.
2. They find a spiritual connection with all things.
3. The roots of Druidry are originally a British spiritual tradition.

MS

Please describe where you live.
Forest in Dandenong Ranges, Melbourne Victoria.

What is your local Indigenous language group/cultural tribe?
I went on a walk to find out more about the local inhabitants of this area. It was very interesting, but I have forgotten the name of the group.

Do you have any contact with them?
Yes, I have Indigenous friends.

What value might writing a history of Druidry in Australia have?
Yes, it would be a good idea as a lot of the history of past Druids has been lost so it would be good to keep a record.

What should it include?
Indigenous culture, who walked the land before us, native trees and species. Practices during rituals and results.

When did you join OBOD?
Approx a year ago. I had been practising Wicca since I was 17, then joined another group of Druids, *The Australian Order of Hern*. It was more set up for males, but I still go to rituals there as well as my OBOD rituals.

How far along the course are you?
Still doing first year.

Why did you join? Why not some other Druid group? What do you like about OBOD?
I was always interested in Druidry but didn't know it existed much in Australia. I found a great group of people in *The Melbourne Grove* and enjoyed the company, discussions and rituals. I like the formal training which I have never done, also have never liked to join groups much, but I am really enjoying the exercises and meditations and information. It is of great help and interest to me. I value and appreciate it very much.

When did you realise you were a Druid? And how did that feel?
Like welcome home, you have been wandering and now you have felt your true self and what it is like to be of service to others and the wider community and also to preserve the forest for future generations. I made my own robes and when I put them on it felt right and I am very comfortable and happy in my own skin.

I was invited as a guest by Elkie to attend my first blessing of waters for the world at our local well or natural spring. I was nervous but as we got to the site, I felt rather welcome and encompassed by the other women there. I was able to let down my guard and relax and sing to the waters of the world for peace and it changed a lot inside me. Such peace and happiness I have not felt for a very long time and my chanting echoing in the forest was very heart felt. I was holding the peace pipes and they were pulsating in my hands and I could feel pure energy and connection to place and water.

When did you first meet another Druid or member of OBOD? Describe that encounter.
It was my birthday and I decided I didn't want to be alone, so I decided to go and see my favourite artist, Wendy Rule, at a nearby pub. I walked there alone- it took me 40 min - and when I was going in there were some people in front of me - Elkie and Brigit. I asked if I could sit with them as I was alone and didn't know anyone except Wendy Rule. They said sure and that's when I found out that they were Druids. I had been searching for a good grove to join so it was my luck and fortune to find and be directed to the Grove. We were talking about different magical topics and then Elkie invited me to be her guest and we swapped phone numbers.

What do you know about the history of Druidry in Australia?
Only what I have learnt from *The Australian Order of Hern* and most of the teaching is from England and Scotland. I don't know much about Australian Druidry, just that we do things differently for the directions and plants and trees. I am hoping to expand my knowledge and experiences.

Are you involved in any other groups (related to your Druidry or spirituality)?
I used to go to the Theosophical society and was a member there.

Mt Franklin Pagan Gathering
The Australian Order of Hern.

Do you see any link between the Druidry that you practise today and the Druidry that was practised by *The United Ancient Order of Druids* **in the early years of European settlement?**
Protecting the environment.
Planting of trees.
Peace and understanding.
Being of Service to others.
Honouring the seasons.

Why do you think Druidry is becoming more popular in Australia? What do you think people are looking for? Has this changed over the years?
I think people are not so interested in organised religions and going to church. With Druidry it is being close to the earth and the seasons. You can practise it anywhere and it is very personal. I think people are connecting to the earth more and understanding the relevance of conservation and planting of trees for future generations.

What do you think is distinctly Australian in regard to Druidry?
I like the way we are different from England with our native trees and shrubs and that we do things that align us with powerful land connections in our own country. I also like that we observe native culture and give thanks to the traditional owners of the land.

Where do you see Druidry in the future of Australia?
I see it getting bigger and growing more popular. People like to be in touch with like-minded people and enjoy celebrating the seasons and knowledge of local trees, fauna and flora. I think it has been hidden and now it is more open and accessible to more people which is a good thing.

If someone asked you to specify what a Druid is in three sentences, what would your three sentences be?
1. A love of nature and animals.
2. The flowing spirit of Awen.
3. Spiritual experiences for the soul and mind.

Michael V

Please describe where you live.
The bush above Dorrigo, hilly, high rain, river, waterfall.

What is your local Indigenous language group/cultural tribe?
Gumbaynggirr.

Do you have any contact with them?
Yes.

What value might writing a history of Druidry in Australia have?
Our history will not be forgotten and vanish into vague memory, and empty names and Dogma!

Cultural history is our proof of an evolving growing wisdom, the camera of society, changing. All branches of Druidry need to be documented, whatever label you hang around under.

What should it include?
Attitudes that caused it to manifest, effects on society, people, Indigenous communities, how we'll deal with wilful destruction

People, events, skills, arts, problems, successes, what illnesses, healing, rules or laws, the evolving myth of DDU.

When did you join OBOD?
1995.

How far along the course are you?
Beginner? From a million years ago.

Why did you join? Why not some other Druid group? What do you like about OBOD?
Cannot remember! It was complete, course and other groups were more wicca; bits and pieces.

I have never smelt the rank odour of Bourgeoise Attitude in OBOD! No taint of the Freemasons! Bush Ogham!

When did you first meet another Druid or member of OBOD? Describe that encounter.
A Pendragon appeared at a festival, told me to join. A Druid in West Australia (Albany) said he had been going.

When did you realise you were a Druid? And how did that feel?
Silly question! Always was. Always will be. No separation.

What do you know about the history of Druidry in Australia?
I know the spirit of Druidry came over with the first fleet, among the alternative thinkers banished from the Isles of the Mighty. I know many seeded in the local tribes, some of these things I have seen and heard from elders, but names I know not.

Would you be willing to research the history of Druidry in your local area for this project?
I am a man of imagination not tact.

Are you involved in any other groups (related to your Druidry or spirituality – including historical societies, other spiritual groups, environmental groups, and social justice groups)?
Medieval, Viking, OTO, guarding the environment.

Do you see any link between the Druidry that you practise today and the Druidry that was practised by *The United Ancient Order of Druids* in the early years of European settlement?
All they did was talk, read the dry lies of white invaders justifying lying.
I'm sure the practice on the inner level was the same, only the outer shape changes.

Why do you think Druidry is becoming more popular in Australia? What do you think people are looking for? Has this changed over the years?
Yes, the sleeping giants are waking up, so more recognise their soul desert and want an oasis, the practice of the egg and dragon is universal.

The ancient belief of this land is earth based. The convict / guard attitude is based on freedom, which we have in Oz in plenty now.

What do you think is distinctly Australian in regard to Druidry?
The ability to accept different attitudes while holding your own different. Ogham.

Where do you see Druidry in the future of Australia? Or, what do you vision for us in the future? Where would you like it to go? Can you relate your ideas to what Druidry in Australia has been in the past?
As we grow stronger, so more people of power will be practising it. (i.e. Churchill in England). So the attitude of ethics must rise above conceit, Guard a resistance to politics and religion.

Active in teaching what no one teaches, active in politics, active in guardianship of the land.

If someone asked you to specify what a Druid is in three sentences, what would your three sentences be?
1. the Balance of attitude; the skill of using their senses; understanding great obligation
2. not stuck in concrete attitude; holder of 3 specific wisdoms;
3. service to the community.

What further questions would you like to see included in a questionnaire about the history of Druidry in Australia?
What are the family memories of the First Fleet people meeting the land, people and animals? Not the merchants; those who felt and stayed.

Where do practices which come from other belief systems cash in on the word 'Druid' and subvert the paradigm?

How can I write except in a great book, how, what was rejected in one world was accepted in another, how creative the throat (voice), just keeps leading me on! So, cultivation, voice, imagination and ethics seem to be my three jewels!

Morphett Vale

Please describe where you live.
Morphett Vale, South Australia, which was named after Sir John Morphett who arrived in 1836 aboard the Cygnet. Prior to this, its name was Emu Downs, and some of the traditional (Indigenous) names were: Mandarilla; Parnangga; Coorara and Yetto. It is approximately 30 kms from Adelaide CBD. We have the hills to our East, City is to the north, the sea is to the west and to the south we have plains and some more hills. I live beside the Onkaparinga Creek, which really is not a creek but a catchment. The local council have recently pulled out the birch trees which were growing abundantly through there and put in more native species, which are taking quite some time to become established. The great gum that looks over my fence often houses a local koala and the kookaburras are often around too. There are some possums that live in the huge palm tree in a neighbouring house which can make quite a racket.

At the moment (mid-August), many of the fruit trees are in full bloom, and the Golden Wattle is radiant with blossom.

What is your local Indigenous language group/cultural tribe?
Our traditional custodians are the Kaurna people.

Do you have any contact with them?
Unfortunately, I don't.

What value might writing a history of Druidry in Australia have?
It will add to the growing history of our country and allow for a living history to emerge.

What should it include?
The history of Druidry. When and how we acknowledge our seasons. A brief overview of the many Groves and Seed Groups of the States and territories of Australia. Also which of these follow which path OBOD, AOD etc… Not sure what else…

When did you join OBOD?
I joined OBOD in 2015 but had been a non-OBOD member of a Grove in Port Lincoln from 1998-2000. When I moved from Port Lincoln to Morphett Vale in 2000, I had reached the Ovate grade, but had not yet been initiated or become part of OBOD due to financial reasons.

How far along the course are you?
I was initiated as Bard in April (Samhain) 2017 and am in the process of writing my Bardic Grade notes up and getting an OBOD mentor so I am able to move onto my Ovate training.

Why did you join? Why not some other Druid group? What do you like about OBOD?
When I moved to Adelaide, I looked for a Druid group, but could not find one. It hasn't been until recently that the Druid 'movement' has taken off – I think the reason it has is largely due to the embracing of the tradition by our local songstress Adrienne Piggott (Spiral Dance). This finally gave me hope that I might be able to continue with my path, which I did – I joined *The Golden Wattle Seed Group*.

I did not know there were any other Druid Orders out there. I had only been part of OBOD celebrations, and really found that this path was more in keeping with my own lifestyle.

OBOD fits with me because of the nature of the material that is sent out to us. As a teacher, I need to be able to work at my own pace, and the gwersi offer this. Occasionally I do need to have a bit of a prod to get my writing done, and I feel that when I am allocated a mentor that this might be something I request!

When did you realise you were a Druid? And how did that feel?
I think I was always a Druid but did not align myself with that term until 1998 at *Cooringal Grove*. When that 'ah-hah' moment came, it was not a complete surprise, but more of a sense of coming home, belonging and community. The time that I spent away from my Druidic practice (15 years) I followed the magical path of Wicca, but it did not feel completely right for me. The day I was accepted into *The Golden Wattle Seed Group* was wonderful – finally I had found a niche. Just how much I had missed my Druidic family became evident to me when I had my

Bardic Initiation… I had finally come home and I sobbed with the sheer overwhelmingly joyous emotion it stirred in me.

As a possible starting point to the above: when did you first meet another Druid or member of OBOD? Describe that encounter.
I cannot remember how I met Rafayard the first time, but we were part of many of the same groups. I do remember that I felt a kinship with her that was immediate. I felt incredibly blessed that she invited me to her Grove and to take part in the OBOD rituals she was holding. She would often set small tasks, like: create something that you feel about Earth, or one of the other elements to share at the seasonal Eisteddfod. Back then I was always writing poetry, which is what I would share with the Grove.

What do you know about the history of Druidry in Australia?
Unfortunately, I do not know much about the history of Druidry in Australia.

Would you be willing to research the history of Druidry in your local area for this project?
I do not have the contacts to do this.

Are you involved in any other groups (related to your Druidry or spirituality – including historical societies, other spiritual groups, environmental groups, and social justice groups)?
I occasionally take part in some of the Pagan get-togethers that are put on by our local Pagan group (PASA – *Pagan Alliance of South Australia*). With the help of a small group we also host a monthly gathering – *Fleurieu Pagans in the Pub*, where we invite guest speakers to share some of their path or offer a short workshop for the evening.

Do you see any link between the Druidry that you practise today and the Druidry that was practised by *The United Ancient Order of Druids* in the early years of European settlement?
I don't know… I imagine that we are following some of the same seasonal celebrations, but not quite sure.

Why do you think Druidry is becoming more popular in Australia? What do you think people are looking for? Has this changed over the years?

People are looking for a way in which to support and protect the Earth, and due to this they align themselves with more Earth based traditions. In the past, the 'Church' was the way in which people connected to their community and communed with God, but now I think the 'Church' is losing appeal as more and more atrocities are committed in its name, and people are seeking something that brings them closer to the natural world.

What do you think is distinctly Australian in regard to Druidry?
I can only speak from my own experience here. I align my quarters to North being Fire and South being Earth and welcome the native animals and elements when I set the quarters.

If someone asked you to specify what a Druid is in three sentences, what would your three sentences be?
1. Someone who lives in harmony with the natural world.
2. Someone who seeks peace within and understanding of the world around them.
3. Someone who is part of a wider community who shares sacred space, and follows their path with love, strength, understanding, and knowledge, while desiring justice on all levels. (I love that prayer!!)

Murray Barton

Please describe where you live.
Kalamunda Western Australia- suburban fringe with lots of natural bushland within walking distance.

What is your local Indigenous language group/cultural tribe?
Whadjuk Noongar.

Do you have any contact with them?
Nothing directly related to Druidry or spirituality.

What value might writing a history of Druidry in Australia have?
Should be an interesting read and hopefully a good touch point for others in the future coming to the tradition - letting them know that others have been that way and gone through what they are going through (or something like it).

What should it include?
Honestly, I have no idea!

When did you join OBOD?
Late 1995/early 1996.

How far along the course are you?
Completed Druid grade.

Why did you join?
Wanted to find out more about Druidry in a practical (i.e. not out of a book context).

Why not some other Druid group?
OBOD was the biggest around and most accessible. I had read some of Philip Carr-Gomm's books and books by the Matthews who are/were also connected to OBOD and OBOD offered a correspondence course.

What do you like about OBOD?
Open, inclusive, doesn't take itself too seriously.

When did you realise you were a Druid? And how did that feel?
It sounds a bit new-agey but somewhere in the OBOD Druid grade I had a dream where I was bathed in the "golden light" of the Order/Tradition. That's when I knew. Other than that, it was a bit Zen; chop wood carry water. It was deeply profound and at the same time insignificant outside of my own personal context.

As a possible starting point to the above: when did you first meet another Druid or member of OBOD? Describe that encounter.
Can't remember the exact date but it would have been 1996-1997 I went to a gathering with what was to become *The Gaelic Druid Order of the Southern Cross* hosted by Ruiseart and Ceit who were also at the time OBOD members. Their rituals were predominantly in Scots Gaelic and involved an amount of mead drinking as the cup was passed around for the ceilidh.

What do you know about the history of Druidry in Australia?
Other than my own points pretty much covered here and where I overlapped with *The Gaelic Druid Order of the Southern Cross* (now based in Scotland) pretty close to nothing – not a topic that has received a lot of attention as far as I have discovered.

Also, I worked with a group of people to publish the first ever (I think) anthology of Druid writings from the Southern Hemisphere – it was called *Southern Echoes* and published in 2003.

Would you be willing to research the history of Druidry in your local area for this project?
I can help. Not sure what that would look like or how much time it would need but happy to discuss.

Are you involved in any other groups (related to your Druidry or spirituality – including historical societies, other spiritual groups, environmental groups, and social justice groups)?
Member of a Buddhist group.

Do you see any link between the Druidry that you practise today and the Druidry that was practised by *The United Ancient Order of Druids* **in the early years of European settlement?**
Nope. As far as I can tell they didn't practise any kind of Druidry- they were a friendly society.

Why do you think Druidry is becoming more popular in Australia?
I didn't realise it was!

What do you think people are looking for?
People are wearying of the current cultural trend further and further towards materialism and exploitation of the natural world. They are looking for an earth honouring spirituality and a sense of sacred (and sacred feminine) which has also largely disappeared from the mainstream religions.

Has this changed over the years?
I think it is a trend which is only increasing.

What do you think is distinctly Australian in regard to Druidry?
Can you define Australian first? [smiley face image] Druidry is a tradition which honours place, time, tribe, ancestors and one's personal journey so it is at once universal and uniquely Australian. But I might be biased in that regard.

Where do you see Druidry in the future of Australia? Or, what do you vision for us in the future? Where would you like it to go? Can you relate your ideas to what Druidry in Australia has been in the past?
I hope people continue to find the tradition and find in it a spirituality that is resonant with the land, their people (past and present) and their own journey. I think the gatherings and publications which we have had to date have grown organically as people have been inspired and/or filled a need. I hope that it doesn't get any more organised than that.

If someone asked you to specify what a Druid is in three sentences, what would your three sentences be?
1. Druidry is a nature based spiritual tradition originating from the ancient peoples of the British Isles and Europe.

2. Druids come from all walks of life and all cultural and religious backgrounds to honour spirit; in themselves and in earth, sky and sea and all that dwell thereon.
3. It's a tradition which seems to have as many definitions as it has adherents; ultimately it is like a mountain, a forest, a storm-tossed ocean: words offer only the faintest glimpse of its beauty, power and magic.

[Editor's Comment: Murray Barton collected and presented *Southern Echoes: An Anthology of Druid Writing from the Southern Hemisphere* (2003 Paperback)]

Narine

Please describe where you live:
Melbourne, urban / East Gippsland. Rural childhood.

What should a history of Druidry in Australia include?
Documentation, future reference and legacy (and partly confirmation, legitimacy). As much as possible.

When did you join OBOD?
?2014

How far along the course are you?
Pre Ovate.

Why did you join? Why not some other Druid group? What do you like about OBOD?
Accessible, relevant, organised, global, flexible.

What was your first OBOD experience in the Southern Hemisphere? When did you first meet another Druid or member of OBOD? Describe that encounter.
My first *Melbourne Grove* ceremony; a feeling of gears shifting and a sudden rightness of the universe; a sense of finding and coming home spiritually.

When did you realise you were a Druid? And how did that feel?
As a child, but didn't know the term/ group until early 50s.

What do you know about the history of Druidry in Australia?
Very little but prepared to research and contribute.

Are you involved in any other groups (related to your Druidry or spirituality)?
Druid network online, BOD (minimal), *Amnesty*, MSF and *Red Cross*, *Permaculture Victoria*

Do you see any link between the Druidry that you practise today and the Druidry that was practised by *The United Ancient Order of Druids* **in the early years of European settlement?**
I imagine beneficence, altruism, fraternity and goodwill.

Why do you think Druidry is becoming more popular in Australia? What do you think people are looking for? Has this changed over the years?
Nature based spirituality- care for the earth and nature. Dissatisfaction with and disconnection from 'mainstream' monotheistic religion.

What do you think is distinctly Australian in regard to Druidry?
Equality, tolerance, light heartedness, humour.

Where do you see Druidry in the future of Australia? Or, what do you vision for us in the future? Where would you like it to go? Can you relate your ideas to what Druidry in Australia has been in the past?
Growing, strengthening, more confidence and higher profile. I would like to see / develop permanent retreat / residential.

If someone asked you to specify what a Druid is in three sentences, what would your three sentences be?
1. Tolerant, respectful of nature.
2. Free of dogma.
3. Cognisant of culture, wisdom and ancestors, but grounded in the love of now and looking forward.

What further questions would you like to see included in a questionnaire about the history of Druidry in Australia?
Family attitudes and background to Pagan and Druidry religions.

Sandra Greenhalgh

Please describe where you live.
Brisbane, Queensland - I can drive to Mt Coot-tha without going through any traffic lights

What is your local Indigenous language group/cultural tribe?
Turrbul and Jagera people.

Do you have any contact with them?
No – only in a professional / work contact.

What value might writing a history of Druidry in Australia have?
Some of us are getting older. Despite the wonders of social media, and the internet, I'm worried that stories will be lost over time… and Druids love history, so why not be involved in writing their own.

What should it include?
A time line. Personal reflections from people studying Druidry while living in Australia.

When did you join OBOD?
I joined in December 1988.

How far along the course are you?
Druid Grade

Why did you join? Why not some other Druid group?
Because it was literally the first Druid group I'd come across in real life, except for Friendly Society Druids. Though having said that, even if I was starting to learn about Druidry today, I would still join OBOD, due to the wonderful correspondence course format.

What do you like about OBOD?
It's very gentle, yet very deep. Undertaking the course work has an impact on so many levels, from the mundane to the psychological to the spiritual. I really like

the other members of OBOD and have formed many wonderful friendships.

When did you realise you were a Druid? And how did that feel?
It was back in 1986, when I discovered there was much more to life than what met the eye. I did a lot of exploration about different types of spirituality, and Druidry seemed to fit me really well. I have an avid and lifelong love of nature, mythology and poetry: all of these seemed to be core Druidry principles.

What was your first OBOD experience in the Southern Hemisphere?
At first, it felt incredibly lonely and quite bewildering. I formally started my Druid studies with OBOD while I was in England in 1988, and when I returned to Australia in late 1989, there were no other people studying Druidry around me. No one. I felt like I was the 'only Druid in the Village' – to paraphrase the TV show *Little Britain*. As well as experiencing a sense of isolation, it was difficult to relate to Australian flora and fauna after being immersed in English and European landscapes for so long.

My whole Druidic framework had to shift to accommodate the changed seasons, and the vastly different songs of this land. I spent a lot of time reflecting while trying to personally integrate Northern Hemisphere practices into a Southern Hemisphere setting. During this time, I was careful to find my own path through the (Eucalypt rather than Oak) forest, while being respectful and culturally appropriate in regards to the Aboriginal and / or Torres Strait Islander peoples who are the traditional custodians of the land.

Fortunately, in the early 1990s I did meet up with some local people enmeshed with earth-based spirituality, including heaps of Wiccans, witches and a group who studied a different type of Druidry. But it wasn't until the inaugural Australian OBOD Assembly in 1997 when I finally met other Australian OBOD members face to face.

I was thrilled to receive a letter from Akkadia and Zan inviting me to the first Australian OBOD Assembly. After packing every scrap of warm clothing I could find as well as camping gear into the back of my little car, I drove down from Queensland to the hills outside of Sydney, near Wiseman's Ferry. The night before the inaugural Assembly, I had dinner alone at the motel, where I spotted some alternatively dressed people eating together. I wondered if they were my

OBOD-kin, but I was too nervous to speak to them at the time, as I dreaded opening up a conversation with, "Hi! Are you the Druids?"

Sure enough, they were indeed the Druids, and we met properly the next morning in the damp birch forest.

Initially, the Assembly seemed quite chaotic and disorganised to me, but everyone was extremely friendly and tried to make it work. The hardships of camping, sharing food (e.g., waiting for the hot water to boil for coffee!) and the commonality of the spiritual framework of OBOD quickly brought us all together. I loved being involved in the rituals (despite the rainy drizzle) and the sheer camaraderie of the Assembly. It was also reassuring to talk with others who were experiencing similar challenges of mapping Northern Hemisphere traditions onto a Southern Hemisphere land, despite some difference in opinion.

And yes, there was mead to be had, a tradition which has continued over the years into the fabric of Queensland's *Macadamia Grove*. At any event when you meet a group of new people at the same time, you tend to bond more with some than others. Carole Nielsen (who became the first editor of *SerpentStar*) was one of my favourite new friends from the Assembly, and when I left, she pressed a bottle of mead into my hand. We formed a plan that we would have a toast (raise glasses together and then drink a small amount of celebratory alcohol) at a designated time during my trip, so we could have a drink 'together' to celebrate the Assembly. I remember parking my car at the side of the road back to Queensland and taking a sip of the mead straight from the bottle, while experiencing fond memories of the inaugural Australian Assembly.

What do you know about the history of Druidry in Australia?
As a child, I adored stories of all kinds, particularly the Greek myths and the Tales of the Round Table (Arthurian legends). I first physically bumped into Druidry after seeing the grand building of the *Ancient Druid Order* in Western Australia, in the late 1980s. I posed outside the majestic door and declared to my friend; "I'm going to join the Druids!"

We both laughed, as it seemed a good joke at the time. I wasn't aware that there were modern day Druids who were involved with matters other than life insurance.

While working in England in 1988, I noticed an advertisement offering a new course from *The Order of Bards, Ovates and Druids*. I immediately 'knew' that this was something I had to do, and I enrolled straight away. The correspondence I received was inspiring and welcoming and I simply loved it from the very beginning. As OBOD had only just re-opened and was quite small, Philip Carr-Gomm (the OBOD Chosen Chief) was my tutor. He seemed very kind, and gently offered insights into a range of topics. I also remember phoning him to ask him about magical places to visit in Ireland, and he also graciously provided very sound travel advice!

After a while, I plucked up the courage to attend an event hosted by Philip and Stephanie in their home. Before attending, I was really scared to meet these assuredly lofty and amazing people. I was somehow convinced that they could read people's minds and therefore would unearth my deepest darkest thoughts, and feelings of inadequacy.

I rang the doorbell and without any dramatics the door was opened by Philip. My first impressions were of a huge halo of curly hair, a lovely smile and being welcomed gently into the house. My feelings of terror dissipated quite quickly, though I was still cautious, despite being warmly welcomed by Stephanie and the other attendees - approximately ten to fifteen in number.

That night Philip led us on a guided meditation. While I had a few different flashes of visions, one of the quite clear ones included me walking near the front of a big crowd of people, so many in number that they flowed over the hills and behind. I thought 'that's a bit nondescript' and when we recounted our experiences from the meditation, I talked instead about an image of a fountain I had seen, as that seemed to be a common theme. However, when Philip described his vision of leading an enormous group of people over the land, I was blown away. "I was there!" I wanted to declare at the time: "I was with you!" And here I am, over thirty years later.

Nearly a year after that meeting, my time of travelling overseas was finished, and I returned to Queensland in Australia. Then my search for local magically-minded people began. Despite being avowedly introverted, I really love spending time with like-minded folk, and from the early 1990s up until the year 2000 I attended every earth-based spirituality event I possibly could, including Australian

Assemblies. However, in 2000, my life underwent a huge change as I gave birth to my first child, and my focus moved to tending the Hearth-fires and mothering. For the next ten or more years, I rarely attended big events, and kept in contact with other Australian OBODies through the internet and reading newsletters.

I re-joined the OBOD community for the Assembly in 2014. Since then I've been actively involved by re-forming *Macadamia Seed Group* (which had its inception in 1998) with other local OBODies, and it formally became *Macadamia Grove* in 2015. *Macadamia Grove* hosted the 2016 *OBOD Southern Hemisphere Assembly* on Bribie Island, Queensland, which was a simply wonderful experience.

Apart from all the wonderful interactions I've been so fortunate to have been part of, I believe now that my most enduring contribution (apart from editing this book) to Druidry in Australia is creating a new deck of Oracle cards this year (2019). These are called the *Druid Wisdom Oracle*. As an independent self-taught artist and author I drew the images, edited them, wrote the instruction booklet and self-published a limited-edition print run. The inception of these cards came about in an unexpected – and quite shocking - inflow of Awen, and I am proud to have honoured that inspiration right through to being able to hold the finished deck in my hand. As the name indicates, these link to the myths, legends, practices and spirituality of Druidry as I was able to express it within the cards, and I like to think that long after I have passed from this plane, these cards will remain.

Are you involved in any other groups (related to your Druidry or spirituality – including historical societies, other spiritual groups, environmental groups, and social justice groups)?
I've been heavily engaged in earthbased spirituality (often called 'Pagan') groups and events in Australia since the early 1990s, and continue to be so. I have also protested with environmental groups (such as *The Wilderness Society*) against environmental vandalism such as logging old growth forests on Fraser island.

Over the years, I've provided an interface for Druidry in Australia in a variety of ways. I've talked about Druidry on podcasts; with university students for their assignments; been interviewed for radio shows; and presented at public events such as *Beltanefire*. I've contributed to a published anthology; provided responses for *The Wild Hunt* articles; and written articles for *SerpentStar*. I'm also a regular attendee of local and interstate events.

Do you see any link between the Druidry that you practise today and the Druidry that was practised by *The United Ancient Order of Druids* **in the early years of European settlement?**
Not so much. I practise my Druidry within a contemporary context. I live very much within the setting of an urban and corporate world and pretending to be a historical Druid – or Celt- isn't my way.

Why do you think Druidry is becoming more popular in Australia? What do you think people are looking for? Has this changed over the years?
I think that social media, and the easy sharing of information has helped the 'explosion' of Druidry in Australia. Add the yearning of people wanting to connect with a valid source of spirituality that is soul-nourishing and nature-honouring… and you have the perfect fit.

I believe that people, at some level, search for spiritual connections which aren't linked into formal religious structures. Druidry also has the benefit of being more 'socially acceptable' than Witchcraft or other forms of Pagan spirituality, which likely makes this form of spirituality attractive to people. The 'Satanic Panic' is not that far distant, and the risk is always present that people who don't readily identify as Christians may be seen as 'devil worshippers.'

The other big factor is that people studying Druidry are usually nice people. We tend to be less embroiled in personal dramas and inter-factional politics, most likely because of the focus on Peace within our studies. Having said that, Druids can be quite fierce when it comes to social justice and environmental issues!

What do you think is distinctly Australian in regard to Druidry?
The practice of Druidry reminds us to take note of the local landscape and creatures and flora around us. We are shaped by our local environment, more so depending on the level of engagement and involvement we have with it.

Where do you see Druidry in the future of Australia? Or, what do you vision for us in the future? Where would you like it to go? Can you relate your ideas to what Druidry in Australia has been in the past?
I'm a bit concerned that Druidry (as shared in public spaces) may be watered down into generic Pagan practices, and that current, influential traditions such as

Reclaiming may shift practices into something not in alignment with my current understanding of Druidry.

Sometimes, in real life situations and interactions with others, I feel we need to define 'this is Druidry' AND 'this isn't Druidry.' However, I fear that to do this is, actually isn't Druidic… so that's actually quite problematic.

I'm also a bit worried that the practices of Druidry might become 'sexy' and people want to engage in it just because it's a bit cool or popular these days. The danger is that they bring in their own prejudices and don't actually engage with any of the principles. It's hard to learn when you are invested in your own ego, or collection of titles, or self- aggrandizement.

If someone asked you to specify what a Druid is in three sentences, what would your three sentences be?
1. Anchored in Celtic mythology and British history.
2. A nature-based spirituality – we love our trees and the worlds around us, seen and unseen.
3. Focusing on creativity and peace and learning

Vicki Minahan

Please describe where you live.
I live in the Dandenong Ranges Victoria on the edge of a small town on 1.5 acres. Mostly treed with native grasses and plants and many birds, we are on the edge of rainforest and dry forest area.

What is your local Indigenous language group/cultural tribe?
Wurundjeri.

Do you have any contact with them?
No.

What value might writing a history of Druidry in Australia have?
I believe it would help new and more practised Druids/Pagans to focus their practice more on an Australian aspect if that is what they want to do. It is also a way to honour our ancestors in this land.

What should it include?
An explanation of Druidry, how it came to Australia, touch on Aussie seasons and variations across the country, key people who have helped establish Druidry in Australia, how it has changed, where the future may be.

When did you join OBOD?
About 2000.

How far along the course are you?
2nd go at Ovate.

Why did you join? Why not some other Druid group? What do you like about OBOD?
I joined because I found the *Druid Animal Oracle* deck in a shop and pulled a Deerhound 1st up, then some other animal guides I have, researched OBOD and liked that it offered guidance and help without trying to indoctrinate.

When did you realise you were a Druid? And how did that feel?
I think when I found the *Druid Animal Oracle*, it was like the light coming on after years of searching.

As a possible starting point to the above: when did you first meet another Druid or member of OBOD? Describe that encounter.
Elkie and Marigold at William Ricketts. I recognised them immediately, it was very much a homecoming, a day I will always remember as it's been a wild ride since.

What do you know about the history of Druidry in Australia?
I know nothing about the history of Druidry in Australia, this is a bit poor really.

Are you involved in any other groups (related to your Druidry or spirituality – including historical societies, other spiritual groups, environmental groups, and social justice groups)?
I also do spiritual work with a small informal group in Australia and a small informal international online group, as well as local environmental work as shift work allows.

Do you see any link between the Druidry that you practise today and the Druidry that was practised by *The United Ancient Order of Druids* **in the early years of European settlement?**
It seems from the little I know it was originally set up to help those in need and to keep some connection with the home country, something I would think most Druids still aspire to.

Why do you think Druidry is becoming more popular in Australia? What do you think people are looking for? Has this changed over the years?
I think people are becoming more concerned about environmental issues and this can then lead into a spiritual practice, also Australia is more open to alternative practices than 20 or 30 years ago.

I believe people are also looking to slow down their lives and see this as a way to do it as well as offering a full and positive life.

What do you think is distinctly Australian in regard to Druidry?
I think this is a newly emerging aspect of Druidry in Australia as we come to terms more with the many and varied seasons this continent has and that those differences can occur within close proximity. I believe we are becoming better at being in tune with these changes.

Where do you see Druidry in the future of Australia? Or, what do you vision for us in the future? Where would you like it to go? Can you relate your ideas to what Druidry in Australia has been in the past?
I hope that it continues to grow, that in the future more are able to live and breathe the life without the demands of a working life, to have a community healer and/or shaman without the need to go out into the world to work would be awesome. At the same time, I hope the communities remain small but become many, it would be sad to lose the family/village feel we have.

If someone asked you to specify what a Druid is in three sentences, what would your three sentences be?
- Someone who practises nature-based spirituality, encompassing writing, healing, understanding the rules and laws of Druidry.
- A person who has an understanding of the four elements and directions and is able to incorporate them into their practice according to where they live.
- Someone who may or may not be academic, but who is true and genuine in their Druid practice.

What further questions would you like to see included in a questionnaire about the history of Druidry in Australia?
I find this a bit hard at this stage, it would be good to see the draft document and decide from there, there are options given for all to include more if they wish anyway.

United Ancient Order of Druids badge and vest

Photo credit: Elkie White

Part IV

FRATERNAL DRUID LODGES IN AUSTRALIA

AUSTRALIA'S FIRST DRUID LODGES

The following section was compiled by Elkie White in 2019. The sources are drawn from personal research in the *Victorian State Library* and the internet.

Elkie expresses her appreciation to Dr. David Waldron, Senior Lecturer, *Federation University*, for checking the document for accuracy, and for agreeing to keep it "accessible" despite wanting to dive much deeper.

Elkie White

One of the questions in the questionnaire was:

> *"Do you see any link between the Druidry that you practise today and the Druidry that was practised by The United Ancient Order of Druids in the early years of European settlement?"*

A couple of people said "no" and a couple more felt that they had insufficient information to comment. Of the remainder there were three distinct lines of thought.

The first was that in both cases, Druidry provided a meaningful spirituality that arose to meet the times. The same (or similar) myths were used to support the same (or similar) goals. Druidry adapted to the people, the conditions, and the era in which it found itself. One person remarked that on the inner level, it was the same and that only the outer form changed.

An important aspect of this 'meaningful spirituality' was imaging the ancient Druids in a positive light. Thus they became good role models for ourselves in the present. Imagining our ancient Druid ancestors as wise, just, and benevolent, provides modern Druids with a moral compass that can be adhered to in the present. Maybe they were, maybe they were not, and probably some were and some were not, yet it would seem that we share a vision of who we would like our Druid ancestors to have been.

Extending from this, is the fact that most people calling themselves a Druid are community-minded. The original *United Ancient Order of Druids* (UAOD) might have been essentially Christian with a Christian tendency to be charitable, while a couple of centuries on, the majority of Druids may not be Christian, yet still care just as deeply about other people. Being of service to others is something that today's Druids share with members of the original Druid fraternities.

The UAOD Lodges in the emerging States of early Australia were intended to help those in need and to keep some sense of connection with the 'home country'. Most Druids today can relate to such intentions.

The attraction of the Druid Lodges was fourfold:
- Protection in times of hardship and benefits to members at a time when no such benefits existed. These included assistance when sick or unemployed and with funeral expenses.
- Friendship and entertainment: the Druid lodges were born out of a general 'club mania' prevalent in the eighteenth century, and like most fraternal societies at that time, the UAOD in Australia provided an important support network for settlers.
- Care: as friendships deepened, a real sense of caring for each other developed. There are groups who went to war together and there are honour boards in various States naming members who undertook active service in World War I.
- Nostalgia: An interest in the past, particularly in the countries they had left behind, would have helped to off-set homesickness.

A Timeline of Fraternal Druid Lodges in Australia

1781: *The Ancient Order of Druids* (AOD) was founded in London (seven years before the landing of the first fleet in Australia).

1833: *The United Ancient Order of Druids* (UAOD) seceded from the AOD; the UAOD was seeking to become more of a fraternal and benevolent society, while AOD continued to mix fraternalism with mysticism. Both would retain elements of the Masonic tradition. The UAOD would acquire a strong membership in the colonies of the British Empire. By 1895 it had 64,000 members worldwide, of which 25,595 were in Australia.

New South Wales
1846: An advertisement in the *Sydney Morning Herald* for 28 September invited brethren of UAOD to a meeting with a view to forming a Sydney lodge. This initiative could not be maintained due to the gold rush.

1861: The *NSW Ancient Order of Druids* was established in Sydney.
By 1867 there were ten Newcastle lodges with about 1,200 members.

1868: This transitioned to the *United Ancient Order of Druids* (UAOD) *Friendly Society of NSW*. They met at Druids House, 302 Pitt Street, Sydney.

1883: The first meeting of the *NSW UAOD Grand Lodge* was held.

1902: The formation of the first *Ladies Druid Lodge* in NSW.

1927: The UAOD purchased Druids House.

1928: At the time of the Opening Ceremony there were approximately 240,500 members, and they were playing an active role as a Friendly Society in Sydney.

1967: *Druids Court* in Allambie Heights was established as a Home for Aged Members.

2011: The UAOD in NSW changed its name to *Noble Oak Life Limited*.

2013: The building was sold and transformed into a hotel. The Lodge Room on Level 4 is the sole direct reminder of the Druids. It is not heritage protected.

The Druid float was popular in Newcastle at the Kurri Kurri Hospital Sunday fundraising procession in the early 20th Century, where some Druids marched in full formal regalia or wore long white robes with flowing beards, while others rode on horseback beside the float.

South Australia

1850: According to the *Noble Oak Life Limited* website, the first Australian Druids Lodge was established in Adelaide. Every other site claims Victoria founded the first UAOD lodge. It is possible that the South Australian lodge was unofficial in 1850 yet it was recognized in the Annual Report of the *Grand Lodge of Australia* held at the Trades' Hall in Carlton, Victoria, 1950, in the Grand President's Address:

> "*The Grand Lodge of South Australia...celebrated the centenary of the establishment of the first Druids' Lodge in South Australia.*"

The Report of Directors further acknowledged this event, reporting that this foundational lodge was in New Thebarton.

In a Souvenir Booklet handed out at the opening of *Druids House* in Melbourne, the following is written:

> "*The Victorian Grand Lodge...in its early stages had the honour of founding the Order in New Zealand...Queensland, Tasmania and Western Australia...In New South Wales and South Australia, Druidism was not the outcome of Victorian activities, being already in existence.*"

The State Library of South Australia may have further information.

By 1877 there were 862 UAOD members in Adelaide.

1894: The first *Grand Druid Lodge* of South Australia was convened at the Rechabite Hall in Grote Street.

By 1912 there were over thirty lodges in South Australia.
- Sir Lewis Cohen Avenue, named for Sir Lewis Cohen, who was, among many other things, a grand president of the UAOD
- There is a Druid Avenue, lined with oak trees, in Stirling
- *Druids Hall*, 10 Jervois Street, Torrensville is still listed as a place of historical significance.

Victoria

1851: The first UAOD Lodge was founded in Melbourne by Mr Hymen with the authority of the AOD. It could not be maintained due to the gold rush.

1861: A permanent *Grand Lodge* of the UAOD was established in Melbourne.

1886: Juvenile lodges were founded in Prahran, South Melbourne and Footscray but had ceased to exist by 1900.

1897: An oak tree was planted to commemorate the founding of a UAOD Lodge in Hamilton. It now has a plaque.

1900: Melbourne Hospital Bazaar and *United Ancient Order of Druids* 31st Annual Gala and Art Union held at the Exhibition Building, April 14 to 28, with proceeds going to the Melbourne Hospital. First prize: a Golden Druid, valued at 1000 pounds! The Druids Procession was one of the attractions at the annual Easter Monday Parade. Later in the day there were cycling contests including the *Druids Grand Wheel Race*. These Galas raised over 100,000 pounds for charities before being abandoned due to government regulations.

1903: A quote in a 1903 UAOD newsletter from GP Bro W. Lees at the Trafalgar Smoke Night:

> "*Good Druids are as moderate in their speeches as they are in their drinking*!"

1913: The Druid's Wing at St Vincent's Hospital opened on May 11. It housed the hospital's first outpatients department and a residence for nurses-in-training. The building was vacated in 1995 due to a reconstruction program. Heritage pieces, like the foundation stone, were kept to mark its place in St Vincent's Hospital history.

Late 1910s: UAOD ran a Druid's cricket competition. This would evolve into the *Druids Cricket Club* (DCC), which is still active today.

1927: *Druid House* opened on April 4 at 407-9 Swanston Street, as the headquarters of the *Friendly Society* in Melbourne

1934: A neon sign exhorting *Join the Druids* was installed on the side of the building

In 2008, a *Druids Australia* website still listed contact details of the *Druids Lodge* in Queensbury Street, North Melbourne, where there is an Honour Board to past members.

Queensland

It has been difficult to find out when UAOD opened in other States but in a Trove article, 18 Jan 1889, the claim is made that by 1875 there were branches in South Australia, Victoria, New South Wales, Tasmania, and in Queensland.

Resources available in the *State Library of Queensland* include Constitutional Laws (1927), Annual Report of the Grand Lodge of Queensland (periodicals) (1933) and General Laws (1973).

Tasmania

1875: I have been unable to establish a founding date but according to the above Trove article of 18 Jan 1889, there was at least one branch in Tasmania by 1875.

1880: There is a photo on the internet of Druids dressed in long robes and flowing beards processing through Launceston.

1899: The first female lodge (in Australia) was opened in Launceston

1904: *Grand Lodge of Tasmania* UAOD established in Launceston

1938: as reported in *The Advocate*: UAOD, Heart of Oak Lodge Diamond Jubilee, in Launceston (i.e. this lodge began in 1878). In 1938 there were 58 male lodges and seven female lodges in Tasmania.

Western Australia

1891: The first Druid's lodge was established in WA, at Karrakatta in Perth. It was granted dispensation by the Grand Lodge of Victoria (as reported in Western Australia, 19 August 1892)

1895: Geraldton Lodge, UAOD, established at the Club Hotel, Banbury

The signatures of the first 25 members are recorded on a medical certificate signed by a resident doctor who passed them as eligible members of the Lodge (*The Geraldton Guardian and Express*, 28 July 1934, p. 4).

1901: The Grand Lodge in Western Australia, headquartered in Perth, was established.

By 1911 there were 4,000 members in 50 branches, with 30,000 pounds invested.

1925: UAOD building opened at 459 Hay Street, Perth.

1934: *Druid's Hall* was constructed in Geraldton. In the 1990s it was leased to the Salvation Army.

1999: Following Federal legislation for Friendly Societies, the UAOD in Western Australia transferred all business to the Victorian Branch. The changes brought about by the legislation were too great for the society to absorb. The Eastern States managed to update and transfer to the insurance industry.

What became of the AOD and UAOD?

Times have changed and we have *Centrelink* now to provide benefits to those in need of them. The UAOD dissolved in 1999 although Commonwealth Orders of the UAOD, long since independent of the parent body, still have branches in the UK.

1908: Enter the *International Grand Lodge of Druidism* (IGLD). There's plenty of information about them on the internet and their efforts to unite various branches of Druidism, including AOD. The IGLD newsletter of May 2014 reported that only three lodges were still operating in Australia: two in Bunbury, WA, and one in Adelaide, SA. Maybe, as in the UK, these are long-since independent of their UAOD parent body.

The December 2017 IGLD newsletter includes a report from Graeme Foulds, Grand Vice President Australia. He lamented that UAOD South Australia may be closing its doors shortly and expressed the hope that remaining members would be able to transfer to another interstate lodge. Apparently, the Bunbury branch was still going, and Mr Foulds was looking forward to travelling to the 2020 Congress in Sweden along with seven other WA and three Eastern State members and partners.

AOD as a fraternal organization still operates today. It continues to hold ceremonies but has become more of a social and charitable organization. The Masonic character is still present and the Order is still organized in lodges (while other Druids organize themselves into groves), and within AOD most of these are exclusively male. Women members are allowed but their lodges are separate. In *Blood and Mistletoe*, Ronald Hutton remarks that the oldest of them all, the organization founded by Henry Hurle and his friends in 1781, may yet become an Ancient Order in the true sense of the word (page 325).

Druids Cricket Club

The following information, which appears to have been last updated in 2011, was sourced August 2019 from http:/prestonDruidscc.vic.cricket.com.au/content.aspx?file=1192%7C23361d

"Preston Druids Cricket Club in its current form was founded 1926 but has traces going back to the late 1910s. In 1922 Druids were represented at a meeting of five clubs who played regular social cricket in the Jaga district. From this meeting the Jika Cricket Association was inaugurated. Although present at the original meeting and attending subsequent Annual meetings of the Jika Cricket Association, the club did not formerly participate in the competition due to its commitments to the Druids Cricket competition of Melbourne, run by the Ancient Order of Druids.

When the Druids competition floundered in the early 1930s, the club formerly affiliated with the Jika Cricket Association in 1932, winning its first pennant during the war years in 1943/44. In the late 1960s on the back of the baby boomers, the club grew from one senior side to four and introduced juniors for the first time in 1968/69.

Today the club is only one of three original Druids Cricket Clubs in existence in Victoria and offers participation for males at Senior level and supports both male and female participation at the Junior level."

Images of UAOD building in Melbourne

Photo Credit: Elkie White

UAOD Druid's Hall in Geraldton, Western Australia

Druid's Hall (fmr), a Inter-War Stripped Classical style hall built in 1934 with brick walls and corrugated asbestos fibre-cement roof sheeting, has cultural heritage significance for the following reasons:

> the place is one of only a few remaining halls specifically built for the United Ancient Order of Druids in Western Australia, established in 1891, and demonstrates the activities of the Order;
>
> the place is a good example of the Inter-War Stripped Classical style, with a prominent classical façade and ornamental pilasters;
>
> the place is a distinctive landmark building located on a prominent corner site at an intersection in the central area of the City of Geraldton;
>
> the place was constructed for the Geraldton Lodge of the United Ancient Order of Druids, one of the first three Druid lodges established in rural Western Australia, that provided health and welfare benefits for Geraldton members from 1895 for over fifty years;
>
> the place provided a fellowship and social venue highly valued by the members and families of the Geraldton Lodge of the United Ancient Order of Druids, Hibernian Australasian Catholic Benefit Society, and other local branches of different friendly societies; and,
>
> the place demonstrates the growth in membership of Druid's lodges in the early twentieth century in Western Australia.

11. ASSESSMENT OF CULTURAL HERITAGE SIGNIFICANCE

The criteria adopted by the Heritage Council in November 1996 have been used to determine the cultural heritage significance of the place.

PRINCIPAL AUSTRALIAN HISTORIC THEME(S)
- 4.3   Developing institutions
- 8.5.3   Associating for mutual aid

HERITAGE COUNCIL OF WESTERN AUSTRALIA THEME(S)
- 308   Commercial & service industries
- 408   Institutions

11.1 AESTHETIC VALUE*

Druid's Hall (fmr), constructed in 1934, is a good example of Inter-War Stripped Classical style, with a prominent classical façade and ornamental pilasters. (Criterion 1.1)

Image sourced November 2019 from http:/inherit.stateheritage.wa.gov.au/Admin/ api/file/fbddf7fb-33de-80d6-f698-728551871af1

Ancient Order of Druids – a personal connection

Tyna King

PLEASE FIND ATTACHED A COPY of certificates belonging to my paternal grandfather, Ken Sargant and a photo of him when he was young.

The Certificates are from *The United Ancient Order of Druids* in Western Australia, Swan Royal Arch Chapter #6 and the Midland Junction Lodge #411. He obtained his "Opening and Closing" Charge (no date noted), 'Junior Past Arch' Charge (10/03/1949), 'Arch Druid's' Charge (02/06/1949) and 'Past Arch Degree' where he was entitled to rank as Past Arch in the Order.

My grandad, Ken Sargant, was born in Pingelly, WA 21/09/1918 and died Albany, WA 19/07/2002. I remember reading somewhere (though I can't find it) that the UAOD was about service to country and community. I believe my grandad definitely lived up to 'service of'. He was in the Australian Army during WWII in New Guinea first as a butcher, got malaria and medically discharged and then re-enlisted as a machine gunner.

Ken was part of the WA *Volunteer Fire Brigade* from the early 60s and made a life member in 1993, he was with *St John Ambulance* and received their long service medal in 1977 (he was with them from 1958-1980). He was a football trainer for several decades, ending with the Royals in Albany. He also did a lot of fund raising by selling tickets for the *Volunteer Fire Brigade*, *St John Ambulance*, *Flying Doctors* and also, I believe, helping out *The Salvation Army*.

I didn't know my grandad was part of the UAOD until the day after his funeral when I was given a wad of his personal papers to photocopy. Even though I'd been on the Druid path since 1997, I had not really told my family as my mum had thought I was part of a cult. I really do regret not having told my grandfather as we may have been able to have a chat on something else, as he loved chatting to me about all sorts. The spooky thing was the day of his funeral I felt compelled to write out the Druid's Prayer and drop it in on his coffin wrapped around one solitary red rose.

UAOD Arch Druids Charge proficiency certificate

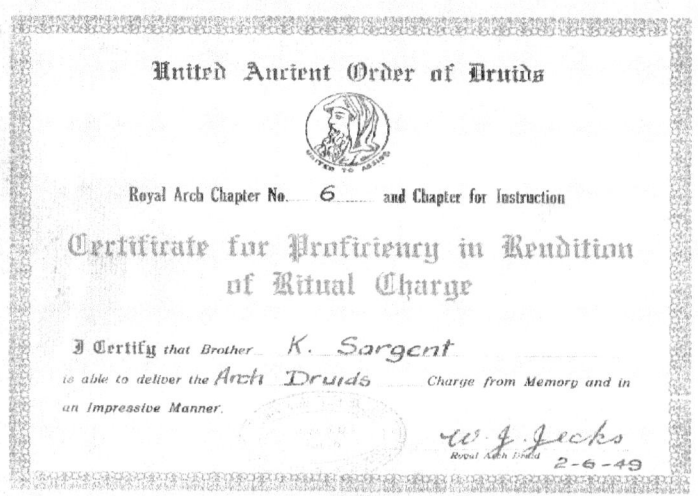

UAOD Grand Lodge Office Past Arch rank certificate

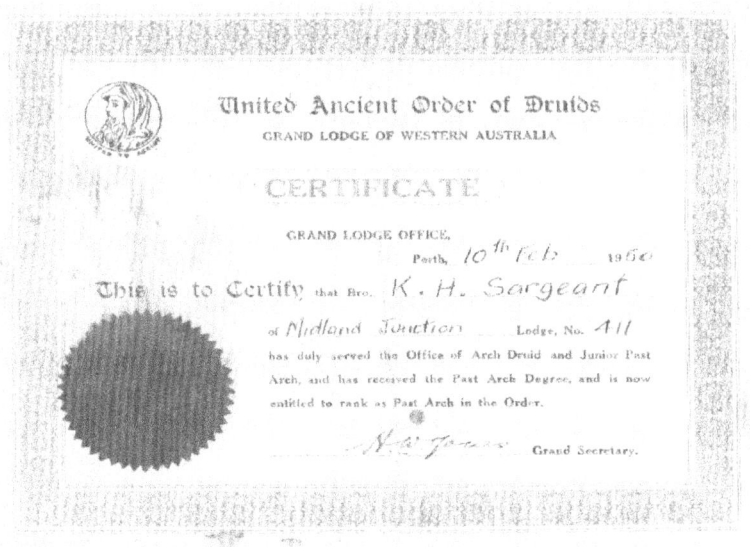

Images credit: Tyna King

Part V

APPENDICES
&
CREDITS

Appendix A: The original *Australian Druid History Project* questionnaire

Towards a History of Druidry in Australia:
The OBOD contribution

Preliminary notes:
Welcome to the Australian Druidry History Project! The catalyst for this project came from several sources including Josie Winter's article for *The Wild Hunt* and Julie Brett's book on *Australian Druidry*. Through this questionnaire, you are invited to include *your* story and perspective. You do not need to answer every question but just the ones that you feel comfortable with or that you feel are important. It is only out of our personal stories that an authentic understanding of Druidry in Australia can emerge. To save paper, the questions have been packed into one sheet of paper. To write more, simply cross-reference to additional sheets. If you prefer, send me an email and ask me to send you the questionnaire in Word format as an attachment. That way you can answer straight into the document.
Please return, with your responses, to Elkie: [email withheld] by December 2018. Thanks.

Your name:
Email contact:
Are you happy to be contacted in regard to this project?

Please describe where you live: city/town/district/State/Territory/general ecology

What is your local indigenous language group/cultural tribe?
Do you have any contact with them?

Generally speaking, do you support the idea of writing a history of Druidry in Australia?
What value might it have?

A HISTORY OF DRUIDRY IN AUSTRALIA

What should it include?

When did you join OBOD?
How far along the course are you?
Why did you join? Why not some other Druid group? What do you like about OBOD?

These 3 questions might link in together but might not:
What was your first OBOD experience in the Southern Hemisphere?

When did you first meet another Druid or member of OBOD? Describe that encounter.

When did you realise you were a Druid? And how did that feel?

What do you know about the history of Druidry in Australia? This is a key question and so please answer it to the best of your ability. Single sentences and full essays are both welcome, and everything in between. Point form is also okay, but for the history-buffs please include names, places, and dates wherever possible.

Would you be willing to research the history of Druidry in your local area for this project?

Are you involved in any other groups (related to your Druidry or spirituality – including historical societies, other spiritual groups, environmental groups, and social justice groups)?

Do you see any link between the Druidry that you practise today and the Druidry that was practised by *The United Ancient Order of Druids* in the early years of European settlement?

Why do you think Druidry is becoming more popular in Australia? What do you think people are looking for? Has this changed over the years?

What do you think is distinctly **Australian** in regard to Druidry?

Where do you see Druidry in the future of Australia? Or, what do you vision for us in the future? Where would you like it to go? Can you relate your ideas to what Druidry in Australia has been in the past?

If someone asked you to specify what a Druid is in three sentences, what would your three sentences be?

As members of OBOD we are not asked to be anything other than that. However some people attach the following words or phrases to Druidry, hence the question: how comfortable are you with the following words? Please rate each from 0-10, with 0 being the least comfortable and 10 the most comfortable.

word	Rating and comments
Druid	
Pagan	
eclectic (Druidry)	
home-grown (Druidry)	
nature-based spirituality	
the word 'religion' (in regard to Druidry)	

Related to the above, do you think that Druidry is worth seeing as distinct to other Pagan groups?

What further questions would you like to see included in a questionnaire about the history of Druidry in Australia?

If your own story is not included in the above questions please feel free to write it on as many extra sheets as you like. Stories, poems, photos, artwork, music and musings are welcome!

Appendix B: Promotion in *SerpentStar* 2017

Introduction to the History Project

The Australian Druidry History Project was launched at the Assembly. The catalyst for this project came from Josie Winter, who instigated the successful *Pagan Collective of Victoria* (PCV) which I have recently been given the honour of joining as a representative of OBOD. Josie was asked to write an article for *The Wild Hunt* on *Druidry in Australia* and needed my answers pronto. The first question was "Tell me about the history of Druidry as a spiritual practice in Australia". Obviously, I could not do justice to such an important question in 24 hours and so I offered to create a questionnaire for the Assembly, with the view that if the interest was there, we could then extend it to other groups and individuals.

Well the interest was there, and I thank-you everyone at the Assembly for their support. I took four completed questionnaires home with me and have been receiving a steady stream of them since. A delightful trend has already emerged in regard to the question: "What do you think is distinctly **Australian** in regard to Druidry?" The responses have embraced not only the physical distinctiveness of Australia (soil, seasons, animals, plants etc) but also its emotional/spiritual distinctiveness (equality, tolerance, light-heartedness, humour, mateship etc). It will be fascinating to see how this develops.

Josie has decided to mostly leave the history question on the back-burner for now but intends to put together a more thorough piece at a later date. I sent her a draft questionnaire for comment, and in response she alerted me to the need for facts and figures for the history nerds, and so I pass on her request, to you, for names, dates and places, wherever possible. I also sent a draft to David Waldron, who is a history lecturer at *Ballarat University*. David replied that it was a good questionnaire, and asked whether Druidry was worth seeing as distinct to other Pagan groups. And so I have included that query in the questionnaire. I sent it to OBOD HQ seeking their support and Philip suggested that we advertise it on the OBOD FB page and in *Touchstone* in order to reach more people. I also wrote to Mandy seeking permission to include her idea for a special edition of *SerpentStar*, which she kindly gave me.

For those of you who weren't at the Assembly here it is, and you are invited to participate - please do! You can photocopy the questions as here presented, or better still, write and ask me to attach the questionnaire to an email. It is in Word and thus very easy to edit, according to your needs. My address is [removed] and I hope to hear from you. Elkie

Appendix C: Additional *SerpentStar* section added to *Australian Druid History Project* questionnaire in 2017

This project ties in with the 20th Anniversary of *SerpentStar*, a newsletter for OBOD members living in the Southern Hemisphere. You can write the answer to this question *and also* submit it for inclusion in the special edition of SS coming out in summer this year. The question is: What was your first OBOD experience in the SH? Or, here's how Mandy put it: At Alban Hefin 1997, our very own *SerpentStar* was born. To celebrate there will be a FIFTH issue this year, released at Alban Hefin, our official 20th birthday. For this special issue I am seeking special content, and the theme is "My first OBOD experience in the Southern Hemisphere". As always, stories, poems, photos, artwork and musings are welcome.

Appendix D: *SerpentStar* update Spring 2018

Update of the History Project, Spring 2018 – for *SerpentStar*

The History of Druidry in Australia Project has been running for a year now and is due to wind up in December, but I'm planning on talking to Philip and Stephanie about it in January and so it might run a little bit beyond that.

The idea is to write a history of Druidry as a spiritual practice in Australia, which Sandra has offered to collate into a book for us. We are hoping that lots of Bards, Ovates, and Druids will participate so that we can cover the rich diversity of expression that Druidry has spawned in Australia. I devised a questionnaire to help the project along and this is still available to anyone who would like to contribute; simply drop me a line at [email withheld].

The questionnaire has undergone a few adjustments along the way but at all stages of its evolution was only intended to act as a springboard that people could use as they wished. You are free to ignore it and write your contribution as an essay with photos, poetry, music and musings, as the Awen moves you. You don't need to be an experienced Druid to have a crack at the questionnaire or your personal essay.

I'm hoping that as well as the personal accounts of individual Druids, we can also include the histories of Australia's various Groves and Seed Groups, *Druids Down Under*, and *Urban Druidry*, all of which are vital expressions of Druidry in Australia.

At the *Golden Wattle* Assembly in August, William gave me two items of regalia that his grandmother found in an op shop in South Australia (see photo). These would have been worn by members of *The United Ancient Order of Druids* (UAOD). According to a similar picture on the internet, this is a photo of an "Australian Druid Past Arch Collar Regalia UAOD". The P. A. on the collar apparently standing for "Past Arch(Druid)".

The black and white photo shows a group of UAOD members wearing such collars; (photo credit: *State Library of South Australia*). As you can see, they are not all the same but there are a few PAs. Maybe the one from the op shop used to belong to one of these people!

Obviously, the more contributions we have, the more accurate our story is likely to be; please get your contribution in by January if you have not already done so.

Elkie

Appendix E: The Wild Hunt responses by Elkie White

The history of Druidry as a spiritual practice in Australia
When did The Melbourne Grove form?

This one is really difficult to answer because Australia is such a massive country and I'm still discovering people who were practising earlier than I was. I joined OBOD in 1995 and started *The Melbourne Grove* of OBOD in 1998. In 1995 I thought I was the only Druid in Melbourne. Just recently I've discovered that *The Australian Order of Herne* might have started earlier than that. I haven't spoken to its founder yet but I would like (us) to. His name is Carlyle and he lives in Preston.

Towards the end of last year I was contacted by a man named Bob who wanted me to conduct a Druid wedding for him. He's not sure but it would seem that he joined OBOD before I did (here in Melbourne). He gave the course up pretty quickly and became an independent Druid.

In a history of Druidry in Australia we must not forget *The United Ancient Order of Druids* (UAOD). They were active in Western Australia, South Australia, Victoria and New South Wales in the early days of settlement. (I don't know about Qld or Tasmania). Theirs was a fraternal society rather than a spiritual path but they deserve a place in the history of Druidry in Australia. They did a lot of good work.

The history of Druidry in Australia is a topic I would love to pursue further, and I know others would too.

How many OBOD groves are there in Australia?

This question is a little easier to answer, particularly as two of our major pipelines are online and are being continually updated: http://www.Druidryaustralia.org and *SerpentStar*, the Southern Hemisphere OBOD newsletter that comes out at the cross-quarters. This year the two have combined in the one website, as given. Yet I must be deliberately vague at this point as to exact numbers because there are some people that I haven't been able to reach yet. In Queensland there is one OBOD Grove: *Macadamia Grove*. In New South Wales there is *Sydney Druids Down Under*, and a Newcastle group called *Wollemi Seed Group*, and the *Song of the Eastern Sea Seed Group* on the Central Coast. In South Australia there is the *Golden Wattle Seed Group* based in Adelaide, and a couple of other groups in the country. In

Western Australia there is the *Dreaming Tree Grove*, who are also affiliated with BDO, and a couple of other groups that I haven't been able to verify. In Victoria there is *The Melbourne Grove*. I don't know about Tasmania or the Territories. Note: there is no such thing as a 'pure' OBOD grove in Australia; they are all inclusive of non-members to varying degrees. Give me a bit more time and there are channels I can use to provide more accurate information.

The current editor of *SerpentStar* has invited its membership to write about their first experience(s) of Druidry in the Southern Hemisphere for its 20-year anniversary at Summer Solstice this year. Interesting information pertaining to the history of OBOD Druidry in Australia is very likely to emerge from this.

Why Druidry over Paganism in general?
Because not all Druids identify as Pagans.

Why OBOD in particular?
For me personally the short, sweet, and accurate answer is that I was led to it, by Life, Spirit, or whatever you want to call it. Speaking more generally, I've noticed that people like the fact OBOD lets you be whatever you want to be. Several members pursue more than one spiritual path; OBOD respects personal choice (and responsibility).

Has there been a rise of interest in Druidry in Australia in recent years?
This is easy to answer – yes - evident in the growth of the *Druids Down Under* Facebook page, which currently has over 2000 members, and the *Silver Birch Grove* of ADF Facebook page, which has over 200 members. OBOD is about to launch its 16th Assembly and there will be over 40 people in attendance, which is a record. I could get exact figures for you from the OBOD office, but I would need more time to do so.

What has led to this?
This is an important question and I would rather not speculate. I would prefer to prepare a questionnaire for the *Druids Down Under* Gathering in March and give each person there an opportunity to contribute to our understanding of what is happening here.

What are the benefits of formal Druidic training over self-taught, eclectic Druidry?

This is the hardest question of all to answer because I have only experienced formal Druidic training. What I have noticed emerging from my Druidic training is a deepening of my inner life. I have gained profound insight from my training but maybe self-taught eclectic Druids have too; I have no way of knowing. But I can personally vouch for the efficacy of the initiatory path that OBOD offers.

A few highlights from the early history of *The Melbourne Grove* **and a <u>very</u> brief update**
Our Grove began at the Spring Equinox in the year 1998, when three members of OBOD met and decided to form a Seed Group for Melbourne members of the Order…

…I need time to complete a full update on our progress since then. For now I will just say that we currently operate on a fully egalitarian basis via a closed Facebook page, and it's working really well! (see *TMG – Past, Present and Future*)

ACKNOWLEDGMENTS AND CREDITS

Thank you to everyone who has contributed their time, energy, words or images. Your generosity, kindness and wisdom are phenomenal. We'd like to give our special thanks and acknowledgments to some people in particular:

- Trudy Richards, Linda Marson, Danuta E. Raine, Akkadia and Zan for their much-valued assistance with editorial support and fact checking.
- Cherry Carroll, whose poem was chosen as winner from a competition hosted on *Druids Down Under* on Facebook. Thanks also to everyone who shared their heartfelt poems.
- Mandy Gibson for actively supporting the project through Serpentstar.
- Julie Brett for allowing us to share information about this project and enabling discussions via *Druids Down Under* on Facebook.
- The three leaders of the largest, international, contemporary Druid groups for each very kindly contributing a Foreword – Philip Shallcrass, a.k.a. Greywolf, Rev. Jean (Drum) Pagano and Philip Carr-Gomm.

The cover design was created by Pro_ebookcovers, using a photo courtesy of Elkie White, which was digitally edited by Sandra Greenhalgh.

The Acknowledgment on page v was modified from reconciliation.org.au

Key Contributors

Listed in alphabetical order by first name:

Adrienne Piggott

Akkadia

Ben Hopkinson

Carole Neilson

Cherry Carroll

Chris Parker

Chris Pingel

Corin Thistlewood

Danuta Electra Raine

Elkie White

GGM Kate Wood-Pahuru

Janine Hartley

Jean (Drum) Pagano

Jeremy Runnalls

John Jordan

Julie Brett

Kacey Stephensen

Lisa Nemeton

MS

Mandy Gibson

Marigold

Michael Vlasto

Morphett Vale

Murray Barton

Narine Efe

Pete B.

Philip Carr-Gomm

Philip Shallcrass, a.k.a. Greywolf

Rafayard

Rebecca Pickard

Rollick

Sandra Greenhalgh

Sarah Marshall

Shaz Cairns

Tiki Swain

Tina Merrybard

Trudy Richards

Tyna King

Vicki Minahan

Vyvyan Ogma Wyverne

Zan

EDITOR BIOGRAPHIES

Sandra Greenhalgh

Sandra is an author, artist and occultist who currently lives in Brisbane, Australia. A long-term participant, student and teacher of Western Mystery traditions, she joined The Order of Bards, Ovates and Druids in 1988, while working in England and Europe.

Growing up in Queensland countryside helped foster her deep love of the wild places of bush, beach and the outback. Whenever possible, Sandra retreats to camping beside the ocean with her extended family and friends. She is also an avid international traveler, in search of mystical and magical places and like-minded people.

Sandra has over thirty years of neopagan community involvement, including leading a women-only spirituality group based in Brisbane. She also particularly enjoys facilitating mid to large size group events and rituals which are layered with mythos and meaning. Tarot and divination are passions, and in 2019 Sandra created a new deck of oracle cards focusing on Druidic lore, called the *Druid Wisdom Oracle*.

Sandra is a Registered Nurse, specializing in innovation and education. She lives with her husband, two teenage children and two cats, and appreciates the loving support her family provides during her exploits and adventures.

Elkie White

Elkie joined *The Order of Bards, Ovates and Druids* (OBOD) in May 1995, finding out recently that she was the 25th Aussie to do so. She moved through the grades of Bard, Ovate, and Druid quite quickly, knowing in her heart that she would one day want to return to them and review them in greater depth.

Becoming an OBOD tutor in 2001 and remaining so until 2013 (and a bit beyond), fulfilled Elkie's desire to return to the course material – old and new – and contemplate it through the eyes of others on the Bardic and Ovate paths.

Elkie felt fortunate to be a tutor/mentor, and also to have been able to attend all of the OBOD Assemblies in Australia, where she could personally meet and befriend some of the people she had assisted with the course-work, (and who had inadvertently helped her), and many more delightful Druidic folks besides.

In 2011, in preparation for her third pilgrimage to the UK and Ireland, Elkie joined the *British Druid Order* (BDO) and the *Irish Druid School* (now called the *Celtic Druid Temple*). Her subsequent pilgrimage in 2013 included re- visiting Wild Ways – a place that is special to both OBOD and BDO – and also Roscommon in Ireland.

In 2017 the Awen took yet another turn; this time to *Ár nDraíocht Féin* (ADF). Elkie studied hard, completed the Dedicant Program, and was expecting to join one of the Guilds, when the Awen evaporated. It was as if the tide had come in, stayed for a while, and then gone out again.

After sitting with that for a while, Elkie was inspired to return to the BDO coursework, which she had left incomplete. Working diligently within these Druidic frameworks was naturally advantageous to her personally, and as her confidence grew, the benefits flowed out into the community through celebrancy and public speaking.

Between 2000 and 2016, Elkie wrote *Pan's Script*, an extensive and accessible book about Astronumerology. She still loves analysing the mystical significance of people's birth data, in that all important quest to "Know Oneself".

Elkie lives in Melbourne with her husband of nearly fifty years. They have two adult children and two young grandchildren.

www.ingramcontent.com/pod-product-compliance
Lightning Source LLC
Chambersburg PA
CBHW070250010526
44107CB00056B/2410